PAINTED LOVE

Painted Love

First edition © The Derek Walcott Press 2008
Selection and Introductions © The Editors 2008
All rights reserved
ISBN 978-1-906038-08-3

Cover art: 'Jimi's Locks' © Suki Dhaliwal 2007
Heaventree logo design by Panna Chauhan

Published in the UK by
The Derek Walcott Press,
a division of The Heaventree Press,
Koco Building, The Arches,
Spon End, Coventry CV1 3JQ

Printed in the UK by
Clifford Press Ltd, Coventry
Perfect-bound by
Coventry Bookbinders Ltd

We are grateful for the financial support of

PAINTED LOVE:
THE LITERATURE OF INTERRACIAL LOVE AND SEX

EDITED BY

Benjamin Zephaniah &
David Dabydeen

WITH

Jonathan Morley
Michael Niblett
Erin Somerville

The Derek Walcott Press

ACKNOWLEDGEMENTS

Thanks to Julia Austin and to Jane Commane for typing out the manuscript, and to John Gilmore for providing a new translation of George Herbert's 'Æthiopissa ambit Cestum Diversi Coloris Virum' .

In the event of modernised or otherwise edited texts, the publishers have made every possible attempt to trace copyight holders: we will endeavour to correct omissions in future editions.

Edward, Lord Herbert of Cherbury
To Mrs. Cecyll   54
Sonnet of Black Beauty   54
The Brown Beauty (all 1665)   55

John Whaley
To a Gentleman in Love with a Negro Woman (1732)   56

Edward Kimber
Fidenia, or The Explanation (1744)   58

Thomas Day
from *The Dying Negro* (1773)   60

"T"
On Seeing a Beautiful Young Lady Kiss a Black Boy (1774)   65

James De-La-Cour
In PRAISE of a NEGRESS (1778)   66

Julius Soubise
Letter from *Nocturnal Revels* (1779)   67

Olaudah Equiano
from Letter to James Tobin (1788)   68

William Blake
The Little Black Boy (1789)   70

John Collins
Conjugal Credulity (1804)   71

Felicia Dorothea Hemans
from *The Siege of Valencia* (1823)   74

Rudyard Kipling
The Ladies (1896)   78

PART II. THE BRITISH IN THE AMERICAS — 81

William Shakespeare
from *The Tempest* (1611) — 89

John Rolfe
Letter to Sir Thomas Dale (1614) — 92

John Dryden
from *The Indian Emperour* (1665) — 97

Aphra Behn
from *The Widow Ranter* (1689) — 102

Stephen Duck
from *Avaro and Amanda* (1734) — 108

Isaac Teale
The Sable Venus (1765) — 117

William Rufus Chetwood
from *The Voyages, Dangerous Adventures, and Imminent Escapes of Captain Richard Falconer* (1766) — 122

John Gabriel Stedman
from *Narrative of a Five Years' Expedition against the Revolted Negroes of Surinam in Guiana on the Wild Coast of South America from the Years 1772 to 1777* (1790) — 131

J. B. Moreton
from *In The West India Islands* (1790) — 146

George Colman
from *Inkle and Yarico* (1796) — 151

Mathew G. Lewis
The Runaway (1845) — 158

Michael Scott
from *Tom Cringle's Log* (1894) — 160

Tekahionwake
A Red Girl's Reasoning (1892)   162

PART III. EXPLORATIONS IN AFRICA & THE NEAR EAST   179

Lady Mary Wortley Montagu
Letter to Lady Mar (1718)   186

William Rufus Chetwood
from *The Voyages, Travels and Adventures of William Owen Gwin Vaughan, Esq.* (1767)   191

Henry Brooke
from *The Fool of Quality* (1770)   195

Georgiana Cavendish, Duchess of Devonshire
A Negro Song (1799)   212

Mungo Park
from *Travels in the Interior Districts of Africa* (1799)   213

George Gordon, Lord Byron
from *Don Juan*, 'Canto V' (1821)   214

H. Rider Haggard
from *King Solomon's Mines* (1885)   227
from *Child of Storm* (1913)   237

INTRODUCTION

Interracial love and sex gets off to a bad start when, in 1593 Aaron, a blackamoor, persuades two Goths to rape a Roman lass, then afterwards cut off her tongue and hands, all this in broad daylight on a public stage in England, in front of dozens of paying customers, all white. A few years later, in 1604, things *really* get out of hand when another blackamoor, Othello, strangles a virginal white lass (whom he had married against her family's wishes), again in similar circumstances (broad daylight, public stage in England, all-white paying customers). Black men had behaved regrettably before, for instance in Thomas Peele's *The Battle of Alcazar* (1594), but none so vilely as Aaron and Othello. And just when you thought that perhaps black men would learn to mend their ways, along comes the monstrous Caliban, in 1611, weaving fantasies of raping the white virginal Miranda. In 1564 Queen Elizabeth I had sponsored a slave-trading expedition to Africa, and England was gearing up for massive profiteering. Aaron, Othello and Caliban would have helped to justify the enslavement of black people. They were mindless, brutish, naturally violent. They needed to be whipped into shape, to be tamed, to be civilised, to have their tallywackers trussed up and their Marys fig-leaved. Above all, they had to be taught the virtues of an honest day's work (though they didn't as yet deserve an honest day's wage).

Suffering was to be the fate of countless enslaved Africans for centuries to come, the most honourable men in the motherland dipping their quills in poison and writing about the necessity for ankle-chains and barracoons. In the eighteenth century Lord Chesterfield, from the plush comfort of his sofa, wrote letters to his son bad-mouthing black people for being as savage as the striped sharp-toothed quadrupeds stalking Africa. If in the medieval period the courtly knight in quest of the Holy Grail was the hero of English Literature, by the eighteenth century he had metamorphosed into a merchant in search of profit. As T. K. Myer has written,

> Literary men of the seventeenth and eighteenth centuries, including Dryden, Pope, Steele, Thomson, most of the Georgic poets and a number of lesser dramatists, essayists and poets did heap high praise upon both the concept of capitalistic business enterprise and upon businessman who practised it…

commerce and industry had caught the literary imagination of the period and represented, for a time at least, the progressive hope of the future.[1] You could have sex with your profits (indeed, children born of unions between white masters and black women increased the stock of slaves) but you couldn't marry them, for how then could you justify having your wife or husband as a slave? And if, as the prevailing literature claimed, black people were like animals, then to marry one of them would be as unacceptable to the Church as if you married one of your horses. Buggery was unlawful, bestiality was unspeakably so. Hence, the body of writing warning of the evils of miscegenation, notably Edward Long's *Candid Reflections* (1772): "The lower class of women in England are remarkably fond of the blacks, for reasons too brutal to mention; they would connect themselves with horses and asses if the laws permitted them."[2]

Human nature being what it is, such warnings were not heeded, hence happy marriages between the African British writer Olaudah Equiano and the Cambridgeshire woman Susanna Cullen in 1792; and between Ukawsaw Gronniosaw (the first African to publish a book in Britain, *Narrative of the Most Remarkable Particulars in the Life of...*, *An African Prince*, c.1770) and Betty, an impoverished English widow, around 1762. Of his marriage to Betty, Gronniosaw wrote: "I never did anything with a better will in all my life, because I firmly believed we should be happy together, and so it proved, for she was given me from the Lord. And I have found her a blessed partner, and we have never repented, though we have gone through many great troubles and difficulties."

On the streets, and in the taverns of London (a visibly multi-ethnic city in the eighteenth century) black people and lower class Whites flirted or made love openly, as evidenced in prints such as William Hogarth's *Noon* (1738). The aristocracy kept their relationships more secret, though the special bond between the Duchess of Queensberry and her African servant Soubise was high society gossip in the 1770s.[3] As to the

---

[1] See Dabydeen, David (ed.), *The Black Presence in English Literature*, Manchester University Press 1985, p.29.
[2] Fryer, Peter, *Staying Power*, Pluto Press 1984, p.157.
[3] Dabydeen, David et al (eds.) *The Oxford Companion to Black British History*, OUP 2007.

hundreds of black women in Britain at the time, their liasons and marriages to white British men remain unrecorded. Who, for instance, was Mr. Davinier, the man who married Dido Elizabeth Lindsay in the late eighteenth century?[4]

The horror of intermarriage and interracial sex persisted in a hundred tracts and pamphlets of the nineteenth century, the Age of Imperialism. Concern shifted to India, the new Jewel in the Crown, and in particular to the British soldiers and administrators who were stationed there, their wives left behind at home. Some commentators, fearing that the climate of India would kill out Europeans within a few generations, argued for a "modification of races, resulting from intermixture and amalgamation through marriage." A new breed of man would be created (with European brains but local resistance to climate).[5] British governance of India would thereby be guaranteed for centuries to come. But decent Christian men and women would have none of it. The Memsahibs were dispatched in their droves to India to keep their men in check, and to keep the Kiplingesque dusky maidens at bay. It didn't help matters much when Queen Victoria went native, not only becoming Empress of India, but also eating curry at Balmoral, taking Hindi and Urdu lessons and, heavens forbid, appointing Abdul Karim (a Muslim!) as her personal assistant. Victoria gave him his own coach, with white servants in attendance, and cottages in the grounds of her royal palaces. The gossip about their relationship was spiced up in the London press, and her leading white courtiers threatened to resign or to force her abdication.

When Victoria died in 1901, her court was purged of colour, all her black and Indian servants dismissed. Antipathy to interracial relationships resumed its normal place in British letters and life. Race riots in Cardiff in 1919, for instance, were partly ignited by white anger at black sailors consorting with white women. That the subject peoples of the Empire were agitating for their independence, was bad enough, but their political leaders went a tad too far when they took up white wives. These leaders (e.g. Cheddi Jagan and Seretse Khama, who each married white women in the 1940s) couldn't be horsewhipped as in the old days, so they were punished by

---

[4] Ibid.
[5] Young, Robert, *Colonial Desire*, Routledge 1995, p.143.

being jailed or sent into exile, thus delaying the granting of Independence. Nehru, it can be argued, gambled with India's Independence by sleeping with Lady Mountbatten, but their adultery remained a secret for decades. Would India have parted from Pakistan in 1947 had Nehru's and Lady Mountbatten's parting of thighs been public knowledge? Would Britain (obsessed as ever with sex and politics) not have delayed Independence, thus allowing Hindus and Muslims a few more crucial years to bond?

We end with this grand question about India's fate – the first country to break from Britain – so as to alert our readers to the fact that an interracial marriage here and there, or a little jukkie-jukkie in the dark, were of global consequence. We, mostly ordinary folk, have fought on the beaches, landing grounds, in fields, in streets and on the hills, to love and/or make love to each other. We will not flag nor fail. We shall go on to the end. We will never surrender. Not to the likes of Edward Long, his forebears and descendents. We have survived slavery, indentureship, Empire. Let's get on with it. Let's get off to a good start, with each other.

God save the Queen!

BZ & DD

I.

THE BLACK PRESENCE IN BRITAIN

Definitions of the "black presence" in British Literature are commonly understood to include the black characters who appear in the works of whites such as Shakespeare, Hogarth and Blake. Although in the eighteenth century a few black writers – most notably Olaudah Equiano (c.1745-1797) – were to bring greater representative balance to literary production itself, the focus of this section must naturally be more towards blacks when they are imagined by the white gaze as the subjects of erotic encounters. Within this framework, different modes appear for writing a "black presence" into the corpus, dependent on Britain's changing historical circumstances and the ideological assumptions that arise. Racial prejudices, it will be seen, often coexist with those of gender and class.

The earliest black lovers were stage villains created by Shakespeare and Thomas Dekker; their amorous (or lustful) exertions were usually directed at the worst sort of women imaginable ("Goths" and "lascivious" Spanish dames) and were part of a wider tendency towards devilish behaviour, also present in less sexually charged black characters such as Muly Hamet in Robert Peele's *The Battle of Alcazar* (1594). These black Machiavels, whose painted faces would have instantly marked them out on the Elizabethan stage, are crowd-pleasing tricksters, extravagant stereotypes comparable to those in anti-Semitism. Indeed, in 1596 and again in 1601, Queen Elizabeth I attempted to expel the "negars" from England, writing to the Mayor of London that "there are divers Blackamoors brought into this realm, of which kinde of people there are already here too manie." Despite the personal profits she enjoyed from being a shareholder in slave-trading voyages, her employment at court of black trumpeters, and even the appeal of a "lytle Blackamore" for whom she purchased an expensive coat in 1577, Elizabeth could, when an enemy within the state was needed on whom to shift the blame for food and labour shortages, adopt the rhetoric of contemporary racism: "manie for wante of service and means to set them on work fall on idleness and to great extremity… those kinde of people should be sent forth of the land."[1] Aaron and Eleazar, with the howls of hatred and derision their behaviour would have provoked in London audiences,

---

[1] See Dabydeen et al (eds.) *The Oxford Companion to Black British History*, OUP 2007.

complemented the royal scapegoating of black people.

Nevertheless there is a certain dramatic glory in the very outrageousness of these characters' evildoing. Eleazar describes himself as "this black temple" and dies vowing to wreak revenge on his Spanish captors, "out-act[ing] you all in perfect villainy." Shakespeare, furthermore, could not only create the dastardly Aaron, who, consumed by lust for Tamora, instructs her sons to rape and mutilate the innocent Lavinia, but would also idealise an apparently black or mulatto woman in his *Sonnets* (perhaps a mixed-race prostitute, a type common in London of the period, the novelist William Boyd has speculated) – she betrays him for a friend. The noble Othello, who shows without a doubt that Shakespeare was interested in the psychology of racial difference, is a further development, and becomes the model for another black paradigm in literature: the honourable free Black, gripped by forces beyond his control, his role being ultimately sacrificial (a character who recurs not just in abolitionist tracts of the eighteenth century but also continues to fall on his sword in today's sci-fi and gangster films and TV crime dramas). Perhaps Ben Jonson's River Niger is correct to suggest that Renaissance conceptions of blackness were dependent on the whims of "brain-sick" poets.

Jonson, with the *Masque of Blackness*, performed in the lavish costumes of Inigo Jones by Queen Anne and her ladies to mark Twelfth Night in 1605, ushers in a more decorative tradition, where black skin is held up to the light as a new ideal of beauty, the daring clash of colours comprising part of the erotic charge – the entwined limbs of black and white lovers are figured as a chequerboard, a printing press, or a dark shop commending its dainty chinaware, in the conceits of the group of mid-century poets such as Henry King, John Cleveland and Eldred Revett, who imitated and at times pirated each others' work. Phineas Fletcher (a well-known playwright) and George Herbert (a major Metaphysical poet) praise black beauty in translation, and as the seventeenth century progresses paeans to "Brown", or mixed-race, subjects become a more prominent feature; Edward Herbert's ode to the "Phaie", for example, eulogises such racial mixing as being opposed to the "extreams" of controversy and conflict.

Edward Kimber, who in 1744 prefixed the following note to his 'Fidenia, or, the Explanation', is the first writer to question the slave trade in a love poem.

> A very beautiful Negro Girl, aged 16, from James River in Guinea, who by every superior Accomplishment, seems far beyond any of her Kind. She learnt the English Tongue in three Months Time, and in four, read the Spectators and Tatlers with inimitable Grace. She has endear'd herself to a grateful Master by her Fidelity and Affection, tho' he has been much censured for his Regard to her.[2]

Although he does not go so far as to purchase the release of this delightful creature, in Kimber's poem the imagery of "chains", "Afric's shore", the "inchanting slave" and her "happy master" collude to make a protest against the system of enslavement – though Fidenia must, of course, be educated out of her benighted ways in order to be truly free. Love poems were only a small part of abolitionist literature, and their transgressive subject is often overwhelmed by other features of the genre – equally present in works such as Thomas Day's *The Dying Negro* (an eighteenth-century bestseller, going through numerous print runs as the campaign to end the human traffic in Britain's colonies gathered momentum in the 1770s) are the piteous passivity of the enslaved, the heart-rending cruelty of West Indian planters, and the technical struggle to move on from a Miltonic register as evidenced in other writers of the period (notably Wordsworth). "Armed with thy sad last gift, the pow'r to die," the Dying Negro can do only that, never *achieve*. Liberty becomes, under the whiggish gaze of the eighteenth-century middle classes, "less dear than love"; and love itself was still subject to the prurient, more or less bewildered fascination of John Collins and his ilk.

In this historical climate, the nonconformist message of the great prophet of love, William Blake, takes on an intense radicalism: as well as asserting the equality of his black and white boys before God in the poem included here, Blake described the "clanking chains" of the Middle Passage in *America: a Prophecy* and provided provocative illustrations to John Gabriel Stedman's *Expedition to Surinam*. But for less outspoken contributors to the *London Magazine* such as James De-La-Cour or "T", the mercantilist reality, that Britain's increasing wealth depended on her trade in Africans, is kept far

---

[2] First printed in the *London Magazine*. See Basker, James G. (ed.) *Amazing Grace: An Anthology of Poems About Slavery 1660-1810*, Yale University Press, 2002, p.89.

from view. For a more radical interracial literature in this period, one needs to look to black British writers themselves – Olaudah Equiano, the famous campaigner, adventurer and man of letters, and the foppish Soubise, lover of the Duchess of Queensberry – who introduce a more outspoken and ironic mode in defence of their sexual conduct.

Sexual (and, in Blake, religious) love are not the only forms of love included, and the excerpt from Felicia Dorothea Hemans' late Romantic verse drama shows paternal love, again filtered through the tragic lens of racial enmity. Hernandez' son has "for the dark eye of a Moorish maid / Abjured his faith" and is slain by his father, showing once again that, regardless of whether writers knowingly embraced the concept of interracial love or frowned upon it, such literary liasons tended to come to a sticky end. The section ends with Rudyard Kipling's 'The Ladies', a soldier's tale of sexual conquest across several continents. Whether Kipling was an apologist for empire or its critic is still debated; it is perhaps safe to note that Kipling's "tommies", with their often ironic folk wisdom and dialect poetry, seem wiser than their generals. Whether a similar model of subalternity can be applied to his colonised women as to his working class heroes is the question for readers here.

WILLIAM SHAKESPEARE

FROM *TITUS ANDRONICUS*

from ACT I SCENE I

Aaron
Now climbeth Tamora Olympus' top,
Safe out of fortune's shot, and sits aloft,
Secure of thunder's crack or lightning flash,
Advanced above pale envy's threatening reach.
As when the golden sun salutes the morn
And, having gilt the ocean with his beams,
Gallops the zodiac in his glistering coach
And overlooks the highest-peering hills,
So Tamora.
Upon her wit doth earthly honour wait,
And virtue stoops and trembles at her frown.
Then, Aaron, arm thy heart and fit thy thoughts
To mount aloft with thy imperial mistress,
And mount her pitch whom thou in triumph long
Hast prisoner held, fettered in amorous chains
And faster bound to Aaron's charming eyes
Than is Prometheus tied to Caucasus.
Away with slavish weeds and servile thoughts!
I will be bright, and shine in pearl and gold
To wait upon this new-made empress.
To wait, said I? – to wanton with this queen,
This goddess, this Semiramis, this nymph,
This siren that will charm Rome's Saturnine
And see his shipwreck and his commonweal's.
Hallo, what storm is this?

from ACT II SCENE II

Tamora
My lovely Aaron, wherefore look'st thou sad
When everything doth make a gleeful boast?
The birds chant melody on every bush,
The snake lies rolled in the cheerful sun,
The green leaves quiver with the cooling wind
And make the chequered shadow on the ground.

WILLIAM SHAKESPEARE

Under their sweet shade, Aaron, let us sit,
And whilst the babbling echo mocks the hounds,
Replying shrilly to the well-tuned horns
As if a double hunt were heard at once,
Let us sit down and mark their yellowing noise;
And after conflict such as was supposed
The wandering prince and Dido once enjoyed,
When with a happy storm they were surprised
And curtained with a counsel-keeping cave,
We may, each wreathed in the other's arms,
Our pastimes done, possess a golden slumber,
Whiles hounds and horns and sweet melodious birds
Be unto us as is a nurse's song
Of lullaby to bring her babe asleep.

Aaron
Madam, though Venus govern your desires,
Saturn is dominator over mine.
What signifies my deadly-standing eye,
My silence and my cloudy melancholy,
My fleece of woolly hair that now uncurls
Even as an adder when she doth unroll
To do some fatal execution?
No, madam, these are no venereal signs;
Vengeance is in my heart, death in my hand,
Blood and revenge are hammering in my head.
Hark, Tamora, the empress of my soul,
Which never hopes more heaven than rests in thee,
This is the day of doom for Bassianus,
His Philomel must loose her tongue today,
Thy sons make pillage of her chastity
And wash their hands in Bassianus' blood.
Seest thou this letter? Take it up, I pray thee, [*Gives letter*]
And give the king this fatal-plotted scroll.
Now question me no more: we are espied.
Here comes a parcel of our hopeful booty,
Which dreads not yet their lives' destruction.

Tamora
Ah, my sweet Moor, sweeter to me than life!

THOMAS DEKKER

FROM *LUST'S DOMINION, OR THE LASCIVIOUS QUEEN*

[*Eleazar, a Moor, married to Maria, is having an affair with Eugenia, the old King of Spain's wife*]

from ACT I SCENE I

Queen Mother
Why is my love's aspect so grim and horrid?
Look smoothly on me:
Chyme out your softest strains of harmony,
And on delicious Musick's silken wings
Send ravishing delight to my love's ears,
That he may be enamoured of your tunes.
Come let's kisse.

Eleazar
Away, away.

Queen Mother
No, no, says I; and twice away says stay:
Come, come, I'le have a kiss, but if you strive,
For one denial you shall forfeit five.

Eleazar
Nay prithee good Queen leave me,
I am now sick, heavie, and dull as lead.

Queen Mother
I'll make thee lighter by taking something from thee.

Eleazar
Do: take from me
This Ague: and these fits that hanging on me
Shake me in pieces, and set all my blood
A boiling with the fire of rage: away, away;
Thou believ'st I jest:
And laugh'st, to see my wrath wear antick shapes:
Be gone, be gone.

THOMAS DEKKER

Queen Mother
What means my love?
Burst all those wires! Burn all those Instruments!
For they displease my Moor. Art thou now pleas'd,
Or wert thou now disturb'd? I'le wage all Spain
To one sweet kisse, this is some new device
To make me fond and long. Oh! you men
Have tricks to make poor women die for you.

Eleazar
What, die for me; away.

Queen Mother
Away, what way? I prithee speak more kindly;
Why do'st thou frown? At whom?

Eleazar
                                At thee.

Queen Mother
                                        At me?
Oh why at me? for each contracted frown
A crooked wrinkle interlines my brow:
Spend but one hour in frowns, and I shall look
Like to a Beldam of one hundred years:
I prithee speak to me and chide me not,
I prithee chide if I have done amiss,
But let my punishment be this, and this.
I prithee smile on me, if but a while,
Then frown on me, I'le die: I prithee smile:
Smile on me, and these two wanton boys,
These pretty lads that do attend on me,
Shall call thee Jove, shall wait upon thy cup
And fill thee Nectar: their enticing eyes
Shall serve as chrystal, wherein thou mayst see
To dress thyself, if thou wilt smile on me.
Smile on me, and with coronets of pearle,
And bells of gold, circling these pretty arms
In a round Ivorie fount these two shall swim,
And dive to make thee sport:

THOMAS DEKKER

Bestow one smile, one little little smile,
And in a net of twisted silk and gold
In my all-naked arms, thy self shalt lie,

Eleazar
Why, what to do? Lust's arms do stretch so wide,
That none can fill them! I'le lay there? Away.

Queen Mother
Where has thou learn'd this language, that can say
No more but two rude words? Away, away:
Am I grown ugly now?

Eleazar
          Ugly as hell.

Queen Mother
Thou lovd'st me once.

Eleazar
          That can thy bastards tell.

Queen Mother
What is my sin? I will amend the same.

Eleazar
Hence strumpet, use of sin makes thee past shame.

Queen Mother
Strumpet.

Eleazar
    Aye, Strumpet.

Queen Mother
          Too true 'tis, woe is me;
I am a Strumpet, but made so by thee.

Eleazar
By me?
No, no; by these young bawds; fetch thee a glasse

THOMAS DEKKER

And thou shalt see the balls of both thine eyes
Burning in fire of lust; by me? there's here
Within this hollow cistern of thy breast
A spring of hot blood: have not I to cool it
Made an extraction to the quintessence
Even of my soul: melted all my spirits,
Ravish'd my youth, deflour'd my lovely cheeks,
And dried this, this to an anatomy
Only to feed your lust, (these boys have ears):
Yet wouldst thou murther me.

Queen Mother
I murder thee?

Eleazar
I cannot ride through the Castilian streets
But thousands eyes through windows, and through doors
Throw killing looks at me, and every slave
At Eleazar darts a finger out,
And every hissing tongue cries, There's the Moor,
That's he that makes a Cuckold of our King,
There go's the Minion of the Spanish Queen;
That's the black Prince of Divels, there go's hee
That on smooth boys, on Masks and Revellings
Spends the Revenues of the King of Spain.
Who arms this many headed beast but you,
Murder and Lust are twins, and both are thine;
Being weary of me thou woudst worry me,
Because some new love makes thee loath thine old.

Queen Mother
Eleazar!

Eleazar
Harlot! I'le not hear thee speak.

Queen Mother
I'le kill myself unless thou hear'st me speak.
My husband King upon his death-bed lies,
Yet have I stole from him to look on thee:
A Queen hath made her self thy Concubine;

THOMAS DEKKER

Yet do'st thou now abhor me. Hear me speak!
Else shall my sons plague thy adult'rous wrongs,
And tread upon thy heart for murd'ring me,
Thy tongue hath murd'red me. (Cry murder boys!)

2 Boys
Murder! the Queen's murd'red!

Eleazar
Love! Slaves, peace!

2 Boys
Murder! The Queen's murd'red!

Eleazar
                    Stop your throats!
Hark, hush you Squalls; dear love look up:
Our Chamber window stares into the Court,
And every wide mouth'd cur, hearing this news
Will give Alarum to the cuckold King.
I did dissemble when I chid my love,
And that dissembling was to try thy love.

Queen Mother
Thou call'dst me strumpet.

Eleazar
                    I'le tear out my tongue
From this black temple for blaspheming thee.

Queen Mother
And when I woo'd thee but to smile on me,
Thou cri'dst, away, away, and frown'dst upon me.

Eleazar
Come now I'le kiss thee, now I'le smile upon thee;
Call to thy ashy cheeks their wonted red:
Come frown not, pout not, smile, smile but upon me,
And with my poniard will I stab my flesh,
And quaffe carowses to thee of my blood,
Whil'st in moist Nectar kisses thou do'st pledge me.

THOMAS DEKKER

[... *Zarack and Balthasar, Eleazar's black slaves, announce the king to be dying*]

Eleazar
Seek no Queens here, I'le broach them if they do,
Upon my falchion's point. Again more knocking!

Zarack
Your father is at hand, my gracious Lord.

Eleazar
Lock all the doors, bar him out you apes.
Hither, a vengeance; stir *Eugenia*,
You know your old walk under ground, away
So, down, hye to the King, quick, quick, you Squalls
Crawle with your Dam, i'th dark. Dear love, farewell,
One day I hope to shutt you up in hell. [*He shuts them in.*]

Enter *Alvero.*

Alvero
Son *Eleazar*, saw you not the Queen?

Eleazar
Hah!

Alvero
Was not the Queen here with you?

Eleazar
                      Queen with mee;
Because my Lord I'm married to your daughter,
You (like your daughter) will grow Jealious:
The Queen with me, with me, a Moore, a Devill,
A slave of *Barbary*, a dog; for so
Your silken Courtiers christen me, but father
Although my flesh be tawny, in my veines
Runs blood as red, and royal as the best
And proud'st in *Spain*, there does old man:
My father, who with his Empire, lost his life,
And left me captive to a Spanish Tyrant, oh!

THOMAS DEKKER

Go tell him! Spanish Tyrant! tell him, do!
He that can loose a kingdom and not rave,
He's a tame jade, I am not, tell old *Philip*
I call him Tyrant! [...]

Alvero
Watch fitter hours to think on wrongs then now,
Death's frozen hand holds Royal *Philip*'s heart, [...]
Come and take leave of him before he dye.

Eleazar
I'le follow you; now purple villany,
Sit like a Roab imperiall on my back,
That under thee I closelyer may contrive
My vengeance; foul deeds hid do sweetly thrive:
Mischief erect thy throne and sit in state
Here, here upon this head; let fools fear fate,
Thus I defie my starrs, I care not I
How low I tumble down, so I mount high.
Old time I'le wait bare-headed at they heels,
And be a foot-boy to thy winged hours;
They shall not tell one Minute out in sands,
But I'le set down the number, I'le still wake
And waste these balls of sight by tossing them,
In busie observations upon thee.
Sweet opportunity I'le bind myself
To thee in base apprentice-hood so long,
Till on thy naked scalp grow hair as thick
As mine, and all hands shall lay hold on thee:
If thou wilt lend me but thy rusty scythe,
To cut down all that stand within my wrongs,
And my revenge. Love dance in twenty formes
Upon my beauty, that this Spanish dame
May be bewitch'd, and dote; her amorous flames
Shall blow up the old King, consume his Sons,
And make all *Spain* a bonefire.

from ACT II SCENE III

[*Philip dies, upon which Eleazar secures his place at court through the petition of his virtuous wife, Maria; his enemies, the young Prince*

THOMAS DEKKER

Philip and Cardinal Mendoza, are cast out. But his patrons attempt their own schemes: King Fernando has designs on Maria, and Eugenia wants her out of the way so she can have the Moor all to herself.]

Fernando
That Cardinall, is all ambition,
And from him doth our Brother gather heart.

Queen Mother
Th'ambition of the one infects the other,
And in a word they both are dangerous;
But might your mother's counsel stand in force,
I would advise you send the trusty Moor
To fetch them back, before they had seduc'd
The squint ey'd multitude from true allegiance,
And drawn them to their dangerous faction.

Fernando
It shall be so, therefore my State's best prop,
Within whose bosome I durst trust my life,
Both for my safety and thine own discharge,
Fetch back those traitors, and till your return
Our self will keep your Castle.

Eleazar
My Leige; the tongue of true obedience
Must not gainsay his Soveraign's impose;
By heaven, I will not kiss the cheek of sleep,
Till I have fetch'd those traitors to the Court.

Fernando [aside]
Why; this sorts right; he gone, his beauteous wife
Shall sail into the naked arms of love.

Queen Mother [aside]
Why, this is as it should be, he once gone,
His wife that keeps me from his marriage bed,
Shall by this hand of mine be murthered.

Fernando
This storm is well nigh past, the swelling clouds

29

THOMAS DEKKER

That hang so full of treason, by the wind
In awfull Majestie are scattered.
Then each man to his rest; good night sweet friend.
[*Aside*] Whil'st thou persu'st the traitors that are fled,
Fernando means to warm thy marriage bed.

Exeunt. [Manet Eleazar]

Eleazar
Many good nights, [*aside*] consume and dam your souls.
I know he means to Cuckold me this night;
Yet do I know no means to hinder it.
Besides, who knows whether the lustful King,
Having my wife and Castle at command,
Will ever make surrender back again:
But if he do not, with my falchion's point
I'le lance those swelling veins in which hot lust
Does keep his Revels, and with that warm blood
Where *Venus*'s bastard coold his sweltering spleen,
Wash the disgrace from *Eleazar*'s brows.

Enter Maria.

Maria
Dear *Eleazar* –

Eleazar
    If they lock the gates
I'le tosse a ball of wild-fire o're the walls.

Maria
Husband, sweet husband –

Eleazar
    Or else swim o're the moat,
And make a breach through the flinty sides
Of the rebellious walls –

Maria
    Hear me, dear heart.

THOMAS DEKKER

Eleazar
Or undermine the chamber where they lie,
And by the violent strength of gunpowder,
Blow up the Castle, and th'incestuous couch,
In which lust wallows; but my labouring thoughts,
Wading too deep in bottomless extreams;
Do drown themselves in their own stratagems.

Maria
Sweet husband! Dwell not upon circumstance,
When weeping sorrow like an Advocate
Importunes you for aid; look in mine eyes,
There you shall see dim grief swimming in tears,
Invocating succor. Oh succor!

Eleazar
Succor. Zounds, for what?

Maria
To shield me from Fernando's unchaste love,
Who with uncessant prayers importun'd me.

Eleazar
To lie with you; I know't.

Maria
            Then seek some means
How to prevent it.

Eleazar
          'Tis impossible;
For to the end that his unbridled lust
Might have more free accesse unto thy bed,
This night he hath enjoined me
To fetch back *Philip* and the Cardinall.

Maria
Then this ensuing night shall give an end
To all my sorrows, for before foul lust
Shall soil the fair complexion of mine honour,
This hand shall rob *Maria* of her life.

THOMAS DEKKER

Eleazar
Not so dear soul, for in extremities
Choose out the least, and ere the hand of death
Should suck this Ivorie palace of thy life,
Imbrace my counsel, and receive this poison:
Which in the instant he attempts thy love,
Then give it him: do, do,
[*aside*] Do; poison him, he gone, thou'rt next.
Be sound in resolution; and farewell;
[*aside*] By one, and one, I'le ship you all to hell.
Spain I will drown thee with thine own proud blood,
Then make an ark of carcasses: farewell.
Revenge and I will sail in blood to hell!

from ACT III SCENE I

Queen Mother
Fair eldest child of love, thou spotlesse night,
Empresse of silence, and the Queen of sleep;
Who with thy black cheeks' pure complexion,
Mak'st lovers eyes enamour'd of thy beauty:
Thou art like my Moor, therefore I will adore thee
For lending me this opportunity,
Oh with the soft skin'd Negro! Heavens keep back
The saucy staring day from the world's eye,
Untill my *Eleazar* make return;
Then in his Castle shall he find his wife,
Transform'd into a strumpet by my son;
Then shall he hate her whom he would not kill!
Then shall I kill her whom I cannot love!
The King is sporting with his Concubine.
Blush not my boy, be bold like me thy mother.
But their delights torture my soul like Devills,
Except her shame be seen.

from ACT V SCENE III

[*Maria does not kill the amorous king; instead she administers him a sleeping potion, whereupon she is murdered by the Queen Mother. Eleazar uses this as an opportunity to stab Fernando and seize the throne of Spain. He is eventually unseated by the machinations of*

THOMAS DEKKER

Philip's family, who trick and kill his Moorish slaves, then dress up in blackface to lull Eleazar into a game of charades that results in his imprisonment and death, and the banishment of the Moors from Spain.]

Eleazar
Villains, slaves, am I not your Lord the Moor,
And *Eleazar*?

Queen Mother
     And the Devill of hell,
And more than that, and *Eleazar* too.

Eleazar
And Devill's dam, what do I here with you?

Queen Mother
My tongue shall torture thee.

Eleazar
     I know thee then,
All women's tongues are tortures unto men.

Queen Mother
Spaniards this was the villain, this is he
Who through enticements of alluring lust,
And glory, which makes silly women proud
And men malicious, did incense my spirit
Beyond the limits of a womans mind,
To wrong my self and that Lord Cardinall;
And that which sticks more near unto my blood,
He that was nearest to my blood, my son;
To dispossesse him of his right by wrong.
Oh! that I might embrace him on this breast,
Which did enclose him when he first was born.
No greater happinesse can heaven showre upon me
Than to circle in these arms of mine
That son whose Royall blood I did defame,
To Crown with honour an ambitious Moor.

THOMAS DEKKER

Philip
Thus then thy happinesse is complete,
Behold thy *Philip* ransom'd from that prison
In which the Moor had cloistered him.

Hortenzo
And here's *Hortenzo*.

Eleazar
                    Then am I betray'd
And cozen'd in my own designs: I did
Contrive their ruine, but their subtil policie
Hath blasted my ambitious thoughts:
Villains! Where's *Zarack*? Where is *Baltazar*?
What have you done with them.

Philip
They're gone to *Pluto*'s kingdom to provide
A place for thee, and to attend thee there;
But least they should be tired with too long
Expecting hopes, come brave spirits of *Spain*,
This is the Moor, the actor of these evills:
Thus thrust him down to act amongst the devils! [*Stabs him.*]

Eleazar
And am I thus dispatch'd;
Had I but breath'd the space of one hour longer,
I would have fully acted my revenge.
But oh! now pallid death bids me prepare,
And haste to *Charon* for to be his fare.
I come, I come, but ere my glasse is run,
I'le curse you all, and cursing end my life.
Maist thou, Lascivious Queen whose damned charms,
Bewitch'd me to the circle of thy arms,
Unpitied die, consumed with loathed lust,
Which thy venereous mind hath basely nurst.
And for you *Philip*, may your days be long,
But clouded with perpetuall misery,
May thou *Hortenzo* and thy *Isabell*,

THOMAS DEKKER

Be fetch'd alive by Furies into hell,
There to be damn'd for ever. Oh! I faint;
Devills come claim your right, and when I am
Confin'd within your kingdom then shall I
Out-act you all in perfect villainy. [*Dies.*]

WILLIAM SHAKESPEARE

FROM *OTHELLO, THE MOOR OF VENICE*

from ACT I SCENE III

[*Othello is accused of using witches' potions to steal Brabantio's daughter*]

Othello
Most potent, grave, and reverend signiors,
My very noble and approved good masters:
That I have ta'en away this old man's daughter
It is most true; true, have I married her.
The very head and front of my offending
Hath this extent, no more. Rude am I in my speech
And little blest with the soft phrase of peace,
For since these arms of mine had seven years' pith
Till now some nine moons wasted, they have used
Their dearest action in the tented field,
And little of this great world can I speak
More than pertains to feats of broil and battle,
And therefore little shall I grace my cause
In speaking for myself. Yet, by your gracious patience,
I will a round unvarnished tale deliver
Of my whole course of love, what drugs, what charms,
What conjuration and what mighty magic –
For such proceeding I am charged withal –
I won his daughter.

[…]

Duke
          Say it, Othello.

Othello
Her father loved me, oft invited me,
Still questioned me the story of my life
From year to year – the battles, sieges, fortunes
That I have passed.
I ran it through, even from my boyish days
To th' very moment that he bade me tell it,

WILLIAM SHAKESPEARE

Wherein I spake of most disastrous chances,
Of moving accidents by blood and field,
Of hair-breadth scapes i'th' imminent deadly breach,
Of being taken by the insolent foe
And sold to slavery; of my redemption thence
And portance in my travailous history;
Wherein of antres vast and deserts idle,
Rough quarries, rocks and hills whose heads touch heaven
It was my hint to speak – such was my process –
And of the cannibals that each other eat,
The Anthropophagi, and men whose heads
Do grow beneath their shoulders. This to hear
Would Desdemona seriously incline,
But still the house affairs would draw her thence,
Which ever as she could with haste dispatch
She'd come again, and with a greedy ear
Devour up my discourse; which I, observing,
Took once a pliant hour and found good means
To draw from her a prayer of earnest heart
That I would by all my pilgrimage dilate,
Whereof by parcels she had something heard
But not intentively. I did consent,
And often did beguile her of her tears
When I did speak of some distressful stroke
That my youth suffered. My story being done
She gave me for my pains a world of sighs,
She swore in faith 'twas strange, 'twas passing strange,
 'Twas pitiful, 'twas wondrous pitiful;
She wished she had not heard it, yet she wished
That heaven had made her such a man. She thanked me
And bade me, if I had a friend that loved her,
I should but teach him how to tell my story
And that would woo her. Upon this hint I spake:
She loved me for the dangers I had passed
And I loved her that she did pity them.
This only is the witchcraft I have used:
Here comes the lady, let her witness it.

BEN JONSON

FROM *THE MASQUE OF BLACKNESS*

SONG
Sound, sound aloud
The welcome of the orient flood,
    Into the west;
Fair Niger, son to great Oceanus,
        Now honoured thus
    With all his beauteous race;
    Who, though but black in face,
        Yet are they bright,
    And full of life and light.
    To prove that beauty best,
Which, not the colour, but the feature
    Assures unto the creature.

Oceanus
Be silent, now the ceremony's done,
And, Niger, say how it comes it, lovely son,
That thou, the Æthiop's river, so far east,
Art seen to fall into the extremest west
Of me, the king of floods, Oceanus,
And in mine empire's heart, salute me thus?
My ceaseless current now amazed stands
To see thy labour through so many lands
Mix thy fresh billow with my brackish stream;
And in the sweetness stretch thy diadem
To these far distant and unequalled skies,
This squared circle of celestial bodies.

Niger
 Divine Oceanus, 'tis not strange at all
That since th' immortal souls of creatures mortall
Mix with their bodies, yet reserve for ever
A power of separation, I should sever
My fresh streams from thy brackish, like things fixed,
Through with thy powerful saltness thus far mixed.
"Virtue, though chained to earth, will still live free:
And hell itself must yield to industry."

BEN JONSON

Oceanus
But what's the end of thy Herculean labours,
Extended to these calm and blessed shores?

Niger
To do a kind and careful father's part,
In satisfying every pensive heart
Of these my daughters, my most loved birth:
Who, though they were the first formed dames of earth,
And, in whose sparkling and refulgent eyes
The glorious sun did still delight to rise;
Though he, the best judge, and most formal cause
Of all dames' beauties, in their firm hues, draws
Signs of his fervent'st love; and thereby shows
That in their black the perfect'st beauty grows;
Since the fixt colour of their curled hair,
Which is the highest grace of dames most fair,
No cares, no age can change; or there display
The fearful tincture of abhorred gray;
Since death herself (herself being pale and blue)
Can never alter their most faithful hue;
All which are arguments to prove how far
Their beauties conquer in great beauty's war;
And more, how near divinity they be,
That stand from passion or decay so free.
Yet since the fabulous voices of some few
Poor brain-sick men, styled poets here with you,
Have, with such envy of their graces, sung
The painted beauties other empires sprung;
Letting their loose and winged fictions fly
To infect all climates, yea, our purity;
As of one Phaeton that fired the world,
And that, before his heedless flames were hurled
About the globe, the Æthiops were as fair
As other dames; now black with black despair:
And in respect of their complexions changed,
Are eachwhere since for luckless creatures ranged;
Which when my daughters hears (as women are
Most jealous of their beauties), fear and care
Possessed them whole; yea, and believing them,
They wept such ceaseless tears into my stream,

BEN JONSON

That it hath thus far overflowed his shore
To seek them patience: who have since, e'ermore
As the sun riseth, charged his burning throne
With volleys of revilings; 'cause he shone
On their scorched cheeks with such intemperate fires,
And other dames made queens of all desires,
To frustrate which strange error, oft I sought.

WILLIAM SHAKESPEARE
FROM *SHAKESPEARE'S SONNETS*

127.

In the old age black was not counted fair,
Or if it were, it bore not beauty's name;
But now is black beauty's successive heir,
And beauty slander'd with a bastard shame:
For since each hand hath put on nature's power,
Fairing the foul with art's false borrow'd face,
Sweet beauty hath no name, no holy bower,
But is profan'd, if not lives in disgrace.
Therefore my mistress' brows are raven black,
Her eyes so suited, and they mourners seem
At such who, not born fair, no beauty lack,
Sland'ring creation with a false esteem:
  Yet so they mourn, becoming of their woe
  That every tongue says beauty should look so.

128.

How oft, when thou, my music, music play'st,
Upon that blessed wood whose motion sounds
With thy sweet fingers, when thou gently sway'st
The wiry concord that mine ear confounds,
Do I envy those jacks that nimble leap
To kiss the tender inward of thy hand,
Whilst my poor lips, which should that harvest reap,
At the wood's boldness by thee blushing stand!
To be so tickled, they would change their state
And situation with those dancing chips,
O'er whom thy fingers walk with gentle gait,
Making dead wood more blest than living lips.
  Since saucy jacks are so happy in this,
  Give them thy fingers, me thy lips to kiss.

130.

My mistress' eyes are nothing like the sun;
Coral is far more red than her lips' red;
If snow be white, why then her breasts are dun;
If hair be wires, black wires grow on her head.
I have seen roses damask'd, red and white,

WILLIAM SHAKESPEARE

But no such roses see I in her cheeks;
And in some perfumes is there more delight
Than in the breath that from my mistress reeks.
I love to hear her speak, yet well I know
That music hath a far more pleasing sound;
I grant I never saw a goddess go;
My mistress, when she walks, treads on the ground:
  And yet, by heaven, I think my love as rare
  As any she beli'd with false compare.

131.

Thou art as tyrannous, so as thou art,
As those whose beauties proudly make them cruel;
For well thou know'st to my dear doting heart
Thou art the fairest and most precious jewel.
Yet, in good faith, some say that thee behold
Thy face hath not the power to make love groan:
To say they err I dare not be so bold,
Although I swear it to myself alone.
And, to be sure that is not false I swear,
A thousand groans, but thinking on thy face,
One on another's neck, do witness bear
Thy black is fairest in my judgement's place.
  In nothing art thou black save in thy deeds,
  And thence this slander, as I think, proceeds.

132.

Thine eyes I love, and they, as pitying me,
Knowing thy heart torments me with disdain,
Have put on black and loving mourners be,
Looking with pretty ruth upon my pain.
And truly not the morning sun of heaven
Better becomes the grey cheeks of the east,
Nor that full star that ushers in the even
Doth half that glory to the sober west,
As those two mourning eyes become thy face.
O, let it then as well beseem thy heart
To mourn for me, since mourning doth thee grace,
And suit thy pity like in every part.
  Then will I swear beauty herself is black
  And all they foul that thy complexion lack.

WILLIAM SHAKESPEARE

133.

Beshrew that heart that makes my heart to groan
For that deep wound it gives my friend and me!
Is't not enough to torture me alone,
But slave to slavery my sweet'st friend must be?
Me from myself thy cruel eye hath taken,
And my next self thou harder hast engrossed:
Of him, myself, and thee, I am forsaken;
A torment thrice threefold thus to be crossed.
Prison to my heart in thy steel bosom's ward,
But then my friend's heart let my poor heart bail;
Whoe'er keeps me, let my heart be his guard;
Thou canst not then use rigour in my gaol:
   And yet thou wilt; for I, being pent in thee,
   Perforce am thine, and all that is in me.

144.

Two loves I have of comfort and despair,
Which like two spirits do suggest me still:
The better angel is a man right fair,
The worser spirit a woman colour'd ill.
To win me soon to hell, my female evil
Tempteth my better angel from my side,
And would corrupt my saint to be a devil,
Wooing his purity with her foul pride.
And whether that my angel be turn'd fiend
Suspect I may, yet not directly tell;
But being both from me, both to each friend,
I guess this one angel in another's hell:
   Yet this shall I ne'er know, but live in doubt,
   Till my bad angel fire my good one out.

PHINEAS FLETCHER
FROM THE GREEK OF ASCLEPIADES

She's black: what then? so are dead coales, but cherish,
    And with soft breath them blow,
And you shall see them glow as bright and flourish,
    As spring-borne Roses grow.

GEORGE HERBERT

ÆTHIOPISSA AMBIT CESTUM DIVERSI COLORIS VIRUM

Quid mihi si facies nigra est? hoc, Ceste, colore
    Sunt etiam tenebrae, quas tamen optat amor.
Cernis ut exustâ semper sit fronte viator;
    Ah longum, quae te deperit, errat iter.
Si nigro sit terra solo, quis despicit aruum?
    Claude oculos, & erunt omnia nigra tibi:
Aut aperi, & cernes corpus quas proijcit umbras;
    Hoc saltem officio fungar amore tui.
Cùm mihi sit facies fumus, quas pectore flammas
    Iamdudum tacitè delituisse putes?
Dure, negas? O fata mihi praesaga doloris,
    Quae mihi lugubres contribuere genas!

A BLACK WOMAN WOOS CESTUS, A MAN OF A DIFFERENT COLOUR

What if my face is black? See how the night
Of like hue is, in which Love takes delight.
The traveller is ever burnt of face,
And she who woos thee, runs a weary race.
The blackest soil bears many a fruitful tree;
But close thine eyes, and all is black to thee.
Ope them again, and see thy shadow there –
To be thy shadow is mine only prayer.
And if my face with smoke or soot is drest,
What flames have longtime lurked within my breast?
Dost spurn me, cruel one? All hope must fade –
The future well they saw, the Fates who made
My gloomy cheeks to be of sorrow's shade!

JOHN CLEVELAND

A FAIR NYMPH SCORNING A BLACK BOY COURTING HER

Nymph
Stand off, and let me take the air.
Why should the smoke pursue the fair?

Boy
My face is smoke, thence may be guessed
What flames within have scorched my breast.

Nymph
The flame of love I cannot view
For the dark lantern of thy hue.

Boy
And yet this lantern keeps Love's taper
Surer than yours that's of white paper.
Whatever midnight hath been here,
The moonshine of your light can clear.

Nymph
My moon of an eclipse is 'fraid,
If thou should'st interpose thy shade.

Boy
Yet one thing, Sweetheart, I will ask;
Take me for a new fashioned mask.

Nymph
Yes, but my bargain shall be this,
I'll throw my mask off when I kiss.

Boy
Our curled embraces shall delight
To checker limbs with black and white.

Nymph
Thy ink, my paper, make me guess
Our nuptial bed will prove a press,

JOHN CLEVELAND

And in our sports, if any came,
They'll read a wanton epigram.

Boy
Why should my black thy love impair?
Let the dark shop commend thy ware;
Or, if thy love from black forbears,
I'll strive to wash it off with tears.

Nymph
Spare, fruitless tears, since then thou must needs
Still wear about thee mourning weeds.
Tears can no more affection win
Than wash thy Ethiopian skin.

ELDRED REVETT

THE INVERSION

Nymph
Stand off fair Boy, thou wilt affright
My solitude with sudden light.

Boy
My face is light, thence may be guest
The truth of my transparent brest.

Nymph
The truth of Love I cannot view,
For the full lustre of thy hew.

Boy
The lustre's sooner pervious made
Then your impenitrable shade;
What-ever Noon my day doth trim,
Your thick how-ever Mist may dim.

Nymph
My Mist would fear to break away,
If you should intermix your ray.

Boy
Our curled embraces shall delight
With Limbs to shuffle day and night:

Nymph
Thy light, my darkness make me fear
Our bed a Chaos would appear;
And in our sports, did any pass,
They'd see the indigested Mass.

Boy
Yet one thing sweet-heart let me crave,
Me for a new-false mirror have;

Nymph
Yes, but my bargain must request,
I throw my glass by, when undrest:

Boy
Why should my hue thee less delight,
Let the Star-foyles set off the night:
Or if thy love from light forbeares,
I'le strive to put it out with teares.

Nymph
Spare fruitless teares, since thou must needs
Still have on thy Transfigur'd weeds,
Teares can no more affection win
Than over-cast thy Angell skin.

ONE ENAMOUR'D ON A BLACK-MOOR

What a strange love doth me invade,
Whose fires must cool in that dark shade!
Round her such solitudes are seen
As she were all retir'd within,
And did in hush't up silence lye,
(Though single) a Conspiracy.
How did my passion find her out,
That is with Curtains drawn about?
And though her eyes do sent'nel keep
She is all over else asleep.
And I expect when she my sight
Should strike with universal light.
A scare seen thing she glides, were gon
If touch'd, an Apparition,
To immortality that dip't
Hath newly from her Lethe slip't.
No feature here we can define
By this, or that illustrious line,
Such curiosity is not
Found in an un-distinguisht blot:
This beauty puts us from the part

ELDRED REVETT

We all have tamely got by hart,
Of Roses here, there Lilies grow,
Of Saphyre, Corall, Hills of snow;
These Rivulets are all ingrost
And all in one Black Ocean lost.
The treasures lock't up we would get
Within the Ebon Cabinet;
And he that ravishes must pick
Open the quaint Italian Trick.
She is her own close mourning in
(At Nature's Charge) a Cypress skin.
Our common Parent else to blot
A moal, on the white mold, a spot,
Dropt it with her own Statute Ink,
And the new temper'd Clay did sink:
So the fair figure doth remain,
Her ever since Record in grain.
Ixion's sometime armfull might
Swell with, perhaps, a fleece more bright;
But she as soft might be allow'd
The goddesse's deputed cloud,
Though sure from our distinct embrace
Centaurs had been a dapple Race.
Thou pretious Night-piece that art made
More valuable in thy shade,
From which when the weak tribe depart,
The skilful Master hugs his art.
Thou dost not to our dear surprise
Thine own white marble statue rise;
And yet no more a price dost lack,
Clean built up of the polish't black.
Thou like no Pelops hast supply
Of any one joynt by Ivory
But art miraculously set
Together totally with Jet.
Nor can I count that bosome cheap,
That lyes not a cold winter heap:
Where pillow yet I warmly can,
In down of the contrary swan.
Let who will wilde enjoyments dream,
And tipple from another stream;

Since he with equall pleasure dwells,
That lyes at these dark fontinells;
These fair, round, sphears contemplate on
So just in the proportion,
And in the lines of either breast,
Find the rich countries of the East.
They not as in the milkie hue,
Are broke into raw streaks of blew,
But have in their more-lived stains,
The very Violets of Veins;
They rise the Double-headed Hill,
Whose tops shade one another still;
Between them lyes the spicy Nest,
That the last Phoenix scorch'd, and blest.
What falls from her is rather made
Her own just picture, than her shade:
And where she walks the Sun doth hold
Her pourtrai'd in a frame of gold.

A BLACK NYMPH SCORNING A FAIR BOY COURTING HER

Nymph
Fond Boy, thy vain pursuit give o're,
Since I thy shadow go before.

Boy
Ah fly not Nymph! we may pursue,
And shadowes overtake like you.

Nymph
I pass howe're in course away
The night to thy succeeding day.

Boy
If night thou art, oh! be not gone,
Till thou have stood a triple one:
Though Jove, I fear, would then invade,
Not his Alcmena, but the shade.

ELDRED REVETT

Nymph
So should the thunderer embrace,
A cloud in his own goddess' place.

Boy
So let us but commix a while,
Distinguish one another's foyl;
That to advantage we may tell,
How either beauty doth excel.

Nymph
I need not thy betraying light,
To shew how far I am from white;
And to the piece that nature made,
I dare be no improving shade.

Boy
Then my dark Angell, I can charm
Thee (circled) in mine either arm.

Nymph
See! from thy slight embraces broke
Secure I vanish in my smoke.

HENRY KING

A BLACKAMOOR MAID TO A FAIR BOY

Stay, lovely boy! why fly'st thou me,
Who languish in these flames for thee?
I'm black, 'tis true – why, so is night,
Yet love does in its shades delight!
One moment close thy sparkling eye,
The world shall seem as black as I;
Or look – and see how black a shade
Is by thy own white body made!
That follows thee where'er you go,
(Ah! who allow'd would not do so!)
O let me then that shadow be,
No maid shall then be blest like me!

THE BOY'S ANSWER

Black maid, complain not that I fly,
When fate demands antipathy!
How monstrous would that union prove,
Where night and day should mingled move!
And the conjunction of our lips,
Not kisses make, but an eclipse!
In which the black shading the white,
Portends more terror than delight!
Yet if my shadow thou wilt be,
Enjoy my shadow's property;
Which, tho' attendant on my eye,
Yet hastes away as I come nigh;
Else stay 'till death has struck me blind,
And then at will thou may'st be kind.

EDWARD, LORD HERBERT OF CHERBURY

TO MRS. DIANA CECYLL

Diana Cecyll, that rare beauty thou dost show
      Is not of Milk, or Snow,
   Or such as pale and whitely things do ow.
But an illustrious Oriental Bright,
Like to the Diamond's refracted light,
Or early Morning breaking from the Night.

Nor is thy hair and eyes made of that ruddy beam,
      Or golden-sanded stream,
   Which we find still the vulgar Poets' theme,
But reverend black, and such as you would say,
Light did but serve it, and did shew the way,
By which at first night did precede the day.

Nor is that symmetry of parts and form divine
      Made of one vulgar line,
   Or such as any know how to define,
But of proportions new, so well exprest,
That the perfections in each part confest,
Are beauties to themselves, and to the rest.

Wonder of all thy Sex! let none henceforth inquire
      Why they so much admire,
   Since they that know thee best ascend no higher;
Only be not with common praises woo'd
Since admiration were no longer good,
When men might hope more then they are understood.

SONNET OF BLACK BEAUTY

Black beauty, which above that common light,
   Whose Power can no colours here renew
   But those which darkness can again subdue,
Do'st still remain unvary'd to the fight,

And like an object equal to the view,
   Art neither chang'd with day, nor hid with night;

When all these colours which the world call bright,
And which old Poetry doth so pursue,

Are with the night so perished and gone,
   That of their being there remains no mark,
Thou still abidest so intirely one,
   That we may know thy blackness is a spark
Of light inaccessible, and alone
   Our darkness which can make us think it dark.

THE BROWN BEAUTY

While the two contraries of Black and White,
In the Brown *Phaie* are so well unite,
That they no longer now seem opposite,
   Who doubts but love, hath this his colour chose,
   Since he therein doth both th' extremes compose,
   And as within their proper Centre close?

Therefore as it present not to the view
That whitely raw and unconcocted hue,
Which Beauty Northern Nations think the true;
   So neither hath it that adust aspect,
   The *Moor* and *Indian* so much affect,
   That for it they all other do reject.

Thus while the White well shadow'd doth appear,
And black doth through his lustre grow so clear,
That each in other equal part doth bear;
   All in so rare proportion is combin'd,
   That the fair temper, which adorns her mind,
   Is even to her outward form confin'd.

Phaie, your Sex's honour, then so live,
That when the World shall with contention strive
To whom they would a chief perfection give,
   They might the controversie so decide,
   As quitting all extreams on either side,
   You more than any may be dignify'd.

JOHN WHALEY

TO A GENTLEMAN IN LOVE WITH A NEGRO WOMAN

(in Imitation of Horace, Lib. 2. Od. 4)

Don't Blush, dear Sir, your Flame to own,
   Your sable Mistress to Approve;
Thy Passion other Breasts have known,
   And Heroes justify your Love.

By *Æthiopian* Beauty mov'd,
   Perseus was clad in Martial Arms
And the World's Lord too feeble prov'd
   For *Cleopatra*'s jetty Charms.

What tho' no sickly White and Red,
   With short liv'd Pride adorn the Maid?
The deeper YEW, its LEAVES ne'er Shed,
   While ROSES and while LILIES Fade.

What tho' no conscious blush Appear;
   The Tincture of a guilty Skin?
Her's is a Colour that will wear,
   And honest Black ne'er harbours Sin.

Think'st thou such Blood, in Slaves can roll,
   Think'st thou such Ligtnings can arise,
Such Pow'r was lodg'd to pierce the Soul,
   In vulgar and Plebeian Eyes?

No, Sir, by Air, and Form, and Dress,
   Thy Fusca, of uncommon Race,
No doubt an *Indian* Princess is;
   And swarthy Kings her Lineage Grace.

Such decent Modesty and Ease! –
   But, least my Rapture be Suspected,
Cease, prying jealous Lover, cease,
   Nor judge the Muse too much Affected.

JOHN WHALEY

Me paler Northern Beauties move,
  My Bosom other Darts receives,
Think not I'll Toast an *Indian* Love,
  While *Fielding* or a *Shirley* Lives.

EDWARD KIMBER
FIDENIA OR, THE EXPLANATION

1.
Ye fair, whose worth I so esteem,
   Who sport on *Britain*'s vivid plains,
Still may your smiles upon me gleam,
   For still your lover wears your chains.
Think not, tho' longer I endure
   This tedious absence from your eyes,
That time, or distance, e'er can cure
   Those passions that from you take rise.

2.
Tho' sweet *Fidenia*, born of kings,
   From *Afric*'s shores, attracts my sight;
What tho' her praise, your *Strephon* sings
   And eager graps the new delight?
What tho' her soft and jetty hue
   Gives yet unfelt, untested joy?
Remembrance speaks such charms in you,
   As all her blandishments destroy.

3.
Tho' *Amblerena* spread her snare,
   And caught me in the am'rous vein;
Her vicious soul, her gloating air,
   The thrilling ecstacies restrain.
Unhappy females, loosely bold,
   Where southern climates raise desire,
Your faint attractions ne'er will hold,
   Where reason sprinkles but the fire.

4.
Rather let me, where *Gambia* flows,
   With black *Fidenia* spend my days,
Than tempt those arms, where lust all glows,
   And mingle with the curs'd embrace.
See! With what majesty she walks!
   What modesty adorns her mien!
How simply innocent she talks,
   Inchanting slave! My *Indian* queen!

5.

E'er my exalted, matchless friend
  Had sav'd me from the enraged deep,
With what sad cries, thou wail'dst my end,
  And how my faithful slave did weep!
How shouts broke forth, with joy replete,
  When sav'd, they cast me on the shore!
With rapture, how you hugg'd my feet,
  And all thy gods, how didst implore!

6.

For this, I'll grateful, thee convey,
  Whence ev'ry precept shall combine,
To chace the savage quite away,
  And all thy motions to refine.
And ev'ry maid, and ev'ry swain,
  Shall melt at thy uncommon tale,
With admiration, tell thy name,
  And me, thy happy master, hail!

7.

Nor you, ye fair ones, will condemn
  A grateful mind, for acts like these;
Nor such a tenderness arraign,
  Where sense, and wit, and prudence please,
Thou, my *Maria*, shall embrace
  Fidenia, with a glad surprise;
Hortenisa too, her beauties trace,
  And own the lustre of her eyes.

THOMAS DAY
FROM *THE DYING NEGRO*

– O my lov'd bride! – for I have call'd thee mine,
Dearer than life, whom I with life resign,
For thee ev'n here this faithful heart shall glow,
A pang shall rend me, and a tear shall flow.
How shall I soothe thy grief, since fate denies
Thy pious duties to my closing eyes?
I cannot clasp thee in a last embrace,
Nor gaze in silent anguish on thy face;
I cannot raise these fetter'd arms for thee,
To ask that mercy heav'n denies to me;
Yet let thy tender breast my sorrows share,
Bleed for my wounds, and feel my deep despair.
Yet let thy tears bedew a wretch's grave,
Whom Fate forbade thy tenderness to save.
Receive these sighs – to thee my soul I breathe,
Fond love in dying groans is all I can bequeath.

    Why did I, slave, beyond my lot aspire?
Why didst thou fan the inauspicious fire?
For thee I bade my drooping soul revive;
For thee alone I could have borne to live;
And love, I said, shall make me large amends,
For persecuting foes, and faithless friends:
Fool that I was! enur'd so long to pain,
To trust to hope, or dream of joy again.
Joy, stranger guest, my easy faith betray'd,
And love now points to death's eternal shade;
There, while I rest from mis'ry's galling load,
Be thou the care of ev'ry pitying God;
Nor may that Daemon's unpropitious pow'r,
Who shed influence on my natal hour,
Pursue thee too with unrelenting hate,
And blend with mine the colour of thy fate.
For thee may those soft hours return again,
When pleasure led thee smiling o'er the plain.
Ere, like some hell-born spectre of dismay,
I cross'd thy path, and darken'd all the way.

THOMAS DAY

[... The "Dying Negro" recounts how he was sold into slavery]

Ye Gods of Afric! in that dreadful hour
Where were your thunders and avenging pow'r!
Did not my pray'rs, my groans, my tears invoke
Your slumb'ring justice to direct the stroke?
No pow'r descended to assist the brave,
No lightnings flash'd, and I became a slave.
From lord to lord my wretched carcase sold,
In Christian traffic, for their sordid gold:
Fate's blackest clouds were gather'd o'er my head;
And, bursting now, they mix me with the dead.

    Yet when my fortune cast my lot with thine,
And bade beneath one roof our labours join,
Surpriz'd I felt the tumults of my breast,
Lull'd by thy beauties to unwonted rest.
Delusive hopes my changing soul enflame,
And gentler transports agitate my frame.
What tho' obscure thy birth, superior grace
Shone in the glowing features of thy face.
Ne'er had my youth such winning softness seen,
Where Afric's sable beauties dance the green,
 When some sweet maid receives her lover's vow,
And binds the offer'd chaplet to her brow.
While on thy languid eyes I fondly gaze,
And trembling meet the lustre of their rays,
Thou, gentle virgin, thou didst not despise
The humble homage of a captive's sighs.
By heav'n abandon'd, and by man betray'd
Each hope reign'd of comfort or of aid,
Thy gen'rous love could ev'ry sorrow end,
In thee I found a mistress and a friend:
Still as I told the story of my woes,
With heaving sighs thy lovely bosom rose:
The trickling drops of liquid crystal stole
Down thy fair cheek and mark'd thy pitying soul:
Dear drops! upon my bleeding heart, like balm
They fell, and soon my tortur'd mind grew calm;
Then my lov'd country, parents, friends forgot,

THOMAS DAY

Heav'n I absolv'd, nor murmur'd at my lot;
Thy sacred smiles could ev'ry pang remove,
And liberty became less dear than love.

    -- And I have lov'd thee with as pure a fire,
As man e'er felt, or woman could inspire:
No pangs like these my pallid tyrants know,
Not such their transports, and not such their woe.
Their softer frames a feeble soul conceal,
A soul unus'd to pity or to feel;
Damp'd by base lucre, and repell'd by fear,
Each nobler passion faintly blazes here.
Not such the mortals burning Afric breeds,
Mother of virtues and heroic deeds!
Descended from yon radiant orb, they claim
Sublimer courage, and a fiercer flame.
Nature has there, unchill'd by art, imprest
 Her awful majesty on ev'ry breast.
Where'er she leads, impatient of controul,
The dauntless Negro rushes to the goal;
Firm in his love, resistless in his hate,
His arm is conquest, and his frown is fate.

    What fond affection in my bosom reigns!
What soft emotions mingle with my pains!
Still as thy form before my mind appears,
My haggard eyes are bath'd in gushing tears;
Thy lov'd idea rushes to my heart,
And stern despair suspends the lifted dart –
O could I burst these fetters which restrain
My struggling limbs, and waft thee o'er the main
To some far distant shore, where Ocean roars
In horrid tempests round the gloomy shores;
To some wild mountain's solitary shade,
Where never European faith betray'd;
How joyful could I, of thy love secure,
Meet ev'ry danger, ev'ry toil endure!
For thee I'd climb the rock, explore the flood,
And tame the famish'd savage of the wood.
When forthcoming summer drinks the shrinking streams,
My care should screen thee from its sultry beams;

THOMAS DAY

At noon I'd crown thee with the fairest flowers,
At eve I'd lead thee to the safest bowers;
And when bleak winter howl'd around the cave,
For thee his horrors and his storms I'd brave;
Nor snows nor raging winds should damp my soul,
Nor such a night as shrouds the dusky pole:
O'er the dark waves my bounding skiff I'd guide,
To pierce each mightier monster of the tide;
Thro' frozen forests force my dreadful way,
In their own dens to rouse the beasts of prey;
Nor other blessing ask, if this might prove
How fix'd my passion, and how fond my love.
– Then should vain fortune to my sight display
All that her anger has now snatch'd away;
Treasures more vast than Av'rice e'er design'd
In midnight visions to a Christian's mind;
The Monarch's diamed, the Conqu'ror's meed,
That empty prize for which the valiant bleed;
All that ambition strives to snatch from fate,
All that the Gods e'er lavish'd in their hate;
Not these should win my lover from my arms,
Or tempt a moment's absence from thy charms;
Indignant would I fly these guilty climes,
And scorn their glories as I hate their crimes!

      But whither does my wand'ring fancy rove?
Hence ye wild wishes of desponding love!
– Ah! where is now that voice which lull'd my woes;
That Angel-face, which sooth'd me to repose?
By Nature tempted, and with passion blind,
Are these the joys Hope whisper'd to my mind?
Is this the end of constancy like thine?
Are these the transports of a love like mine?
My hopes, my joys, are vanish'd into air,
And now of all that once engag'd my care,
These chains alone remain, this weapon and despair.

      – So be thy life's gay prospects all o'ercast,
All thy fond hopes dire disappointment blast!
Thus end thy golden visions, son of pride!
Whose ruthless ruffians tore me from my bride;

THOMAS DAY

That beauteous prize Heav'n had reserv'd at last,
Sweet recompence for all my sorrows past.
O may thy harden'd bosom never prove
The tender joys of friendship or of love!
Yet may'st thou, doom'd to hopeless flames a prey,
In unrequited passion pine away!
May ev'ry transport violate thy rest,
Which tears the jealous lover's gloomy breast!
May secret anguish gnaw thy cruel heart,
'Till death in all his terrors wing the dart;
Then, to complete the horror of thy doom,
A favour'd rival smile upon thy tomb!

      Why does my ling'ring soul her flight delay?
Come, lovely maid, and gild the dreary way!
Come, wildly rushing with disorder'd charms,
And clasp thy bleeding lover in thy arms;
Close his sad eyes, receive his parting breath,
And sooth him sinking to the shades of death!
O come – thy presence can my pangs beguile,
And bid th'inexorable tyrant smile;
Transported will I languish on thy breast,
And sink enraptur'd to eternal rest:
The hate of men, the wrongs of fate forgive,
Forget my woes, and almost wish to live.
– Ah! rather fly, lest ought of doubt controul
The dreadful purpose lab'ring in my soul;
Tears must not bend me, nor thy beauties move,
This hour I triumph over fate and love.

"T"

ON SEEING A BEAUTIFUL YOUNG LADY KISS A BLACK BOY

Whoever saw a contrast half so true?
The spotless ivory with the ebon view!
Was such Adonis when the Queen of Love
Prais'd all his charms – and did his form approve?
Thrice happy boy, to riot in such bliss,
And take from beauty's lips a virgin kiss!
To have the sweet distinction, I would be
As Æthiop black; – O to be kiss'd by thee
Is such a rapture, that by Jove I'd part
With every worth – since I have pledg'd my heart.
Thus *Cato*'s daughter, in the day of Rome,
On black *Numidia*'s prince bestow'd her bloom;
Juba with rapture took the patriot maid,
And bless'd his *Marcia* in the rural shade.
More black than *Juba* is thy Æthiop boy,
And thou more fair than *Marcia* crown'st his joy.
Thrice happy boy – with such a mistress kind,
With spotless manners, and the purest mind.

JAMES DE-LA-COUR

IN PRAISE OF A NEGRESS

What shape I have, that form is all my own,
To art a stranger, and to modes unknown;
To paint or patches, perfum'd fraud, no friend,
Nor know what stays or honey-water mend:
No spotted moons deform my jetty face,
I would be blacker than that speckled race!
My simple lotion is the purer rain,
And e'en that wash is labour took in vain.
But my pearl teeth, without tobacco's aid,
On snow or Indian iv'ry cast a shade!
My eyes eclipse the stars in all their flame,
Such as may not e'en Albion's daughters shame!
My softer skin with the mole's velvet vies,
Ah! who will on these altars sacrifice?
But if I please less in the sultry day,
My colour with the candle dies away;
Since to our hue the light is deem'd a foe,
Night will a THAIS in my charms bestow.

JULIUS SOUBISE
LETTER, FROM *NOCTURNAL REVELS*

DEAR MISS,

    I HAVE often beheld you in public with rapture; indeed it is impossible to view you without such emotions as must animate every man of sentiment. In a word, Madam, you have seized my heart, and I dare tell you I am your *Negro Slave*. You startle at this expression, Madam; but I love to be sincere. I am of that swarthy race of ADAM, whom some despise on account of their complexion; but I begin to find from experience, that even this trial of our patience may last but for a time, as Providence has given such knowledge to Man, as to remedy all the evils of this life. There is not a disorder under the sun which may not, by the skill and industry of the learned, be removed: so do I find, that similar applications in the researches of medicine, have brought to bear such discoveries, as to remove the tawny hue of any complexion, if applied with skill and perseverance. In this pursuit, my dear Miss, I am resolutely engaged, and hope, in a few weeks, I may be able to throw myself at your feet, in as agreeable a form as you can desire; in the mean time, believe me with the greatest sincerity,
    Yours most devotedly,
        My Lovely Angel,
            S——SE.

OLAUDAH EQUIANO
FROM A LETTER TO JAMES TOBIN

In a word, the public can bear testimony with me that you are a malicious slanderer of an honest, industrious, injured people!

From the same source of malevolence the freedom of their inclinations is to be shackled – it is not so sufficient for their bodies to be oppressed, but their minds must also? Iniquity in the extreme! If the mind of a black man conceives the passion of love for a fair female, he is to pine, languish, and even die, sooner than an intermarriage be allowed, merely because the complexion of the offspring should be tawney – a more foolish prejudice than this never warped a cultivated mind – for as no contamination of the virtues of the heart would result from the union, the mixture of colour could be of no consequence. God looks with equal good-will on all his creatures, whether black or white – let neither, therefore, arrogantly condemn the other.

The mutual commerce of the sexes of both Blacks and Whites, under the restrictions of moderation and law, would yield more benefit than a prohibition – the mind free would not have such a strong propensity toward the black females as when under restraint: Nature abhors restraint, and for ease either evades or breaks it. Hence arise secret amours, adultery, fornication and all other evils of lasciviousness! Hence that most abandoned boasting of the French Planter, who, under the dominion of lust, had the shameless impudence to exult at the violations he had committed against Virtue, Religion, and the Almighty – hence also spring actual murders on infants, the procuring of abortions, enfeebled constitutions, disgrace, shame, and a thousand other horrid enormities.

Now, Sir, would it not be more honour to us to have a few darker visages than perhaps yours among us, than inundation of such evils? and to provide effectual remedies, by a liberal policy against evils which may be traced to some of our most wealthy Planters as their fountain, and which may have smeared the purity of even your own chastity?

As the ground-work, why not establish intermarriages at home, and in our Colonies? and encourage open, free, and generous love upon Nature's own wide and extensive plan, subservient only to moral rectitude, without distinctions of the colour of a skin?

OLAUDAH EQUIANO

That ancient, most wise, and inspired politician, Moses, encouraged strangers to unite with the Israelites, upon this maxim, that every addition to their number was an addition to their strength, and as an inducement, admitted them to most of the immunities of his own people. He established marriage with strangers by his own example – the Lord confirmed them – and punished Aaron and Miriam for vexing their brother for marrying the Ethiopian. Away then with your narrow impolitic notion of preventing by law what will be a national honour, national strength, and productive of national virtue – Intermarriages!

Wherefore, to conclude in the words of one of your selected texts, "If I come, I will remember the deeds which he doeth, prating against us with malicious words."

I am Sir,
Your fervent Servant,
GUSTAVUS VASSA, the Ethiopian
and the King's late Commissary for the African Settlement.
Baldwin's Garden, Jan.1788.

WILLIAM BLAKE
THE LITTLE BLACK BOY

MY mother bore me in the southern wild,
    And I am black, but O, my soul is white!
White as an angel is the English child,
    But I am black, as if bereaved of light.

My mother taught me underneath a tree,
    And, sitting down before the heat of day,
She took me on her lap and kissèd me,
    And, pointing to the East, began to say:

"Look at the rising sun: there God does live,
    And gives His light, and gives His heat away,
And flowers and trees and beasts and men receive
    Comfort in morning, joy in the noonday.

"And we are put on earth a little space,
    That we may learn to bear the beams of love;
And these black bodies and this sunburnt face
    Are but a cloud, and like a shady grove.

"For when our souls have learn'd the heat to bear,
    The cloud will vanish; we shall hear His voice,
Saying, 'Come out from the grove, my love and care,
    And round my golden tent like lambs rejoice.' "

Thus did my mother say, and kissèd me,
    And thus I say to little English boy.
When I from black and he from white cloud free,
    And round the tent of God like lambs we joy,

I'll shade him from the heat till he can bear
    To lean in joy upon our Father's knee;
And then I'll stand and stroke his silver hair,
    And be like him, and he will then love me.

JOHN COLLINS

CONJUGAL CREDULITY
(Founded on Fact)

Blind Wittols will wink at their Spouses' defects,
When as plain as the sun at noon day;
And suppose Madam's honour their temples protects,
From the weapons of Bucks when at bay.

Thus a Planter, who liv'd in Antigua's warm isle,
Whose Wife took a Black to her bed;
With Raleigh's fam'd plant all his cares would beguile,
While She planted Horns on his head.

For he smok'd it by night and he smok'd it by day,
From his pipe never wishing to stir;
And though He, for her jigging, the piper must pay,
'Tis certain he never smok'd Her.

When at length pregnant symptoms of danger appear'd,
Which, in less than nine months must make known,
Whether young Pickaninny, with Sable besmear'd,
The good man would embrace as his own.

Such a plight to be in, she perceiv'd with alarm,
When on taking the Midwife aside,
She thought the best way to prevent future harm,
Was in her secret faith to confide.

So the whole truth came out, who the brat had begot,
And what colour of course he must be;
When the matron heard all, and surpis'd not a jot,
Reply'd, "Leave the matter to me:

I'll make old Corunto leap out of his skin,
Or near it, for joy of an heir,
And all ears to remove, a fine tale will I spin,
Which to swallow, I'm sure he won't spare.

For you're Longing for Charcoal's the thing I'll avow,
And in secret you've told it to me;

JOHN COLLINS

That you've got a strange whim, and 'tis strange I'll allow,
To devour it where no one can see."

The scheme thus concerted, Old Goody repair'd
To the husband, to wish him much joy;
"For," says she, "my good Sir, all your pray'rs have been heard,
And you'll soon have a fine chopping Boy:

Or suppose it a Girl, 'tis your own flesh and blood,
And you'll not want an heir for your wealth;
But I've found out a thing that must not be withstood,
And the thing must be done, too, by stealth.

Madam's longing for Charcoal, and, wond'rous to tell,
Though miscarriage and death should ensue,
If not plac'd in the dark at her bedside, – full well
I'm assured, not a grain will she chew.

But I'll undertake, if you'll say but the word,
That when you fast asleep seem to lie,
She'll crunch it and munch it, so sharply she's spurr'd,
Her capricious odd gust to supply."

"Eat Charcoal! Lord, Lord, (says the husband) how strange!
The thought fills me full of dejection."
"Phoo, phoo, (replies Goody) at worst 'twill but change
The young Hans in Kelder's complexion.

And what if it does, be the Bairn fair or brown,
'Tis better than no Bairn at all;
For if still-born the Babe, 'twill be murder you'll own,
If as white as a Greenland snowball."

With reluctance the Husband his doubts did dismiss,
And the Charcoal was plac'd as directed,
For Madam to munch in the dark, – but mark this –
Sugar Candy the business effected.

So forth from her pocket the sweetmeat she drew,
And she crunch'd it with glee in the dark,

JOHN COLLINS

While in pocket, the Charcoal was hid from all view,
When at morn rose the old doting spark.

Yet so stinted the medicine was every night,
That the Midwife betrayed many fears;
If the poor little thing should at last see the light,
That 'twould live but a very few years.

"May be so," says the Husband, "but this I'll be sworn,
Long or short let its life be ordain'd,
I'd rather 'twould kick up as soon as 'twas born,
Than my wife should with slander be stain'd.

For the neighbours will say, if I give her too much,
Being ignorant all of the cause,
When they see a black dye the young bantling besmutch,
That the mother has made some Fore Paws.

And crouds after crouds, then to scandal's foul school,
Will, to make game of me, every one go;
Saying, she's a young strumpet, and I an old fool,
That have got for an heir a young Mungo."

When, the sequel to wind up, on one Monday morn,
And a black Monday 'twas to be sure,
Young Snowball as black as an Æthiop was born,
And his colour no washing could cure.

"Look you there," says the midwife, "I knew how 'twould be,
Had you given her Charcoal enough,
Instead of this sable complexion you see,
You had saved the young gentleman's buff."

"Hold your tongue, you damn'd jade," says the Husband, quite mad,
"'Tis the Charcoal has caus'd all this evil,
And I'm sure if a single grain more she had had,
My poor boy had been black as the devil."

FELICIA DOROTHEA HEMANS
FROM *THE SIEGE OF VALENCIA*

Hernandez
Read you no records in this mien, of things
Whose traces on man's aspect are not such
As the breeze leaves on the water? – Lofty birth,
War, peril, power? – Affliction's hand is strong,
If it erase the haughty characters
They grave so deep! – I have not always been
That which I am. The name I bore is not
Of those which perish! – I was once a chief –
A warrior! – nor, as now, a lonely man!
I was a father!

Elmina
                 Then thy heart can *feel*!
Thou wilt have pity!

Hernandez
                 Should I pity *thee*?
Thy sons will perish gloriously – their blood –

Elmina
Their blood! My children's blood! – Thou speak'st as 'twere
Of casting down a wine-cup, in the mirth
And wantonness of feasting! – My fair boys!
– Man! Hast *thou* been a father?

Hernandez
                 Let them die!
Let them die *now*, thy children! So thy heart
Shall wear their beautiful image all undimm'd
Within it, to the last! Nor shalt thou learn
The bitter lesson, of what worthless dust
Are framed the idols, whose false glory binds
Earth's fetter on our souls! – Thou think'st it much
To mourn the early dead; but there are tears
Heavy with deeper anguish! We endow
Those who we love, in our fond passionate blindness,
With power upon our souls, too absolute

FELICIA DOROTHEA HEMANS

To be a mortal's trust! Within their hands
We lay the flaming sword, whose stroke alone
Can reach our hearts, and *they* are merciful,
As they are strong, that wield it not to pierce us!
– Aye, fear them, fear the loved! – Had I but wept
O'er my son's grave, as o'er a babe's where tears
Are as spring dew-drops, glittering in the sun,
And brightening the young vedure, I might still
Have loved and trusted!

Elmina (disdainfully)
                        But he fell in war!
And hath not glory medicine in her cup
For the brief pangs of nature?

Hernandez
                        Glory! – Peace,
And listen! – By my side the stripling grew,
Last of my line. I rear'd him to take joy
I' th' blaze of arms, as eagles train their young
To look upon the day-king! – His quick blood
Ev'n to his boyish cheek would mantle up,
When the heavens rang with trumpets, and his eye
Flash with the spirit of a race whose deeds –
But this availeth not! – Yet he *was* brave.
I've seen him clear himself a path in fight
As lightning through a forest, and his plume
Waved like a torch, above the battle-storm,
The soldier's guide, when princely crests had sunk,
And banners were struck down. – Around my steps
Floated his fame, like music, and I lived
But in the lofty sounds. But when my heart
In one frail ark had ventur'd all, when most
He seem'd to stand between my soul and heaven,
– Then came the thunder-stroke!

Elmina
                    'Tis ever thus!
And the unquiet and foreboding sense
That thus 'twill ever be, doth link itself

FELICIA DOROTHEA HEMANS

Darkly with all deep love! He died?

Hernandez
                                                    Not so!
– Death! Death! – Why, earth should be a paradise,
To make that name so fearful! – Had he died,
With his young fame about him for a shroud,
I had not learn'd the might of agony,
To bring proud natures low! – No! he fell off –
Why do I tell thee this? – What right hast *thou*
To learn how pass'd the glory from my house?
Yet listen! – He forsook me! – He, that was
As mine own soul, forsook me! trampled o'er
The ashes of his sires! – Aye, leagued himself
E'en with the infidel, the curse of Spain,
And, for the dark eye of a Moorish maid,
Abjured his faith, his God! – Now, talk of death!

Elmina
Oh! I can pity thee –

Hernandez
                        There's more to hear.
I braced the corslet o'er my heart's deep wound,
And cast my troubled spirit on the tide
Of war and high events, whose stormy waves
Might bear it up from sinking –

Elmina
                                And ye met
No more?

Hernandez
                Be still! – We did! – we met *once more*.
God had his own high purpose to fulfil,
Or think'st thou that the sun in his bright heaven
Had look'd upon such things? – We met once more.
– That was an hour to leave its lightning-mark
Sear'd upon brain and bosom! – there had been
Combat on Ebro's banks, and when the day

FELICIA DOROTHEA HEMANS

Sank in red clouds, it faded from a field
Still held by Moorish lances. Night closed round,
A night of sultry darkness, in the shadow
Of whose broad wing, e'en unto death I strove
Long with a turban'd champion; but my sword
Was heavy with God's vengeance – and prevail'd.
He fell – my heart exulted – and I stood
In gloomy triumph o'er him – Nature gave
No sign of horror, for 'twas Heaven's decree!
He strove to speak – but I had done the work
Of wrath too well – yet in his last deep moan
A dreadful something of familiar sound
Came o'er my shuddering sense. – The moon look'd forth,
And I beheld – speak not! – 'twas he – my son!
My boy lay dying there! He raised one glance,
And knew me – for he sought with feeble hand
To cover his glazed eyes. A darker veil
Sank o'er them soon. – I will not have thy look
Fix'd on me thus! – Away!

RUDYARD KIPLING

THE LADIES

I've taken my fun where I've found it;
    I've rogued an' I've ranged in my time;
I've 'ad my pickin' o' sweet'earts,
    An' four o' the lot was prime.
One was an 'arf-caste widow,
    One was a woman at Prome,
One was the wife of a *jemadar-sais*,
    An' one is a girl at 'ome.

CHORUS
Now I aren't no 'and with the ladies,
    For, takin' 'em all along,
You never can say till you've tried 'em,
    An' then you are like to be wrong.
There's times when you'll think that you mightn't,
    There's times when you'll know that you might;
But the things you will learn from the Yellow an' Brown,
    They'll 'elp you a lot with the White!

I was a young un at 'Oogli,
    Shy as a girl to begin;
Aggie de Castrer she made me,
    An' Aggie was clever as sin;
Older than me, but my first un –
    More like a mother she were –
Showed me the way to promotion an' pay,
    An' I learned about women from 'er!

CHORUS
Now I aren't no 'and with the ladies,
    For, takin' 'em all along, &c.

Then I was ordered to Burma,
    Actin' in charge o' Bazaar,
An' I got me a tiddy live 'eathen
    Through buyin' supplies off 'er pa.
Funny an' yellow an' faithful –
    Doll in a teacup she were,

But we lived on the square, like a true-married pair,
   And I learned about women from 'er!

CHORUS
Now I aren't no 'and with the ladies,
   For, takin' 'em all along, &c.

Then we was shifted to Neemuch
   (Or I might ha' been keepin' 'er now)
An' I took with a shiny she-devil,
   The wife of a nigger at Mhow;
Taught me the gipsy-folks' bolee;
   Kind o' volcano she were,
For she knifed me one night 'cause I wished she were white,
   And I learned about women from 'er!

CHORUS
Now I aren't no 'and with the ladies,
   For, takin' 'em all along, &c.

Then I come 'ome in the trooper,
   'Long of a kid o' sixteen –
Girl from a convent at Meerut,
   The straightest I have ever seen.
Love at first sight was 'er trouble.
   She didn't know what it were;
An' I wouldn't do such, 'cause I liked 'er too much,
   But – I learned about women from 'er!

CHORUS
Now I aren't no 'and with the ladies,
   For, takin' 'em all along, &c.

I've taken my fun where I've found it,
   An' now I must pay for my fun,
For the more you 'ave known o' the others
   The less you will settle for one;
An' the end of it's sittin' and thinkin',
   An' dreamin' Hell-fires to see;
So be warned by my lot (which I know you will not)
   An' learn about women from me!

II.

THE BRITISH IN THE AMERICAS

The discovery of Christopher Columbus on a beach in the Bahamas in 1492 by the native Taino inhabitants precipitated a cataclysmic transformation of the continent that would come to be known as America – or 'the Americas' as it is more often referred to now, due to the United States' appropriation for itself of the term America. In the centuries that followed those Tainos' first encounter with the sailor who designated them 'Indians' on account of his faulty grasp of geography, the continent – soon recognised by the Europeans to be not in fact India but a (to them) 'New World' – was conquered by rival colonial powers, its peoples exterminated and enslaved. Lands were settled by colonialists and natural resources expropriated and shipped back across the Atlantic. From the sixteenth century the drive to produce staples for expanding markets in Europe resulted in the establishment of plantation agriculture in parts of South and Central America, across the Caribbean, and in the southern area of North America. Initially, enslaved native peoples and indentured Europeans were used as labour, but the demands of the plantation regime meant the colonists soon turned to Africa in their efforts to secure an expanded workforce. By the late nineteenth century more than ten million Africans had been forcibly transported to the 'New World', many others having died en route amidst the horrendous conditions on board the slave ships. Once there they were consumed by the plantation system, their labour swallowed up in the production of commodities including sugar, tobacco, coffee, and cotton.[1]

With the initial conquest of the continent had come an avalanche of explorers, adventurers, and missionaries, soon followed by a slew of botanists, ethnographers, anthropologists, biologists, cartographers, geographers and other travellers. As this swarm descended under the signs of the cross and sword – or the market and the taxonomic grid – to colonise, brutalise, categorise, and chronicle the native inhabitants of the Americas, they became physically, culturally, and discursively entangled with those whose lives they were subjecting to violent and often fatal disruption. Similarly, the growth of plantation slavery meant not only further travelogues and treatises concerning (and usually attempting to justify) the circumstances of the enslaved; it also placed the coloniser in close proximity to the

---

[1] See Sidney Mintz, *Sweetness and Power: The Place of Sugar in Modern History* (New York: Penguin, 1985).

colonised within a framework of domination that bred the conditions for the systematic sexual abuse of African women. The diaries of Thomas Thistlewood, for example, a planter and overseer in Jamaica in the eighteenth century, record his ferocious sexual exploitation of female slaves, as well as the perverse methods of torture he invented to punish his labourers, during the years 1750 to 1786. The atrocities recounted by Thistlewood are such that they might appear the aberrations of a singularly grotesque sadist; yet as James Walvin points out, Thistlewood in fact may "have been no worse, no more violent or predatory, than many other whites who masterminded the slave societies of the Americas; what distinguished Thistlewood from the thousands of other men like him was the simple fact that he kept a diary".[2]

The sexual abuse of the enslaved came to be condemned by some colonists, not out of any sympathy with the oppressed (indeed, many contemporary commentators such as Edward Long blamed the 'licentious' ways of the black woman[3]) but because such practices raised the spectre of miscegenation. In addition to fuelling fears over biological and cultural 'contamination' and 'degeneration' brought on by contact with other races, miscegenation threatened to collapse the hierarchies of colour erected by the Europeans to justify their subordination of black and brown peoples. However – perhaps, as we will see in a moment, because of the need to preserve these hierarchies by mystifying them – there were explorers and colonists who represented the sexual relations between masters and slaves, or settlers and natives, not in their brutal reality but in terms of a romantic union (indeed, one of the extraordinary things about Thistlewood's diaries is that alongside his appalling sexual abuses they also document his seemingly genuine and longstanding romantic affection for one of his slaves, Phibbah, whom he took as his common law wife in 1754). These romantic depictions of interracial contact are obviously highly problematic: not only do they frequently reduce the native or the enslaved to an exotic stereotype or alluring fantasy of

---

[2] James Walvin, *The Trader, The Owner, The Slave* (London: Jonathan Cape, 2007), pp. 172-73. See also Douglas Hall, *In Miserable Slavery: Thomas Thistlewood in Jamaica 1750-86* (Kingston: University of the West Indies Press).
[3] Edward Long, The History of Jamaica (1774; rpt London: Frank Cass, 1970), Vol. II.

Otherness, but also they work to occlude the real power relations and conditions of exploitation under which such 'romances' were conducted. A common ploy, for instance, is for the colonial representation to speak not of the physical chains of slavery but of the affective bonds of love, thereby portraying the domination of the colonised by the coloniser as willing submission on the part of the former.[4]

This section presents a selection of accounts by British travellers and colonists in the Americas, which reflect this romanticising and mystification of the colonial encounter. Included here also are extracts from writers who never visited the 'New World' but whose fictions draw on the travellers' tales being sent back from across the Atlantic as well as on fantasies of the exotic Other and fears over miscegenation. However, a handful of the selected texts complicate this picture through their recording – or, more accurately, their representation – of the voice of the colonised in the form of songs sung by the enslaved. While these representations clearly translate, distort, edit, and censure the words of the colonised, nevertheless they point to a subversive oral tradition that sought to resist the stereotypes and ideological frameworks imposed by the coloniser. As Jean D'Costa and Barbara Lalla observe, even in "the novels and travelogues written by white visitors survive echoes of the voice of those who, having neither quill nor printing press, left the mark of their exile upon the minds of white observers".[5] In fact, the final piece included here departs from our criterion of British writers to include the fiction of an aboriginal Canadian. In 'A Red Girl's Reasoning', Tekahionwake – who was born in 1861 to an English mother and a Native Canadian father – dramatises the tensions in the marriage between the aboriginal Christine and the white Charlie McDonald, ultimately showing Christine re-asserting her agency and cultural history in the face of Charlie's racism: "Why should I" she protests, "recognise the rites of your nation when you do not recognise the rites of mine?"

The opening extract in this section, however, returns us to the initial encounter between settler and native on 'New

---

[4] See Mary Louise Pratt, *Imperial Eyes: Travel Writing and Transculturation* (New York: Routledge, 1992), p.97.

[5] Jean D'Costa and Barbara Lalla, *Voices in Exile: Jamaican Texts of the 18th and 19th Centuries* (Tuscaloosa: University of Alabama Press, 1989), p.8.

World' soil. First performed in 1611, Shakespeare's *The Tempest* draws upon accounts of voyages to the Americas circulating at the time it was written.[6] Although there is some controversy as to where exactly the play is set, the characters of Prospero and Caliban, the exiled European Duke and the native inhabitant of an island now controlled by the former, certainly seem to represent the positions of planter/master and native/slave (indeed, Caliban's name would appear to be an anagram of cannibal, itself a derivative of the word Carib, the name of a native tribe in the Americas).[7] In the passage presented here many key colonial issues are raised: Prospero's appropriation not only of the island, but also of Caliban's knowledge of his mother Sycorax's "charms"; the imposition of colonial culture upon the colonised (specifically here, language – "You taught me language, and my profit on't / Is I know how to curse"); and perhaps most importantly in our context, fears over miscegenation and the threat this could pose to the colonial order (the suggestion that Caliban tried to rape Miranda and his declaration that he should have "peopled else / This isle with Calibans").

The letter from John Rolfe, written in 1614, recounts another relationship that has become paradigmatic of early interracial contact in the Americas, that between Rolfe himself, a colonist and tobacco planter in Jamestown, Virginia, and Pocahontas, a Native American princess, daughter of the leader of the Powhatan federation. Pocahontas was kidnapped by the Jamestown settlers in 1613, eventually learning English and converting to Christianity. She married Rolfe in 1614 and travelled with him to England two years later. The representation of the relationship between the pair has frequently been drawn in those mystifying terms sketched above, with their transracial love becoming a figure for, as Peter Hulme puts it, "the ideal of cultural harmony through romance" – an ideal that tends to occlude the real violence of the colonial encounter.[8]

John Dryden's *The Indian Emperour*, from 1665 presents

---

[6] See Frank Kermode, 'Introduction' in William Shakespeare, *The Tempest* (London: Methuen, 1969), p.xxvii.
[7] Ibid, p.xxiv.
[8] Peter Hulme, *Colonial Encounters: Europe and the Native Caribbean, 1492-1791* (New York: Methuen, 1986), p.141.

a similar colonial-native relationship, albeit a fictional one. Set against the backdrop of the conquest of Mexico by the Spanish in the sixteenth century, the play dramatises the lives of the historical figures Hernán Cortés, the Spanish conquistador, and Montezuma, the Aztec king. However, Dryden fabricates a love story between Cortés and Montezuma's daughter, Cydaria. Again, this romance is used to mystify the violence of conquest, here helping in the construction of a spurious distinction between 'good' and 'bad' colonialisms designed to justify English claims to 'New World' territory over Spanish ones.[9]

Both Aphra Behn's *The Widow Ranter*, a play published posthumously in 1689, and Stephen Duck's *Avaro and Amanda*, published in 1736, present interracial love affairs between Englishmen and Native American women. Behn's hero, Nathanial Bacon (based on an historical figure), becomes dissatisfied with the colonial government in Virginia, believing it to be ineffective at keeping order in the colony. He rebels and launches his own attack on the local native tribes. However, Bacon is also in love with the Indian Queen, Semernia, who likewise loves him yet has been forcibly married to an Indian King. Ultimately Bacon kills Semernia by accident after she enters a battle against him disguised as a man (Semernia had felt duty bound to avenge the death of her husband at the hands of Bacon, despite her feelings for the latter). Duck's long poem is a re-working of the Inkle and Yarico story, also represented here by George Colman's comic opera, first staged in 1787. There are numerous versions of this tale of a love affair between an English trader, Inkle, and an Indian princess, Yarico, most of which derive from Richard Ligon's brief account of the story in his *True and Exact History of the Island of Barbadoes* (1657).[10] In Colman's opera, Inkle and Yarico's relationship is paralleled by that between their respective servants, Trudge and Wowski. Colman also altered the ending of the story from that found in earlier versions: whereas Inkle usually ends up betraying Yarico and selling her into slavery, here he has a change of heart and the pair are reconciled.

---

[9] See Paulina Kewes, "Dryden's Theatre and the Passions of Politics" in Stephen N. Zwicker, *The Cambridge Companion to John Dryden* (Cambridge: Cambridge University Press, 2004), p.137.
[10] See Frank Felsenstein, *English Trader, Indian Maid: Representing Gender, Race, and Slavery in the New World* (Baltimore: Johns Hopkins University Press, 1999).

The 1720 novel *The Voyages, Dangerous Adventures, and Imminent Escapes of Captain Richard Falconer* by the London playwright William Rufus Chetwood likewise features an interracial love affair between an Englishman – in this case, an adventurer, Falconer, who is shipwrecked on his way to Virginia – and a Native American woman. Chetwood's breathless narrative careers through a series of escapades, including marriage to his lover and the latter's death as she tries to protect Falconer from attack by Indians.

Isaac Teale's 'The Sable Venus' is a panegyric to black beauty. Teale was a Church of England clergyman who went to Jamaica and served as teacher and mentor to the white historian Bryan Edwards. The poem was written in 1765 and later included by Edwards in his own collection, *Poems Written Chiefly in the West Indies* (1792). It was, according to Barbara Bush, "one of the most powerful eighteenth-century constructs of African womanhood, which reflected white male obsessions with sexual otherness and exoticism".[11] While the poem "explores the complex nature of black-white romantic relationships in a slave society",[12] it once again mystifies out of the picture the harsh reality of slave labour.

John Gabriel Stedman's depiction of his relationship with the slave Joanna in his *Narrative of a Five Years Expedition Against the Revolted Negroes of Surinam* (1796) performs a similar manoeuvre, only here the tone is more sentimental in comparison to Teale's lusting paean. Stedman went to Surinam in 1772, and his Narrative chronicles not only his experiences there, but also the flora and fauna he encountered, his military campaigns, and his romantic attachment to Joanna. Stedman initially wishes to buy Joanna and return with her to England, but she refuses him. Later she has something of a mysterious change of heart, throwing herself at Stedman's feet (though she still refuses to travel to England). The two settle down together and have a son. When Stedman is recalled to Europe in 1777 he tries once more to persuade Joanna to accompany him, but again she refuses. Stedman leaves, ultimately marrying someone else

---

[11] Barbara Bush, "'Sable Venus', 'She Devil' or 'Drudge'? British Slavery and the 'Fabulous Fiction' of Black Women's Identities, c. 1650-1838", *Women's History Review*, 9:4 (2000), p.770.
[12] James G. Basker, *Amazing Grace, An Anthology of Poetry About Slavery, 1660-1810* (New Haven and London: Yale University Press, 2002), p.146.

in Europe; Joanna stays in Surinam, where she dies five years later, poisoned by jealous rivals in the colony. Although in his *Narrative* Stedman indicted slavery (or, more particularly, the conditions in which slaves in Surinam were kept), the representation of his relationship with Joanna – touching though it might appear at times – seems complicit with the same desire to occlude the concrete power relations underpinning the plantation regime. By representing the relationship between the coloniser and colonised as one of reciprocity and willed submission based on love, the coloniser can attempt to bypass the messy issue of coercion and domination.[13]

The extracts from the works of J. B. Moreton, Mathew G. Lewis, and Michael Scott all feature slave songs that, while distorted by their scribal reproduction by the coloniser, nevertheless provide echoes of the voices of the colonised. Scott's account of the John Canoe (Jonkonnu) song in his novel *Tom Cringle's Log* traces, as Carolyn Cooper puts it, "Massa Buccra's gradual path from the soft, silken dove of his white love, to the brown girl, and, ultimately, we may presume, to the black devil herself."[14] By contrast, the song reproduced by Lewis – author of the infamous Gothic thriller *The Monk* (1796) in addition to being a planter in Jamaica – describes the "black boy" Peter being enticed away by the "white girl" Lilly. In the songs reproduced by Moreton – a British bookkeeper in Jamaica whose *West India Customs and Manners* first appeared in 1790 – we get some sense of the black woman's perception of the sexual labour she is forced to perform, alongside her subversion of the proprieties of colonial manners through the riotous vulgarity of the lyrics. As Cooper observes, "English grammar and metre are imposed on the Jamaican text but the essential meaning of the song – its subversively vulgar intention – seems to have escaped intact".[15] The contrast between this 'vulgarity' and the 'proper' norms upheld by colonialism is underlined by Moreton's attempt to re-contain the sentiments of the Jamaican text through his own poem, which re-frames black sexuality in terms of the familiar colonial narrative tropes of classical beauty (Cleopatra's "jetty charms") and a sentimentalised pastoral playfulness. Moreton's staid verse, however, only highlights the transgressive vibrancy of the songs, which in their 'vulgarity' help to rend the veil cast over black-white relations by colonial romances.

---

[13] See Pratt, op. cit., pp.95-97.
[14] Carolyn Cooper, *Noises in the Blood: Orality, Gender and the 'Vulgar' Body of Jamaican Popular Culture* (London: Macmillan, 1993), p.28.
[15] Ibid. p.22.

WILLIAM SHAKESPEARE
FROM *THE TEMPEST*

Prospero [the right Duke of Milan]
Thou poisonous slave, got by the devil himself
Upon thy wicked dam; come forth!

Enter Caliban [a savage and deformed slave]

Caliban
As wicked dew as ere my mother brushed
With raven's feather from unwholesome fen
Drop on you both. A southwest blow on ye
And blister you all o'er.

Prospero
For this, be sure, tonight thou shalt have cramps,
Side-stitches, that shall pen thy breath up; urchins
Shall forth at vast of night that they may work
All exercise on thee; thou shalt be pinched
As thick as honeycomb, each pinch more stinging
Than bees that made 'em.

Caliban
                    I must eat my dinner.
This island's mine by Sycorax, my mother,
Which thou tak'st from me. When thou cam'st first
 Thou strok'st me and made much of me; wouldst give me
Water with berries in't, and teach me how
To name the bigger light and how the less
That burn by day and night. And then I loved thee
And showed thee all the qualities o'th'isle:
The fresh springs, brine pits, barren place and fertile.
Cursed be I that did so! All the charms
Of Sycorax – toads, beetles, bats – light on you,
For I am all the subjects that you have,
Which first was mine own king; and here you sty me
In this hard rock, whiles you do keep me from
the rest o'th' island.

Prospero
                  Thou most lying slave,

WILLIAM SHAKESPEARE

Whom stripes may move, not kindness; I have used thee
(Filth as thou art) with humane care and lodged thee
In mine own cell, till thou didst seek to violate
  the honour of my child.

Caliban
O ho, O ho! Would't had been done;
Thou didst prevent me, I had peopled else
This isle with Calibans.

Miranda
                      Abhorred slave,
Which any print of goodness wilt not take,
Being capable of all ill; I pitied thee,
Took pains to make thee speak, taught thee each hour
One thing or other. When thou didst not, savage,
Know thine own meaning, but wouldst gabble like
A thing most brutish, I endowed thy purposes
With words that made them known. But thy vile race
(Though thou didst learn) had that in't which good natures
Could not abide to be with; therefore wast thou
Deservedly confined into this rock,
Who hadst deserved more than a prison.

Caliban
You taught me language, and my profit on't
Is I know how to curse. The red plague rid you
For learning me your language.

Prospero
                          Hag-seed, hence:
Fetch us in fuel, and be quick – thou'rt best –
To answer other business. Shrug'st thou, malice?
If thou neglect'st, or dost unwillingly
What I command, I'll rack thee with old cramps,
Fill all thy bones with aches, make thee roar,
That beasts shall tremble at thy din.

Caliban
                         No, pray thee.
[*Aside*] I must obey; his art is of such a power

WILLIAM SHAKESPEARE

It would control my dam's god Setebos,
And make a vassal of him.

Prospero
                        So, slave, hence.

JOHN ROLFE
LETTER TO SIR THOMAS DALE

Honourable Sir, and most worthy Governor:

When your leasure shall best serve you to peruse these lines, I trust in God, the beginning will not strike you into a greater admiration, than the end will give you good content. It is a matter of no small moment, concerning my own particular, which here I impart unto you, and which toucheth mee so neerely, as the tendernesse of my salvation. Howbeit I freely subject myself to your grave and mature judgement, deliberation, approbation, and determination; assuring my selfe of your zealous admonitions, and godly comforts, either perswading me to desist, or incouraging me to persist therin, with a religious feare and godly care, for which (from the very instant, that this began to roote itselfe within the secret bosome of my brest) my daily and earnest praiers have bin, still are, and ever shall be produced forth with as sincere a godly zeale as I possibly may to be directed, aided and governed in all my thoughts, words, and deedes, to the glory of God, and for my eternal consolation, to persevere wherein I never had more neede, nor (till now) could ever imagine to have bin moved with the like occasion.

    But (my case standing as it doth) what better worldly refuge can I here seeke, than to shelter my selfe under the safety of your favourable protection? And did not my ease proceede from an unspotted conscience, I should not dare to offer to your view and approved judgement, these passions of my troubled soule, so full of feare and trembling as hypocrisie and dissimulation. But knowing my owne innocency and godly fervor, in the whole prosecution hereof, I doubt not of your benigne acceptance, and clement construction. As for the malicious depravers, and turbulent spirits, to whom nothing is tastful, but what pleaseth their unsavoury pallat, I passe not for them being well assured in my perswasion (by the often triall and proving of my self, in my holiest meditations and praiers) that I am called hereunto by the spirit of God; and it shall be sufficient for me to be protected by your selfe in all vertuous and pious endevours. And for my more happie proceeding herein, my daily oblations shall ever be addressed to bring to passe so good effects, that your selfe, and all the world may truely say: This is the worke of God, and it is marvelous in our eies.

But to avoid tedious preambles, and to come nearer the matter: first suffer me with your patience, to sweepe and make cleane the way wherein I walke, from all suspicions and doubts, which may be covered therein, and faithfully to reveale unto you, what should move me hereunto.

Let therefore this my well advised protestation, which here I make betweene God and my own conscience, be a sufficient witnesse, at the dreadfull day of judgement (when the secret of all men's harts shall be opened) to condemne me herein, if my chiefest intent and purpose be not, to strive with all my power of body and minde, in the undertaking of so mightie a matter, no way led (so farre forth as man's weaknesse may permit) with the unbridled desire of carnall affection: but for the good of this plantation, for the honour of our countrie, for the glory of God, for my owne salvation, and for the converting to the true knowledge of God and Jesus Christ, an unbeleeving creature, namely Pokahuntas, to whom my hartie and best thoughts are, and have a long time bin so intangled, and inthralled in so intricate a laborinth, that I was even awearied to unwinde my selfe thereout. But almighty God, who never faileth his, that truly invocate his holy name hath opened the gate, and led me by the hand that I might plainly see and discerne the safe paths wherein to treade.

To you therefore (most noble Sir) the patron and Father of us in this countrey doe I utter the effects of this settled and long continued affection (which hath made a mightie warre in my meditations) and here I doe truely relate, to what issue this dangerous combate is come unto, wherein I have not onely examined, but throughly tried and pared my thoughts even to the quick, before I could finde any fit wholesome and apt applications to cure so daungerous an ulcer. I never failed to offer my daily and faithfull praiers to God, for his sacred and holy assistance. I forgot not to set before mine eies the frailty of mankinde, his prones to evill, his indulgencie of wicked thoughts, with many other imperfections wherein man is daily insnared, and oftentimes overthrowne, and them compared to my present estate. Nor was I ignorant of the heavie displeasure which almightie God conceived against the sonnes of Levie and

JOHN ROLFE

Israel for marrying strange wives, nor of the inconveniences which may thereby arise, with other the like good motions which made me looke about warily and with good circumspection, into the grounds and principall agitations, which thus should provoke me to be in love with one whose eduction hath bin rude, her manners barbarous, her generation accursed, and so discrepant in all nurtriture from my selfe, that oftentimes with feare and trembling, I have ended my private controversie with this: surely these are wicked instigations hatched by him who seeketh and delighteth in man's destruction; and so with fervent praiers to be ever preserved from such diabolical assaults (as I tooke those to be) I have taken some rest.

Thus when I thought I had obtained me peace and quietnesse, beholde another, but more gracious tentation hath made breaches into my holiest and strongest meditation; with which I have bin put to a new triall, in a straighter manner than the former; for besides the many passions and sufferings which I have daily, hourely, yea and in my sleep indured, even awaking mee to astonishment, taxing mee with remisnesse, and carelessness, refusing and neglecting to performe the duetie of a good Christian, pulling me by the eare, and crying: why dost not thou indevour to make her a Christian? And these have happened to my greater wonder, even when she hath bin furthest separated from me, which in common reason (were it not an undoubted worke of God) might breed forgetfulnesse of a farre more worthie creature. Besides, I say the holy spirit of God often demaunded of me, why was I created? if not for transitory pleasures and worldly vanities, but to labour in the Lord's vineyard, there to sow and plant, to nourish and increase the fruites thereof, daily adding with the good husband in the Gospell, somewhat to the tallent, that in the end the fruites may be reaped, to the comfort of the labourer in this life, and his salvation in the world to come? And if this be, as undoubtedly this is, the service Jesus Christ requireth of his best servant: wo unto him that hath these instruments of pietie put into his hands and wilfilly despiseth to worke with them. Likewise, adding hereunto her great appearance of love to me, her desire to be taught and instructed in the knowledge of God, her capablenesse of understanding, her aptnesse and willingnesse to receive anie good impression, and also the spirituall, besides her

JOHN ROLFE

own incitements stirring me up hereunto.

What should I doe? Shall I be of so untoward a disposition, as to refuse to leade the blind into the right way? Shall I be so unnaturall, as not to give bread to the hungrie? or uncharitable, as not to cover the naked? Shall I despise to actuate those pious dueties of a Christian? Shall the base feares of displeasing the world, overpower and with holde mee from revealing unto man these spirituall workes of the Lord, which in my meditations and praiers, I have daily made knowne unto him? God forbid. I assuredly trust hee hath thus delt with me for my eternall felicitie, and for his glorie: and I hope so to be guided by his heavenly graice, that in the end by my faithfull paines, and christianlike labour, I shall attaine to that blessed promise, pronounced by that holy Prophet Daniell unto the righteous that bring many unto the knowledge of God, namely, that they shall shine like the starres forever and ever. A sweeter comfort cannot be to a true Christian, nor a greater incouragement for him to labour all the daies of his life, in the performance thereof, nor a greater gaine of consolation, to be desired at the hour of death, and in the day of judgement.

Againe by my reading, and conference with honest and religious persons, have I received no small encouragement, besides serena mea conscientia, the cleereness of my conscience, clean from the filth of impurity, quoe est instar muri ahenei, which is unto me, as a brazen wall. If I should set down at large, the perturbations and godly motions, which have striven within mee, I should but make a tedious and unnecessary volume. But I doubt not these shall be sufficient both to certifie you of my tru intents, in discharging of my dutie to God, and to your selfe, to whose gracious providence I humbly submit my selfe, for his glory, your honour, our Countrey's good, the benefit of this Plantation, and for the converting of one unregenerate, to regeneration; which I beseech God to graunt, for his deere Sonne Christ Jesus his sake.

Now if the vulgar sort, who square all men's actions by the base rule of their owne filthinesse, shall taxe or taunt me in this my godly labour: let them know, it is not any hungry appetite, to gorge my self with incontinency; sure (if I would, and were so sensually inclined) I might satisfie such desire, though not without a seared conscience, yet with Christians more pleasing to the eie, and lesse fearfull in the offence unlawfully committed. Nor am I in so desperate an estate, that I regard not what becommeth of mee; nor am I out of hope but one day to see my Country, nor so void of friends, nor mean in birth, but there to obtain a match to my great content: nor have I ignorantly passed over my hopes there, or regardlessly seek to loose the love of my friends, by taking this course: I know them all, and have not rashly overslipped any.

But shal it please God thus to dispose of me (which I earnestly desire to fulfil my ends before sette down) I will heartely accept of it as a godly taxe appointed me, and I will never cease (God assisting me), until I have accomplished, and brought to perfection so holy a worke, in which I will daily pray God to blesse me, to mine, and her eternall happiness. And thus desiring no longer to live, to enjoy the blessings of God, then this my resolution doth tend to such godly ends, as are by me before declared: not doubting of your favourable acceptance, I take my leave, beseeching Almighty God to raine downe upon you, such plenitude of his heavenly graces, as your heart can wish and desire, and so I rest,

At your command most willing to be disposed of,

John Rolfe

JOHN DRYDEN

FROM *THE INDIAN EMPEROUR*

CORTEZ TO CYDARIA

Cydaria
My Father's gone, and yet I cannot go,
Sure I have something lost or left behind!

Cortez
Like Travellers who wander in the Snow,
I on her beauty gaze till I am blind.

Cydaria
Thick breath, quick pulse, and heaving of my heart,
All signs of some unwonted change appear:
I find myself unwilling to depart,
And yet I know not why I would be here.
Stranger, you raise such torments in my breast,
That when I go, if I must go again,
I'le tell my Father you have robb'd my rest,
And to him of your injuries complain.

Cortez
Unknown, I swear, those wrongs were which I wrought,
But my complaints will much more just appear,
Who from another world my freedom brought,
And to your conquering Eyes have lost it here.

Cydaria
Where is that other world from whence you came?

Cortez
Beyond the Ocean, far from hence it lies.

Cydaria
Your other world, I fear, is then the same
That souls must go to when the body dies.
But what's the cause that keeps you here with me?
That I may know what keeps me here with you?

JOHN DRYDEN

Cortez
Mine is a love which must perpetual be,
If you can be so just as I am true.

[*Enter Orbellan.*]

Orbellan
Your Father wonders much at your delay.

Cydaria
So great a wonder for so small a stay!

Orbellan
He has commanded you with me to go.

Cydaria
Has he not sent to bring the stranger too?

Orbellan
If he tomorrow dares in sight appear,
His high plac'd Love, perhaps may cost him dear.

Cortez
Dares – that word was never spoke to *Spaniard* yet
But forfeited his Life who gave him it;
Hast quickly with thy pledge of safety hence,
Thy guilt's protected by her innocence.

Cydaria
Sure in some fatal hour my Love was born,
So soon o'rcast with absence in the morn!

Cortez
Turn hence those pointed glories of your Eyes,
For if more charms beneath those Circles rise,
So weak my Vertue, they so strong appear,
I shall turn ravisher to keep you here.

JOHN DRYDEN

from ACT II

Cortez
Methinks like two black storms on either hand,
Our *Spanish* Army and your *Indians* stands;
This only space betwixt the Cloud, is clear,
Where you, like day, broke loose from both, appear.

Cydaria
Those closing Skies might still continue bright,
But who can help it if you'll make it night?
The gods have given you power of Life and Death,
Like them to save or scatter with a breath.

Cortez
That power they to your Father did dispose,
'Twas in his choice to makes us Friends or Foes.

Alibech
Injurious strength would rapine still excuse,
By off'ring terms the weaker must refuse:
And such as these your hard conditions are,
You threaten Peace, and you invite a War.

Cortez
If for myself to Conquer here I came,
You might perhaps my actions justly blame:
Now I am sent, and am not to dispute
My Prince's orders, but to execute.

Alibech
He who his Prince so blindly does obey,
To keep his Faith his Vertue throws away.

Cortez
Monarchs may err, but should each private breast
Judge their ill Acts, they would dispute their best.

Cydaria
Then all your care is for your Prince I see,
Your truth to him out-weighs your love to me;

JOHN DRYDEN

You may so cruel to deny me prove,
But never after that, pretend to love.

Cortez
Command my Life, and I will soon obey,
To save my Honour I my Blood will pay.

Cydaria
What is this Honour which does Love controul?

Cortez
A raging Fit of Vertue in the Soul;
A painful burden, which great minds must bear,
Obtain'd with danger, and possess'd with fear.

Cydaria
Lay down that burden, if it painful grow,
You'll find, without it, Love will lighter go.

Cortez
Honour once lost is never to be found.

Alibech
Perhaps he looks to have both passions Crown'd:
First dye his Honour in a Purple Flood.
Then Court the Daughter in the Father's Blood.

Cortez
The edge of War I'le from the Battel take,
And spare her Father's Subjects for her sake.

Cydaria
I cannot love you less when I'm refuse'd,
But I can dye to be unkindly us'd;
Where shall a Maid's distracted heart find rest,
If she can miss it in her Lover's breast?

Cortez
I till to morrow will the fight delay:
Remember you have conquer'd me today.

JOHN DRYDEN

Alibech
This grant destroys all you have urg'd before,
Honour could not give this, or can give more;
Our Women in the foremost ranks appear,
March to the Fight, and meet your Mistress there:
Into the thickest Squadrons she must run,
Kill her, and see what Honour must be won.

Cydaria
I must be in the Battel; but I'le go
With empty Quiver, and unbended Bow;
Not draw an Arrow in this fatal strife,
For fear its point should reach your Noble Life.

[*Enter Pizarro.*]

Cortes
No more, your kindness wounds me to the death,
Honour, be gone, what art thou but a breath?
I'le live, proud of my infamy and shame,
Grac'd with no Triumph but a Lover's name;
Men can but say Love did his reason blind,
And Love's the noblest frailty of the mind.
Draw off my Men, the War's already done.

Pizarro
Your Orders come too late, the Fight's begun.

APHRA BEHN

FROM *THE WIDOW RANTER*

from ACT II SCENE I

[*A pavilion. Discovers the Indian King and Queen sitting in state, with guards of Indians, men and women attending; to them Bacon richly dressed, attended by Daring, Fearless, and other Officers; he bows to the King and Queen who rise to receive him.*]

Cavarnio [*the Indian King*]
I am sorry, sir, we meet upon these terms, we who so often have embraced as friends.

Bacon [*General of the English: based on Nathaniel Bacon, a Virginian 'leveller' who seized control of Jamestown in 1676*]
[*Aside*] How charming is the queen? War, sir, is not in my business nor my pleasure. Nor was I bred in arms; my country's good has forced me to assume a soldier's life. And 'tis with much regret that I employ the first effects of it against my friends; yet whilst I may – whilst this cessation lasts, I beg we may exchange those friendships, sir, we have so often paid in happier peace.

King
For your part, sir, you've been so noble, that I repent the fatal difference that makes us meet in arms. Yet though I'm young I'm sensible of injuries; and oft have heard my grandsire say – that we were monarchs once of all this spacious world, till you an unknown people landing here, distressed and ruined by destructive storms, abusing all our charitable hospitality, usurped your right, and made your friends your slaves.

Bacon
I will not justify the ingratitude of my forefathers, but finding her my inheritance, I am resolved still to maintain it so; and by my sword which first cut out my portion, defend each inch of land with my last drop of blood.

Semernia [*the Indian Queen*]
[*Aside*] Even his threats have charms that please the heart

King
Come sir, let this ungrateful theme alone, which is better disputed in the field.

Queen
Is it impossible there might be wrought an understanding betwixt my lord and you? 'Twas to that end I first desired my truce, myself proposing to be mediator, to which my Lord Cavarnio shall agree, could you but condescend – I know you're noble; and I have heard you say our tender sex could never plead in vain.

Bacon
Alas! I dare not trust your pleading mouth, madam. A few soft words from such a charming mouth would make me lay the conqueror at your feet as a sacrifice for all the ills he has done you.

Queen
[*Aside*] How strangely I am pleased to hear him talk

King
Semernia, see – the dancers do appear.
[*To Bacon*] Sir, will you take your seat?

[*He leads the Queen to a seat, they sit and talk.*]

Bacon
Curse on his sports that interrupted me; my very soul was havering at my lip, ready to have discovered all its secrets. But oh! I dread to tell her of my pain, and when I would, an awful trembling seizes me, and she can only from my dying eyes, read all the sentiments of my captive heart. [*Sits down; the rest wait.*]

[*Enter Indians that dance antics; after the dance the King seems in discourse with Bacon, the Queen rises, and comes forth.*]

Queen
The more I gaze upon this English stranger, the more confusion struggles in my soul; oft have I heard of love, and oft this gallant

man (when peace had made him pay his idle visits) has told a thousand tales of dying maids. And ever when he spoke, my panting heart, with a prophetic fear in sighs replied, I shall fall such a victim to his eyes.

[Enter an Indian.]

Indian
[To the King] Sir, here's a messenger from the English council desires admittance to the general.

Bacon
[To the King] With your permission sir, he may advance.

Re-enter Indian with Dunce, and a letter.

Dunce *[a farrier, fled from England, and Chaplain to the Governor]*
All health and happiness attend your Honour, this from the Honourable Council.

King
I'll leave you till you have dispatched the messenger, and then expect your presence in the royal tent.

[Exeunt, King, Queen and Indians]

Bacon
Lieutenant, read the letter.

Daring
"Sir, the necessity of what you have acted makes it pardonable, and we could wish we had done the country and ourselves so much justice as to have given you that commission you desired. – We now find it reasonable to raise more forces, to oppose these insolences, which possibly yours may be too weak to accomplish, to which end the council is ordered to meet this evening, and desire you will come and take your place there, and be pleased to accept from us a commission to command in chief in this war. – Therefore send those soldiers under your command to their respective houses, and haste, sir, to your affectionate friends –"

[... *While Bacon reads the letter again, to him the Indian Queen, with women waiting.*]

Queen
Now while my lord's asleep in his pavilion I'll try my power with the general, for an accommodation of peace: the very dreams of war fright my soft slumbers that used to be employed in kinder business.

Bacon
Ha! – the queen – What happiness is this presents itself which all my industry could never gain?

Queen
[*Approaching him*] Sir –

Bacon
Pressed with the greatest extremes of joy and fear I trembling stand, unable to approach her.

Queen
I hope you will not think it fear in me, though timorous as a dove, by nature framed; nor that my lord, whose youth's unskilled in war, can either doubt his courage, or his forces, that makes me seek a reconciliation on any honourable terms of peace.

Bacon
Ah madam! If you knew how absolutely you command my fate I fear but little honour would be left of me, since whatsoe'er you ask me I should grant.

Queen
Indeed I would not ask your honour, sir, that renders you too brave for my esteem. Nor can I think that you would part with that. No, not to save your life.

Bacon
I would do more to serve your least commands than part with trivial life.

Queen
Bless me! Sir, how came I by such power?

Bacon
The gods, and Nature gave it you in your creation, formed with all the charms that ever graced your sex.

Queen
Is it possible? Am I so beautiful?

Bacon
As heaven, or angels there.

Queen
Supposing this, how might my beauty make you so obliging?

Bacon
Beauty has still a power over great souls, and from the moment I beheld your eyes, my stubborn heart melted to compliance, and from a nature rough and turbulent, grew soft and gentle as the god of love.

Queen
The god of love! What is the god of love?

Bacon
'Tis a resistless fire, that's kindled thus – [*Takes her by the hand and gazes on her.*] At every gaze we take from fine eyes, from bashful looks, and such soft touches – it makes us sigh – and pant as I do now, and stops the breath when e'er we speak of pain.

Queen
[*Aside*] Alas for me if this should be love!

Bacon
It makes us tremble, when we touch the fair one, and all the blood runs shivering through the veins, the heart's surrounded with a feeble languishment, the eyes are dying, and the cheeks are pale, the tongue faltering, and the body fainting.

Queen
[*Aside*] Then I'm undone, and all I feel is love. If love be catching, sir, by looks and touches, let us at distance parley – [*Aside*] or rather let me fly, for within view is too near –

Bacon
Ah! She retires – displeased I fear with my presumptuous love – Oh pardon, fairest creature. [*Kneels.*]

Queen
I'll talk no more, our words exchange our souls, and every look fades all my blooming honour, like sunbeams, on unguarded roses. – Take all our kingdoms – make our people slaves, and let me fall beneath your conquering sword. But never let me hear you talk again or gaze upon your eyes – [*Goes out.*]

Bacon
She loves! By heaven she loves! And has not art enough to hide her flame though she have cruel honour to suppress it. However, I'll pursue her to the banquet. [*Exit.*]

STEPHEN DUCK

FROM *AVARO AND AMANDA*

CANTO II

ALL Night in Tears, the pensive Merchant lay,
And often wished, and fear'd the coming Day;
Till, on the Hills, the rising Sun display'd
His golden Beams, and chas'd away the Shade:
Harmonious Birds salute his chearful Rays,
And hail the rosy Morn with joyful Lays;
While, stretch'd upon the Ground, AVARO moans,
answ'ring their tuneful Songs with piercing Groans.
      Not distant far from where the Youth was laid,
A purling Stream, in pleasing Murmurs, play'd:
And, by the Margin of the crystal Flood,
 Two Rows of Trees in beauteous Order stood;
Whose Branches form'd a pendant Arch above,
Diffusing gloomy Verdure o'er the Grove.
An *Indian* Princess hither daily came,
Pleas'd with the grateful Shade, and cooling Stream:
She now was walking to her lov'd Retreat
And heard the mourning Youth lament his Fate:
Fix'd in Amaze a-while she list'ning stood;
Then twixt approach'd him, rushing thro' the Wood.
Th'affrighted Merchant rose with gazing Eyes,
And tim'rous Looks, that testify'd Surprize:
Backward he starts; the Dame, with equal Fears,
Recedes as fast, and wonders what appears;
Yet, bolder grown, she soon advanc'd again,
Smit with the Beauty of the Godlike Man:
His Dress, and fair Complexion, charm'd her Sight;
Each glowing Feature gave her new Delight;
While Love and Pity both arose within,
And kindled in her Soul a Flame unseen.
With equal Joy AVARO now survey'd
The native Graces of the *Negro* Maid:
He view'd her Arms, with various Ribbands bound;
Her downy Head, with painted Feathers crown'd;
With Beades, and lucid Shells, in Circles strung,
Which shone refulgent, as they round her hung.
      As when, in splendid Robes, a courtly Maid

108

STEPHEN DUCK

Begins the Dance at Ball or Masquerade;
The Pearls and Di'monds shine with mingled Light,
And Glitt'ring Pendants blaze against the Sight.
    So shone the beauteous Shells around her Waist,
And sparkling Gems, that deck'd her jetty Breast;
All which AVARO's gazing Eyes pursue,
Charm'd with her lovely Shape, disclos'd to View:
Each Limb appears in just Proportion made,
With Elegance thro' ev'ry Part display'd:
And now his Cares dissolve, new Passions move;
And Nature intimates, the Change is LOVE.
    Not far remote, a cooling Grot was made,
In which the Virgin often sought a Shade:
Thick Shrubs, and fruitful Vines around it grew;
And none, except herself, the Mansion knew.
To this obscure Recess the Royal Dame,
Rejoicing, with her lovely Captive came:
Then, from the Branches, with officious Haste,
She plucks the Fruits, which yield a sweet Repast:
That done, she, with her Bow, explores the Wood;
Pierc'd with her Shaft, the Fowl resigns his Blood
Then back she hastens to her cool Retreat,
And for AVARO dress'd the grateful Meat:
To slake his Thirst, she next directs his Way,
Where crystal Streams in wild Meanders stray,
Nor lets him there, expos'd to Foes, remain;
But to the Cave conducts him safe again.
    So doats AMANDA on the Merchant, while
She scorns the Lovers of her native Isle:
For all the Heroes of her Country strove,
With Emulation, to attract her Love;
And, when they could the painted Fowls insnare,
Or pierce the savage Beast in sylvan War,
The Skins and Feathers, Trophies of their Fame,
They gave for Presents to the Royal Dame;
All which she to her lov'd AVARO brought,
And with them gayly deck'd his shining Grot:
The spotted Panther here she hung; and there,
With Paws extended, frown'd the shaggy Bear;
Here gaudy Plumes appear, in Lustre bright;
There Shells and Pearls diffuse a sparkling Light.

STEPHEN DUCK

    As when, to grace some Royal Prince's Hall,
The skilful Painter animates the Wall;
Here warlike Heroes frown in martial Arms,
There a soft Nymph displays her blushing Charms;
A pleasing Landscape next invites our Eye,
And the Room glows with sweet Variety.
    Yet, still to give her Lover more Delight,
(Lest what he daily saw, should pall the Sight)
When SOL with Purple cloath'd the Western Sky,
And Shades extended shew'd the Ev'ning nigh,
She to some verdant Grove the Youth convey'd,
Where Nightingales harmonious Music made:
Soft Flow'rets were their Couch; and, all around,
Diffusive Sweets perfum'd the fragrant Ground.
There oft she would his snowy Bosom bare,
Oft round her Fingers wind his silver Hair;
Charm'd with the Contrast, which their Colours made,
More pleasing than the Tulip's Light and Shade.
Nor was the Youth insensible; but soon
Repaid her Love by shewing of his own:
Oft would his Bosom heave with speaking Sighs;
Oft would he gaze, and languish with his Eyes;
Now on her panting Breasts his Head repose,
To meet his Head her panting Breast arose;
While in her Soul ecstatic Raptures glow'd,
And her fond Arms believ'd they clasp'd a God.
    So liv'd the happy Pair, observ'd by none,
Till both had learn'd a Language of their own;
In which the Youth, one Ev'ning in the Shade,
Beguiles the harmless unsuspicious Maid;
Leans on her Breast, and, with a Kiss, betrays;
Then vents his specious Fraud in Words like these:
    "Witness, ye Gods, and all ye bless'd above,
(For ye can witness best, how well I love)
If e'er among our blooming Nymphs, I knew
Such Pleasures, as my Soul receives from you?
O dear AMANDA! I could but, with thee,
Once more my happy native Country see,
You should not there in lonely Caves retreat,
Nor trace the burning Sands with naked Feet;
Your Limbs, which now the Sun and Wind invade,

STEPHEN DUCK

Should neatly be in softest Silks array'd;
In gilded Coaches gayly should you ride,
By Horses drawn, which prancing Side by Side,
Neigh, foam, and champ the Bit with graceful Pride;
Our Time, in Pomp and Peace, should slide away,
And blooming Pleasures crown the smiling Day;
And when the setting Sun forsook the Skies,
Approaching Night should but increase our Joys:
We would not on the chilling Ground embrace,
Nor Foes, as now, should interrupt our Peace;
But both reposing on some easy Bed,
Soft, as the fleecy Down, that decks thy Head,
The sportive God of Love should round us Play,
While we, in Raptures, pass'd the Night away:
Then let us carefully, my dear, explore
The Haven, where I first approach'd the Shore.
Perhaps we shall some floating Ship survey,
Safe to conduct us o'er the watry Way:
Nor let the foaming Waves your Steps retard;
I'll guard you o'er, and be a faithful Guard."
    How oft, alas! is Innocence betray'd,
When Love invites, and Flatterers persuade?
How could the Dame, a Stranger to Deceit,
Imagine such a heavenly Form a Cheat?
She paus'd, she sigh'd; then with pensive Look,
Half loth, and half consenting, thus she spoke:
    "Once has AVARO 'scap'd the raging Main:
Why would you tempt the fickle Seas again?
To seek new Dangers, when in Safety here,
Would but provoke the Deities you fear –
Sometimes, I own, we've been supriz'd by Foes,
Whose nightly Walks have wak'd you from Repose:
Yet still I guard your sacred Life secure,
And always will – What can AMANDA more?"
    Thus said, she clasp'd him in her loving Arms,
Embrac'd his Neck, and doated on his Charms:
And now both shew their Passions in their Look,
And now Connubial HYMEN both invoke;
In sportive Joys they clos'd the genial Day,
While PHILOMELA sung the Nuptial Lay;
Till soon the Youth reclin'd upon her Breast,

STEPHEN DUCK

And golden Slumbers seal'd their Eyes to Rest.

CANTO IV

Farewel, bright Goddess of th'*Idalian* Grove;
Farewel, ye sportive Deities of LOVE!
No longer I your pleasing Joys rehearse;
A rougher Theme demands my pensive Verse;
A Scene of Woes remains to be display'd,
Indulgent Love with Slavery repaid:
Ingratitude, and broken Vows, and Lies,
The mighty Ills that spring from Avarice,
Provoke my Lays: Your Aid, ye Muses, bring;
Assist my Tragic Numbers, while I sing.
Say, what ensu'd, when, on the briny Deep,
The watchful Dame beheld a floating ship?
She call'd, and beckon'd to it from the Shore;
Then to the Youth the grateful Tidings bore;
And said, "I something see like winged Trees,
(Strange to behold!) fly swiftly o'er the Seas;
Their bulky Roots upon the Billows float:
Say is not this the Ship, you long have sought?
Or I mistake, or, by the Gods' Command,
This comes to bear us to your native Land:
Then hasten, see the Partner of your Heart,
With You, her Guide, is ready to depart;
My Father, Mother, Friends, I bid Adieu,
Friends, Father, Mother, not so dear as *You*."
    To whom the Youth, with smiling Brow, reply'd:
"O thou true Pattern of a faithful Bride!
Who dar'st thy Father, Mother, Friends resign;
And risque thy own dear Life, to rescue mine! –
If I forget the Debt I owe to *Thee*,
May all the Gods forget their Care of *Me*.
In more wild Desarts let me rove again;
Nor find a Friend, like *Thee*, to ease my Pain!
There let the Vultures, Wolves, and Tigers tear
This Body, *Thou* hast kindly nourish'd here!
    So saying, to the Beach he straight descends:
And, by the Flag discerns the Crew his Friends:
And now his Heart exults within his Breast;

STEPHEN DUCK

His loving Mate an equal Joy confest;
She, with him, gladly ventures on the Main,
Unthinking of her future Toil and Pain.
    So, to the Plough, the Heifer, yet unbroke,
Walks cheerful on, nor dreads th'impending Yoke;
Till, in Fields, urg'd with the piercing Goad,
She groans, and writhes, reluctant with her Load.
    The *British* Bark was to *Barbadoes* bound:
Th'expected Shore the Sailors quickly found;
Where, safe from Danger, now the perjur'd Youth,
False to his former Vows of sacred Truth,
Reflecting, counts the Int'rest he had lost,
While Fate detain'd him on the *Indian* Coast:
The frugal Thoughts suppress his am'rous Flame,
And prompt him to betray the faithful Dame.
Yet scare he can the cursed Fact pursue;
But hesitates at what he fain would do:
For, tho his Av'rice moves him to the Ill,
His Gratitude within him struggles still;
And 'twixt two Passions, neither guides his Will.
    As when two Scales, with equal Loads suspend,
Sway to and fro; alternate both descend,
Till, undeclining, each aloft abides;
Nor this, nor that, the doubtful Weight decides.
    So stood the doubtful Youth a-while; nor wou'd
Forsake the Evil, nor pursue the Good;
Till, as the Sailors in the Haven stay,
To purchase Salves, the Planters croud the Key:
One asks, for what the *Negro* may be sold;
Then bids a Price, and shews the tempting Gold:
Which when AVARO views with greedy Eyes,
He soon resolves to gain th'alluring Prize.
Nor Oaths, nor Gratitude, can longer bind;
Her Fate he thus determines in his Mind:
    "Suppose I should conduct this *Indian* o'er;
And thus, instead of Gold, import a *Moor* –
Would not my Sire, with stern contracted Brows
Condemn my Choice, and curse my nuptial Vows?
Was it for this I learn'd the Merchant's Art?
Only to gain a doating *Negroe*'s Heart!
Was it for this the raging Seas I crost?

STEPHEN DUCK

No; Gold induc'd me to the *Indian* Coast;
And Gold is offer'd for this simple Dame;
Shall I refuse it, or renounce my Flame? –
Let am'rous Fools their tiresome Joys renew,
And doat on *Love*, while *Int'rest* I pursue."
He added not; for now, intent on Gold,
And dead to all Remorse, the Dame he sold.
   AMANDA stood confounded with Surprize,
And silently reproach'd him with her Eyes:
She often try'd to speak, but when she try'd
Her Heart swell'd full, her Voice its Aid deny'd;
And, when she made her fault'ring Tongue obey,
These Words, commix'd with Sighs, found out their Way.
   "Who can the mystic Ways of Fate explain?
Am I awake, or do I dream again;
Is *this* the sad Reward for all my Care?
Was it for this I cheer'd thee in Despair?
The Gods above (if any Gods there be)
Witness what I have done to succour thee!
Yet, if my Kindness can't thy Pity move,
Pity the Fruits of our unhappy Love:
Oh! let the Infant in my pregnant Womb,
Excite thee to revoke my threatedn'd Doom!
Think how the future Slave, in Climes remote,
Shall curse the treach'rous Sire, that him begot."
   So spake the mourning Dame, but spake in vain;
Th'obdurate Youth insults her with Disdain;
Not all her Kindness could his Pity move,
Nor yet the Fruits of their unhappy Love.
But, as the Flames, which soften Wax, display
The same warm Force to harden sordid Clay;
That Motive which would melt another Heart,
More harden'd his, and made him act a double Villain's Part.
He, for the Child, demands a larger Sum;
And sells it, while an Embryo in the Womb.
   And now he sternly takes her by the Hand;
Then drags her on, reluctant to the Land;
While, as she walks her dismal Fate she moans,
The rocks around her echo to her Groans:
"O base, ungrateful Youth!" she loudly cries;
"O base, ungrateful Youth!" the Shore replies:

STEPHEN DUCK

"And can'st thou, cruel, perjur'd Villain! leave
Thy tender Infant too, an abject Slave,
To toil, and groan, and bleed beneath the *Rod*?
Fool, that I was, to think thou wert a God!
Sure from some savage Tiger art thou sprung –
No! Tigers feed, and fawn upon their Young:
But thou despisest all paternal Cares,
The Fate of Infants, and their Mothers Pray'rs."
      In vain she does her wretched State deplore;
Pleas'd with the Gold, he gladly quits the Shore;
The ruffling Winds dilate the Sails, the Ship
Divides the Waves, and skims along the Deep.
Three Days the bellying Canvas gently swells,
Clear shines the Sun, and friendly blow the Gales;
Then frowning Clouds invest the vaulted Sky,
And hollow Winds proclaim a Tempest nigh:
Fierce BOREAS loudly o'er the Ocean roars,
Smoke the white Waves, and sound the adverse Shores;
While, to increase the Horrors of the Main,
Descends a Deluge of impetuous Rain.
The giddy Ship on circling Eddies rides,
Toss'd and re-toss'd, the Sport of Winds and Tides.
Redoubled Peals of roaring Thunder roll
And Flames, conflicting, flash from Pole to Pole,
While guilty Thoughts distract AVARO's Soul.
Of Life despairing, tho' afraid to die,
One fatal Effort yet he means to try:
While all the busy Crew, with panting Breath,
Were lab'ring to repel the liquid Death;
AVARO from the Stern the Boat divides,
And yields up to the Fury of the Tides:
Toss'd on the boist'rous Wave, the Vessel flies,
Now sinking low, now mounting to the Skies;
Till soon the Storm decreas'd, and, by Degrees,
Hush'd were the Winds, and calm the ruffled Seas;
The Sailors safely steer their Course again,
And leave AVARO floating on the Main;
Who landed quickly on a lonely Isle,
where human Feet ne'er print the baleful Soil;
A dreary Wilderness was all appear'd,
And howling Wolves the only Sound he heard;

STEPHEN DUCK

A thousand Deaths he views before his Eyes,
A thousand Guilt-created Fiends arise;
A *conscious-Hell* within his Bosom burns,
And racks his tortur'd Soul while thus he mourns:
    "Curs'd be the Precepts of my selfish Sire,
Who bad me after fatal Gold aspire!
Curs'd be myself, and doubly curs'd, who sold
A faithful Friend, to gain that fatal Gold! –
O! could these gloomy Woods my Sin conceal,
Or in my Bosom quench this fiery *Hell*;
Here would I pine my wretched Life away,
Or to the hungry Savage fall a Prey –
But can the gloomy Woods conceal my Sin,
Or cooling shadows quench the *Hell* within?
No; like some Spirit banish'd Heav'n, I find
Terrors in ev'ry Place, to rack my Mind;
Tormenting conscious Plagues increase my Care,
And guilty Thoughts indulge my just Despair –
O! Where shall I that piercing Eye evade,
That scans the Depths of *Hell*'s tremendous Shade!"
    So saying, straight he gave a hideous Glare,
With rolling Eyes, that witness'd strong Despair:
Then drew his pointed Weapon from the Sheath,
Confus'dly wild, and all his thoughts on Death;
To pierce his trembling Heart he thrice essay'd,
And thrice his coward Arm deny'd its Aid:
Meanwhile a howling Wolf, with Hunger prest,
Leap'd on the Wretch, and seiz'd him by the Breast;
Tore out his Heart, and lick'd the purple Flood;
For Earth refus'd to drink the Villain's Blood.

ISAAC TEALE

THE SABLE VENUS, AN ODE
(Inscribed to Bryan Edwards, Esq; of Jamaica)

I long had my gay lyre forsook,
But strung it, t'other day, and took,
    T'wards *Helicon* my way.
The muses were together met,
The president himself was set,
    By chance 'twas concert day,

Erato smil'd to see me come,
Ask'd why I staid so much at home;
    I own'd my conduct wrong;
But now, the sable queen of love,
Resolv'd my gratitude to prove,
    Had sent me for a song.

The ladies look'd extremely shy,
Apollo's smile was arch and sly,
    But not one word they said.
I gaz'd, sure silence is consent,
I made my bow, away I went;
    Was not my duty paid?

Come to my bosom genial fire,
Soft sounds, and lovely thoughts inspire,
    Unusual is my theme;
Not such dissolving *Ovid* sung,
Nor melting *Saphho*'s glowing tongue;
    More dainty mine I deem.

Sweet is the beam of morning bright,
Yet sweet the sober shade of night,
    On rich *Angola*'s shores
While beauty clad in sable dye,
Enchanting fires the wond'ring eye,
    Farewel! ye *Paphian* bow'rs.

O sable queen! thy mild domain
I seek, and court thy gentle reign,

ISAAC TEALE

So soothing soft and sweet:
Where meeting love, sincere delight,
Fond pleasure, ready joys invite,
    And all true raptures meet.

The prating *Frank*, the *Spaniard* proud,
The double *Scot*, *Hibernian* loud,
    And sullen *English* own
The pleasing softness of thy sway,
And here, transferr'd allegiance pay,
    For gracious is thy throne.

From east to west, o'er either Ind
Thy scepter sways, thy pow'r we find
    By both the tropics felt:
The blazing sun, that guilds the zone
Waits but the triumphs of thy throne,
    Quite round the burning belt.

When thou, this large domain to view,
Jamaica's isle, thy conquest new,
    First left thy native shore.
Gay was the morn, and soft the breeze,
With wanton joy the curling seas
    The beauteous burthen bore.

Of iv'ry was the car, inlaid
With every shell of lively shade,
    The throne was burnish'd gold:
The footstool, gay with coral beam'd,
The wheels with brightest amber gleam'd
    And glist'ring round they rowl'd.

The peacock, and the ostrich spread
Their beautous plumes, a trembling shade
    From noon-day's sultry flame.
Sent by their fire, the careful east,
With wanton breezes fan'd her breast,
    And flutter'd round the dame.

The winged fish, in purple trace,

ISAAC TEALE

The chariot drew; with easy grace
    Their azure rein she guides:
And now they fly, and now they swim,
Now o'er the wave they lightly skim,
    Or dart beneath the tides.

Each bird that haunts the rock and bay,
Each sealy native of the sea,
    Came crouding o'er the main:
The dolphin shews his thousand dyes,
The grampus his enormous size,
    And gambol in her train.

Her skin excell'd the raven plume,
Her breath the fragrant orange bloom,
    Her eye the tropic beam:
Soft was her lip as silken down,
And mild her look as ev'ning sun
    That gilds the *Cobre* stream.

The loveliest limbs her form compose,
Such as her sister *Venus* chose,
    In *Florence*, where she's seen:
Both just alike, except the white,
No difference, no— none at night,
    The beauteous dames between.

With native ease, serene she sat,
In elegance of charms compleat,
    And ev'ry heart she won:
False dress, deformity may shade,
True beauty courts no foreign aid;
    Can tapers light the sun?

The pow'r that rules the ocean wide,
'Twas he, they say, had calm'd the tide,
    Beheld the chariot rowl:
Assum'd the figure of a tar,
The Captain of a man-of-war,
    And told her all his soul.

ISAAC TEALE

She smiled, with kind consenting eyes,
Beauty was ever valour's prize;
    He rais'd a murky cloud:
The tritons sound, the sirens sang,
The dolphins dance, the billows rang,
    And joy fills all the crowd.

Blest offspring of the warm embrace!
Gay ruler of the saffron race!
    Tho' strong thy bow, dear boy,
Thy mingled shafts of black and white,
Are wing'd with feathers of delight,
    Their prints are tipt with joy.

But when her step had touch'd the strand,
Wild rapture seiz'd the ravish'd land,
    From every part they came:
Each mountain, valley, plain and grove
Haste eagerly to shew their love,
    Right welcome was the dame.

Port-Royal shouts were heard aloud,
Gay *St Jago* sent a croud,
    Grave *Kingston* not a few:
No rabble rout, I heard it said,
Some great ones join'd the cavalcade –
    I can't indeed say who.

Gay Goddess of the sable smile!
Propitious still, this grateful isle
    With thy protection bless!
Her fix, secure, thy constant throne;
Where all, adoring thee, do one,
    One Deity confess.

For me, if I no longer own
Allegiance to the *Cyprian* throne,
    I play no fickle part.
It were ingratitude to slight
Superiour kindness, I delight
    To feel a grateful heart.

ISAAC TEALE

Then, play goddess! cease to change,
Nor in new beauties vainly range,
    Tho' whatsoe'er thy view,
Try ev'ry form thou canst put on,
I'll follow thee thro' ev'ry one,
    So staunch am I, so true.

Do thou in gentle *Phibba* smile,
In artful *Benneba* beguile,
    In wanton *Mimba* pout;
In sprightly *Cuba*'s eyes look gay,
Or grave in sober *Quasheba*,
    I still shall find thee out.

Just now, in *Auba*'s easy mien;
I think I saw my roving queen,
    I will be sure tonight:
Send *Quako*, gentle girl, from home,
I would not have him see me come;
    Why should we mad him quite?

Thus have I sung, perhaps too gay
Such subject for such time of day,
    And fitter far for youth:
Should then the song too wanton seem,
You know who chose th'unlucky theme:
    Dear BRYAN, tell the truth.

WILLIAM RUFUS CHETWOOD

FROM *THE VOYAGES, DANGEROUS ADVENTURES, AND IMMINENT ESCAPES OF CAPTAIN RICHARD FALCONER*

At last those *Indians* that went hollowing through the Wood seem'd to me to have the worst of it, and were drove by the other Party quite back again; but did not pursue 'em any farther, only let fly their Arrows at 'em; and one of 'em came among the Shrubs where I lay, which startled me, for I was afraid they wou'd come to look for their Arrows, and so find me. After the hurly-burly was over, I resolv'd to go out of the Wood, and follow those *Indians* that were Vanquishers, with this Hope, that they might be of a milder Nature, and not so barbarous as the others who run through the wood, who to my thinking had more stern Looks than those *Indians* I had seen upon that part of the Island where we us'd to Land to get Wood and Water. So as I said, I got up, and directed my Course out of the Wood after the *Indians*, but soon discover'd two *Indian* Men, (which I suppose had hid themselves during the late Conflict). It was to no purpose for me to fly, for they had got sight of me; or if I had, they wou'd have soon sent one of their winged Messengers after me; so I chose boldly to meet 'em. When we were come within forty Paces of one of another, one of the *Indians* was going to shoot at me, but was with-held by one of the Women: As soon as ever I came close to 'em, they look'd upon me with strange Gestures, and distorted Countenances; I put my Hand to my Head and Breast, which is the Token of Submission with the *Indians*; and they let me know by Signs that I must go with them, which I did not deny; for if I had, I knew I shou'd be forc'd; so I went willingly enough. When we had got through the Wood, one of the *Indian* Men wou'd have my Coat and the Wastecoat of, which I durst not refuse: The Coat he put upon his Companion, and the Wastecoat on himself, and strutted strangely. I gave my Handkerchief and Neckcloth to the Woman that hinder'd the *Indian* from shooting at me, who reciev'd it with a great deal of Joy, and seem'd mightily pleas'd with me.

When we arriv'd at their Hutts, there came out at least a Hundred Frightful-looking *Indians*, who came about me, and had a great deal of Talk with those that brought me with 'em; but the two Indians were forc'd to part with their Cloaths they had taken from me, to two of the oldest *Indians*, who immediately put 'em on, and seem'd mighty proud of themselves. They gave me some Rice, and another sort of Victuals boyl'd; but what it was compos'd of, I could never learn, neither did I eat any of the same all the while I was among 'em. When Night came, I was sent into a Hutt by my self, and the Door shut upon me, I had a piece of Mat to lie on, but nothing to cover me. Now I had leasure to reflect upon my Misfortunes, which I cou'd not do before, by reason of the Fears I was in. I thought my Condition was now worse than ever it was, for I really believ'd they design'd to make a Sacrifice of me, for I thought to myself they were Cannibals, or Men-Eaters. I pass'd the Night with a thousand Anxieties and Inquietudes; but nevertheless my Senses were so tyr'd, that I slept whether I wou'd or no; and in the Morning was awak'd by four of the Eldest *Indians* that came to visit me, who made Signs to me to follow 'em, which I did without any hesitation; when I was out in the midst of the plain Place before the Doors of their Hutts, they brought before me several of their Women, and gave me to know by Signs that I shou'd take her to be my Mate, or Bedfellow, or suffer Death. I must confess I was mightily shock'd, but not giving my self much time to weigh, or think of the Matter, I pitch'd upon her that I had given my Neckcloth and Handkerchief to, and immediately all the rest were dismiss'd; and my Bride and I (for it was even so) were conducted to a Hutt, where there was several old *Indians* waiting for me to compleat the Ceremony. When my Bride and I came before 'em, we were order'd to sit down, then both our Feet were wash'd with Water: after that they brought us a piece of their *Indian* Cake, or Bread, on which I was order'd to break off a piece, and give to my Bride. She then came and laid her Head on my Breast; and then, kneeling, put my Right foot upon her Neck; when that was done, she rose and went out, but immediately return'd, and brought me some Flesh broil'd on the Coals, which she tore into Morsels, and put in my Mouth, and stood before me all the while I eat. I must confess I was so hungry, that I had a very good appetite to my Victuals, being I had not eat any Flesh for four Days: But I had no great Stomach to my Bride; although a

WILLIAM RUFUS CHETWOOD

well-featur'd Woman, yet her Complexion did not like me. When I had done Eating, my Bride and I were put into a Hutt, and shut close without any Light; but the old Proverb, *Joan's as good as my Lady in the Dark*, had like to have prov'd no Proverb to me.

In the Morning we were wak'd with a rude Noise round our Tent, which startled me at first; but I found afterwards it was a sort of an *Epithalamium*. When they had made their frightful Noise for sometime, they entered promiscuously Men and Women. The Men came and took hold of me, and the Women of my new Spouse, led us out with Shouts, unpleasing Noises, and antick Gestures: They continu'd it till we came to a River, and then we parted; the Men with me, and the Women with my Wife. They put me into the River, and wash'd me all over, and I suppose the Women did as much by my Tawny Rib. After they had given notice by their shouts, that they had made an End of scowring me, they put on my Shirt and Drawers again, and led me to the Bank where my Spouse waited for me with her She-attendance, and we return'd with the same Noise as we came out. When we came to the Hutts, the old *Indians* met us; the Old Men took me, and the Old Women my Wife, and gave us an Entertainment separably, which lasted two Hours, according to my Computation; when they had made an End, they fetch'd us out of our different Tents, and seated us on a Bank, and then danc'd, and play'd such mad, rude, monkey Gambols, that put me in mind of the mad Feasts of the *Bacchi* in *Virgil*, for they wou'd tear their Faces with their Nails and scratch one another so violently, that one wou'd have thought they had been so many *Bethlemites*, and yet all in Mirth; for they wou'd laugh such Horse-laughs when ever any one of 'em was hurt, that quite stun'd me. When this sport was over, the young *Indians* of both Sexes took my Bride and I into one of their Hutts, and gave us an Entertainment of Fish broil'd upon the Coals, and a pleasant Liquor in a Calabash, that was exceeding strong, which soon got into most of their Noddles; and as fast as they grew a little Tipsie, they reel'd out one by one, and laid themselves before the Door of the Hut, and went to sleep. My good Wife, among the rest, got her Dose too; but was so monstrously loving withall, that I cou'd not tell well what to do with her. When Night came, we retir'd to our Rest as before, and were wak'd next Morning by another kind of Noise that was made, with rude knocking at our Door, or rather Basket, for it was nothing else, and five or six of the old *Indians* came in with Hatchets, and other Instruments, to enable us to get Food for ourselves, as I understood. My wife took me out under the Arm, and carry'd me into the Wood with our Bows and Arrows, and by her Signs gave me to understand that she would bring me where I shou'd kill some Creature. At last we came to the Foot of a Hill, where we ascended with some difficulty; but when we had gain'd the Summit, we discover'd vast Numbers, or Herds of Goats. My Spouse shot, and kill'd on the first time; but I was such a Bungler at it, that I cou'd never do any execution. But my Spouse was very dextrous, as all the *Indians* are in the Island of *Dominico*.

My Wife seem'd to have a great Love for me, and wou'd always make much of me, her Way. When we had skin'd our Goat, we took out our Implements, and made a Fire to broil some of it. When it was ready, I gave my Creator thanks for providing for us poor insignificant Mortals; and looking towards Heav'n, the Residence of him that form'd us all. My Wife fix'd her Eyes upon me, and then look'd upwards too, with a kind of Concern. After we had done, I return'd thanks again in the same manner as before, and my Wife did the same, that is, she star'd upwards again as if she had a mind to see something as she thought I look'd at: And when she found she cou'd not see anything, she came about me, and put her Arm tenderly about my Neck, and with a sort of begging Tone, seem'd to ask me by Signs and Words, which I cou'd not understand, what I meant by looking upwards. I really griev'd to know that I cou'd not make her understand, for I cou'd not learn any of their Speech, but here and there a common Word; neither did I ever perceive they had any manner of Worship to any thing; otherwise if I wou'd have made her comprehend what I meant, I might have found it no hard Matter to have converted her from their abominable Heathenism; for she was of a mighty mild Nature, very Loving and Courteous, and nothing like the rest of the Savage Crew, who were prone to all manner of Wickedness. Her Voice too, differ'd from theirs, for most of the *Indians* pronounc'd their Words in their Throat, as indeed you cou'd not well speak 'em without Gutteral Sound; yet she, whatever was the meaning on't, spake her Words in a different Way from the rest, and had a pleasing manner. I really had begun to love her, and only wish'd she had been my Wife in the usual Forms: She cou'd pronounce any Word in English that I wou'd say to her, but I cou'd never get her to repeat whole Sentences; and all she did was like a Parrot. After we had done our hunting-work, I was for going over the Hill to view the Country, and walk'd up and down a good way; but I observ'd my Wife was very uneasy, but especially when I got to the Brow of the Hill. On the other side (which was about half a League over) I made an Essay to go down; she laid hold of my Arms, and pull'd me back with all her force, and with many supplicating Actions seem'd to beg of me not to go; and when she found I was offering at it again, she screem'd out so dismally, that it frighted me from making any more attempts. I endeavour'd to know what it meant, but cou'd gather nothing from her Words or Actions that cou'd let me into any thing: But she wou'd often handle her Bow and Arrows, and with menacing Actions let me know that there was some Danger. As we went homeward this odd Accident ran very much in my Head, and I was mighty desirous to find out the meaning of it; and every time I went to hunt there with my Wife, I wanted sadly to get down the Hill on the other side.

This Hill was of a vast Length, and extended from East to South-West, almost a-cross the Island. I did not know how to contrive it, but after hunting, I must believe I was very much tyr'd, and laid my self down in order to sleep; and my Wife with her usual good humour, accompany'd me, and in a very little time I found she was in a sound Sleep. I immediately rose, and stole away softly upon my intended Journey. I got away from my Wife without awaking, and came to the Brow of the Hill, which I survey'd, and found no difficulty in the descending. When I got to the Bottom of the Hill, I was mightily pleas'd with the Evenness of the Ground, and the Prospect round me, which I cou'd compare to nothing but the Vale of Esham in England, bating the Houses and Towns in't. I had walk'd up and down the Vale for near an Hour, and was preparing to go back the way I came, when looking back to take my last Survey, I saw a Smoak at a Distance, and it ran in my Mind it was the very place that our Men us'd to go to, from on Board, to truck with the Inhabitants. The thought took up some of my Time; and I believe, if it had not been for a tender Regard for my Wife, I had certainly directed my Course for that Smoak I saw there. But I must confess I cou'd not think of leaving her behind me, but

Curiosity put into my Head to go a little nearer that Smoak I had discover'd: But just I was moving that way, I heard a dreadful Screaming behind me; and turning about, I saw my Wife upon the Brow of the Hill, making the most pitiful Lamentation imaginable. The tender Regard I now began to have for my Wife, made me make all the haste I cou'd to her Relief, as thinking some Mischance might have befell her. When I came to the Bottom of the Hill, I saw several of the *Indians* of our Neighbourhood waiting for me above, and some were coming down. As soon as I had got to the Top of the Hill, I was immediately seiz'd by the *Indians* above, and drag'd along as if I had been the greatest Criminal imaginable, and my poor Wife hanging upon my Arm all drown'd in Tears. I cou'd not imagine what was the Matter, and what cou'd be the Reason of their using me in this manner. I found it must be something extraordinary, by the Grief of my Wife, whose Sorrow increas'd the farther I went towards our Hutts; but e're we cou'd get there, it rain'd and thunder'd so violently, that we were well wash'd before we came to our Journey's End.

When we were within ken of our Hutts, the whole Tribe came near us, some skipping and dancing, as mightily rejoyc'd; others with the Face of Concern, and hanging their Heads in sign of Sorrow, and mightily lamented over my Wife. After the old *Indians* had consulted some time, they ty'd me to a wither'd Tree that stood at the Mouth of the Hutts; then I began to understand what they meant, for I cou'd perceive that they were bringing Boughs of green Wood, in order to burn me. This Sight made my Courage fail me, and it was impossible to express my Despair and Horror. I found now that the last Day of my Life was come, (for it was impossible to see anything to the contrary.) My last Recourse was to the Maker and Giver of all good Things, for I had try'd all other Means in vain; as also had my poor Wife, whose Rage and Despair overcame her; and she was carry'd away by the Women in the utmost Agony. After my Wife was gone, they set fire to the Wood which enclos'd me; which being green and wet with the late Rain, was a great while in Burning; all the while it was kindling, some of the *Indians* jump'd round me, and danc'd after their barbarous manner, while others stood ready with their Bows an Arrows to shoot me (as I suppos'd) if the Fire shou'd burn the Bands that ty'd me, and I shou'd offer to run away. The Wood being green (as I said before) was very stubborn in kindling, which made the Apprehension more dreadful: I made several Essays to break the Bands that held me, but all my Efforts were but in vain; and I observ'd every Time I made my fruitless Endeavours, the barbarous Crew shouted and laugh'd for joy. The Fire encreasing, I pray'd to Almighty God to give me Strength to bear the horrid Pain I was going to suffer; and if it was possible, to go out of the World with the Patience and Fortitude of a good Christian, who was only going to change this troublesome Life for a better. I compar'd my self to a wounded Person, that must bear probing of his Hurts, in order to cure 'em.

    I now had given my self up entirely to my Thoughts of the other World; and this seem'd to me like abandoning a barren Island, in order to go to one where there was plenty of every thing. But before the Fire reach'd me, there fell such a prodigious Showre of Rain, mix'd with Thunder and Lightning, that extinguish'd the Fire. The Storm lasted for several Hours with the utmost Violence, and I remain'd stil ty'd to the Tree. When the Storm was over, they began to renew their Fire, and brought the Wood nearer than before, it being first half a Yard from my Body all round; but now they pil'd it close to me, that the Fire might the sooner be my Executioner, which I wish'd for, as knowing it wou'd put me to a speedier Death. But before they had well plac'd the Wood, they heard Shouts and Noises in the adjacent Woods; upon which the *Indians* immediately ran away from me, and took to their Arms in an Instant, old and young. The Noise came nearer, and nearer still, till at last I cou'd perceive several *Indians* bolt out of the Wood, who were met by our *Indians*, and a bloody Fight ensu'd. The Enemy *Indians* seem'd to have the best on't, by reason of some Fire-Arms that they had, with which they made strange havock with our *Indians*; the Battle continu'd for some Hours with a great deal of Heat, and many of our *Indians* fell. At last the Enemy *Indians* drove ours, even beyond the Hutts, and I cou'd only hear the Noise they made, being I was still fastened to the Tree.

    The Fight continu'd out of sight about half an Hour, when my Wife came running with all the Transports of Joy imaginable; and after having put her Head under my Feet, she unty'd me, and fell upon me with all the Signs of a sincere Love. I must confess I was mightily rejoyc'd to see my self at Liberty, and let what wou'd happen, my Condition cou'd not be worse that it was some Hours ago. I cou'd not forbear expressing my Love to my Wife by Kisses and Embraces. We went to our Hutt, and I took my Sword that had been laid up from my first being amongst 'em. I was going out of my Tent in order to go with my Wife to some other part of the Island, that was not known to the *Indians*: But just as we came among the Tents, three *Indians* met us that had run away from the Fight (as I conjectur'd). As soon as they saw me and my Wife, they came up with a great deal of ill Nature in their Countenances; and after some Talk with my Wife, one of 'em with his wooden Sword, went to make a Blow at me; but my Wife interposing, receiv'd the Blow upon her Head, which struck her to the Ground, bloody and senseless. My Rage rose so high up on this, that I could not contain my self; but I drew my Sword and thrust it up to the Hilt in the Wretch's Body; the other two seeing their Companion's Death, ran upon me with the Rage of Lyons; but I slipping on one side, avoided the Strokes intended me: They turn'd immediately upon me, and let drive at me several Blows, which had the good Fortune not to hit me; but I run one of 'em into the Throat with my Sword; upon which he set up such a Cry that frightened me, and ran away, and was immediately follow'd by the other. I then ran to the Assistance of my Wife, who lay almost strangled in her own Blood. I rais'd her from the Earth, and seated her under the Tree where I was ty'd, and brought her to her self a little, but I found her Skull was crack'd with the Blow the *Indian* gave her, and to my great Grief perceiv'd she was just expiring.

But the Sorrow and Tenderness to part with me, (as I judg'd by her Actions) struck me to the Soul. She laid one Arm about my Waste, and her Head in my Lap, but with such piteous Looks in her Eyes that almost distracted me. She made Signs to me to look upward (as I fancy'd) to pray for her, tho' I cou'd not tell for certain what she meant; but she pronounc'd several Words with Earnestness and Passion; and I really fancy'd, if we cou'd have understood one another, I shou'd have found she shou'd have had some Notions of a supreme Being. Before she expir'd, the Enemy *Indians* return'd with all of our *Indian* Prisoners, I mean all that they had not kill'd; for out of Two Hundred *Indians* of our Party, there was not above Twenty-two left. They were mightily surpiz'd to find me, for many of the Enemy *Indians* knew me; and when I came to examine their Faces, I remembr'd they were the *Indians* that inhabited about the Bay where our Ship lay. One or two of 'em cou'd speak a little *English*, that they learn'd by conversing with the English that usually Anchor'd in the Bay. One of 'em knew my Name, that he had gather'd from our Sailors enquiring for me, when sent by the Captain before the Ship sail'd. Master *Falconer*, says he, me glad to see you, White Men belong to great Ships, come look for you, very Great, and not look you here go away much sorry. My Wife took up all my Thoughts, who was just dying; and though her Strength and Speech fail'd her, yet she endeavour'd to pull down my Face to hers, which she kiss'd; then sunk her Head into my Bosom, and expir'd. I was really as much concern'd, as if I had marry'd one of my own Complexion and Country; for I had great Hopes, if ever I cou'd have made my Escape with her, and cou'd but have taught her *English*, to have made her a good Christian. With the Assistance of my now friendly *Indians* I laid her in the Earth: They told me she was Daughter to one of the Chiefs of their Enemy-Tribe. From these *Indians* I learn'd, that those I had fell amongst were a Tribe of *Indians* that had liv'd on this side of the Ridge of Mountains for many Years, and declar'd open War with those of the other side for holding Correspondence with *Whites*; and were so strict that they put all the *Indians* to Death that ever attempted singly to go over the Mountains, which was the Reason of my Danger of Burning.

JOHN GABRIEL STEDMAN

FROM *NARRATIVE OF A FIVE YEARS' EXPEDITION AGAINST THE REVOLTED NEGROES OF SURINAM IN GUIANA ON THE WILD COAST OF SOUTH AMERICA FROM THE YEARS 1772 TO 1777*

ARRIVAL IN SURINAM

After being confined nearly the whole of sixty-three days within the limits of a small vessel, and upon an element to which few of the troops had been accustomed, it would not be easy to describe the pleasure we experienced on finding ourselves once more on land, and surrounded by a thousand agreeable circumstances.

The town appeared uncommonly neat and pleasing, the shipping extremely beautiful, the adjacent woods adorned with the utmost fragrance, and the whole scene gilded by the rays of an unclouded sun. We did not however take leave of our wooden habitation at this time, but the next day were formally disembarked with a general appearance of rejoicing, all the ships in the roads being in full dress and the guns keeping up an incessant fire till the whole of the troops were landed.

All the inhabitants of Paramaribo were collected to behold this splendid scene, nor were the expectations they had formed disappointed. The corps consisted of nearly five hundred young men (for we had been so fortunate as only to lose one during the voyage), the oldest of whom was scarcely more than thirty, and the whole party neatly clothed in their new uniforms and their caps ornamented with twigs of orange-blossom. We paraded on a large green plain between the town and the citadel, opposite to the Governor's palace, but during the course of the ceremonies several soldiers fainted from the excessive heat. The troops then marched into quarters prepared for their reception, whilst the officers were regaled with a dinner by the Governor, which would have derived a considerable relish from its succeeding the salt provisions to which we had long been confined, had any contrast been necessary to heighten our opinion of its elegance. But the choicest delicacies of America and Europe were united in this repast, and served up in silver; a great variety of the richest wines were poured with profusion; the dessert was composed of the most delicious fruits; and the company were attended by a considerable number of extremely handsome negro and mulatto maids, all naked from the waist upwards, according to the custom of the country, but the other parts of their persons arrayed in the finest India chintzes, and the whole adorned with golden chains, medals, beads, bracelets and sweet-smelling flowers.

After partaking of this superb entertainment until about seven o'clock, I set out in search of the house of Mr Lolkens, the hospitable gentleman who had so obligingly invited me to make it my own. I soon discovered the place, but my reception was so ludicrous that I cannot forbear relating the particulars. On knocking at the door, it was opened by a young female negro, of a masculine appearance, whose whole dress consisted of a single petticoat, and who held a lighted tobacco-pipe in one hand and a burning candle in the other, which she brought close to my face, in order to reconnoitre me. I enquired if her master was at home, to which she replied, but in a language totally unintelligible to me. I then mentioned his name, on which she burst into an immoderate fit of laughter, displaying two rows of very beautiful teeth; at the same time, laying hold of the breast-buttons of my coat, she made me a signal to follow her. I was much at a loss how to act, but went in, and was ushered by the girl into a very neat apartment, whither she brought some excellent fruit and a bottle of Madeira wine, which she placed upon the table. She then, in the best manner she was able, informed me that her new *masera*, with the rest of his family, was gone to spend a few days at his plantation, and that she was left behind to receive an English Captain, whom she supposed to be me. I signified that I was and filled her out a tumbler of wine, which I had the utmost difficulty persuading her to accept, for such is the degrading light in which these unhappy beings are considered that it is accounted a high degree of presumption in them to eat or drink in the presence of a European. I contrived for some time to carry on something like a conversation with this woman, but was soon glad to put an end to it by recurring to the bottle.

Tired with the employments of the day, I longed for some rest, and made a signal to my attendant that I wanted to sleep: but my motion was strangely misconstrued, for she immediately seized me by the neck, and imprinted upon my lips a most ardent kiss. Heartily provoked at this unexpected and (from one of her colour) unwelcome salutation, I disentangled myself from her embraces and angrily flung into the apartment allotted for my place of rest. But here I was again pursued by my black tormentor who, in opposition to all I could say, insisted upon pulling off my shoes and stockings, and in a moment disencumbered me of that part of my apparel. I was extremely chagrined at her conduct though this is an office commonly performed by slaves in Surinam to all ranks and sexes without exception. Nor ought anyone to conceive that this apparently extraordinary conduct resulted from any peculiarity of disposition in the girl; her behaviour was only such as would have been practised by the generality of female negro slaves, and will be found, by all who visit the West India settlements, to be characteristic of the whole dark sisterhood.

SOME ACCOUNT OF A BEAUTIFUL FEMALE SLAVE

Having already stated that from our arrival till February 27th we seemed to be landed in Guiana for little more than idle dissipation; I shall now proceed from the same date, which was about the commencement of the rainy season, when our mirth and conviviality still continued, to present to the reader, as a contrast to the preceding scenes of horror, a description of the most beautiful mulatto maid Joanna. This charming young woman I first saw at the house of a Mr. Demelly, secretary to the Court of Policy, where I daily breakfasted and with whose lady Joanna, but fifteen years of age, was a very remarkable favourite, Rather taller than the middle size, she was possessed of the most elegant shape that nature can exhibit, moving her well-formed limbs with more than common gracefulness. Her face was full of native modesty, and the most distinguished sweetness; her eyes, as black as ebony, were large and full of expression, bespeaking the goodness of her heart; with cheeks through which glowed, in spite of the darkness of her complexion, a beautiful tinge of vermillion, when gazed upon. Her nose was perfectly formed, rather small; her lips a little prominent, which when she spoke, discovered to regular rows of teeth, as white as mountain snow; her hair was a dark brown inclining to black, forming a beautiful globe of small ringlets, ornamented with flowers and gold spangles. Round her neck, her arms, and her ankles, she wore gold chains, rings and medals: while a shawl of India muslin, the end of which was negligently thrown over her polished shoulders, gracefully covered part of her lovely bosom: a petticoat of rich chintz alone completed her apparel. Bareheaded and bare-footed, she shone with double lustre, as she carried in her delicate hand a beaver hat, the crown trimmed round with silver. The figure and appearance of this charming creature could not but attract my particular attention, as they did indeed that of all who beheld her; and induced me to enquire from Mrs. Demelly, with much surprise, who she was, that appeared to be so much distinguished above all others of her species in the colony.

"She is, Sir," replied this lady, "the daughter of a respectable gentleman, named Kruythoff; who had, besides this girl, four children by a black woman called Cery, the property of a Mr. D. B., on his estate called Fauconberg, in the upper part of the river Comewina.

"Some few years since Mr. Kruythoff made the offer of above one thousand pounds sterling to Mr. D. B. to obtain manumission for his offspring; which being inhumanely refused, it had such an effect upon his spirits, that he became frantic, and died in that melancholy state soon after; leaving in slavery, at the discretion of a tyrant, two boys and three fine girls, of which the one now before us is the eldest.

"The gold medals, &c. which seem to surprise you, are the gifts which her faithful mother, who is a most deserving woman towards her children, and of some consequence amongst her caste, received from her father (who she ever attended with exemplary affection) just before he expired.

"Mr. D. B., however, met with his just reward: for having since driven all his best carpenter negroes to the woods by his injustice and severity, he was ruined, and obliged to fly the colony, and leave the estate and stock to the disposal of his creditors; while one of the above unhappy deserters, a *samboe*, has by his industry been the protector of Cery and her children. His name is Jolycoeur, and he is now the first of Baron's captains, whom you may have a chance of meeting in the rebel camp, breathing revenge against the Christians.

"Mrs. D. B. is still in Surinam, being arrested after her husband's debts, till Fauconberg shall be sold by execution to pay them. This lady now lodges at my house, where the unfortunate Joanna attends her, whom she treats with peculiar tenderness and distinction."

Having thanked Mrs. Demelly for her account of Joanna, in whose eye glittered the precious pearl of sympathy, I took my leave, and went to my lodging in a state of sadness and stupefaction. However trifling, and like the style of romance, this relation may appear to some, it is nevertheless a genuine account, and on that score I flatter myself may be not entirely uninteresting to others.

When reflecting on the state of slavery altogether, while my ears were stunned with the clang of the whip, and the dismal yells of the wretched negroes on whom it was exercised, from morning till night; and considering that this might one day be the fate of the unfortunate mulatto I have been describing, should she chance to fall into the hands of a tyrannical master or mistress, I could not help execrating the barbarity of Mr. D. B. for having withheld her from a fond parent, who by bestowing on her a decent education and some accomplishments, would probably have produced, in this foresaken plant, now exposed to every rude blast without protection, an ornament to civilised society.

I became melancholy with these reflections; and in order to counterbalance, though in a very small degree, the general calamity of the miserable slaves who surrounded me, I began to take more delight in the prattling of my poor negro boy, Quaco, than in all the fashionable conversation of the polite inhabitants of this colony: but my spirits were depressed, and in the space of twenty-four hours I was very ill indeed; when a cordial, a few preserved tamarinds, and a basket of fine oranges, were sent by an unknown person. This first contributed to my relief, and losing about twelve ounces of blood, I recovered so far, that on the fifth I was able, for change of air, to accompany a Captain Macneyl, who gave me a pressing invitation to his beautiful coffee plantation, called Sporkesgift, in the Matapaca Creek.

JOANNA

As we were still in a state of inaction, I made another excursion, with a Mr. Charles Ryndorp, who rowed me in his barge to five beautiful coffee estates, and one sugar plantation, in the Matapaca, Paramarica, and Werapa Creeks, the description of which I must defer to another occasion; on one of which, called Schovnort, I was the witness to a scene of such barbarity which I cannot help relating.

The victim of this cruelty was a fine old negro slave who, having been as he thought undeservedly sentenced to receive some hundred lashes by the lacerating whips of two negro drivers, in the midst of the execution pulled out a knife, which, after having made a fruitless thrust at his persecutor the overseer, he plunged up to the haft in his own bowels, repeating the blow till he dropped down at the tyrant's feet. For this crime he was, being first recovered, condemned to be chained to the furnace which distils the *kill-devil*, there to keep in the intense heat of a perpetual fire night and day, being blistered all over, till he should expire by infirmity or old age, of the latter of which however he had but little chance. He showed me his wounds with a smile of contempt, which I returned with a sigh and small donation: nor shall I ever forget the miserable man, who, like Cerberus, was loaded with irons and chained to an everlasting torment. As for everything else I observed in this little tour, I must acknowledge it elegant and splendid, and my reception hospitable beyond my expectation: but these Elysian fields could not dissipate the gloom which the infernal furnace had left upon my mind.

Of the coffee estates, that of Mr. Sims, called Limeshope, was the most magnificent, and may be deemed with justice one of the richest in the colony. We now once more, on the sixth of April, returned safe to Paramaribo, where we found the *Westerlingwerf* man-of-war, Captain Crass, which had arrived from Plymouth in thirty-seven days, into which port he had put to stop a leak, having parted company with us, as already mentioned, off Portland, at the end of December 1772. This day, dining at the house of my friend, Mr. Lolkens, to whom I had been, as I have said, recommended by letters, I was an eye witness of the unpardonable contempt with which negro slaves are treated in this colony. His son, a boy of not more than ten years old, when sitting at table, gave a slap in the face to a grey-headed black woman, who by accident touched his powdered hair as she was serving a dish of kerry. I could not help blaming his father for overlooking the action, but he told me, with a smile, that the child should no longer offend, as he was next day to sail for Holland for education. To this I answered that I thought it almost too late. At the same moment a sailor passing by, broke the head of a negro with a bludgeon, for not having saluted him with his hat. Such is the state of slavery, at least in this Dutch settlement!

About this time, Colonel Fourgeoud made a second excursion, and now departed with a barge, to explore the banks and situation of the river Surinam, as he had never before done, those of Rio Comewina and Rio Cottica.

At this time died Captain Barends, one of the masters of the transports, which were still kept in commission in case they should be wanted for our return to Europe. Five or six sailors belonging to the merchant ships, were now buried every day, whose lamentable fate I cannot pass by unnoticed. They are actually used worse than the negroes in this scorching climate, where, besides rowing large flat-bottomed barges up and down the rivers, day and night, for coffee, sugar, etc. and being exposed to the burning sun and heavy rains, and besides stowing the above commodities in a hold as hot as an oven they are now obliged to row every upstart planter to his estate at a call, which saves the gentleman so many negroes, and for which they receive in return nothing – many times not so much as a mouthful of meat and drink. They palliate hunger and thirst by begging from the slaves a few bananas or plantains, eating oranges and drinking water, which in a little time relieves them from every complaint, by shipping them off to eternity. In every part of the colony they are no better treated, but, like horses, they must (having unloaded the vessels) drag the commodities to the distant storehouses, being bathed in sweat, and bullied with bad language, sometimes with blows. A few negroes are ordered to attend, but not to work, by the direction of their masters, which many would willingly do to relieve the drooping sailors, to whom this usage must be exceedingly disheartening and galling. The planters even employ these men to paint their houses, clear their sash windows, and do numberless other menial services, for which a seaman was never intended. All this is done to save the work of the negroes; while by this usage thousands are swept to the grave, who in the line of their profession alone may have lived many years. Nor dare the West India Captains to refuse the men, without incurring the displeasure of the planters, and seeing their ships rot in the harbour without loading. Nay, I have heard a sailor fervently wish he had been born a negro, and beg to be employed among them in cultivating a coffee plantation.

I now took an early opportunity to enquire of Mrs. Demelly what was become of the amiable Joanna. I was informed that her lady, Mrs. D. B. had escaped to Holland on board the *Boreas* man-of war, under the protection of Captain Van-de-Velde, and that her young mulatto was now at the house of her aunt, a free woman, whence she expected hourly to be sent up to the estate Fauconberg, friendless, and at the mercy of some unprincipled overseer appointed by creditors, who had now taken possession of the plantation and stock, till the whole should be sold to pay the several sums due to them by Mr. D. B. Good god! I flew to the spot in search of poor Joanna: I found her bathed in tears. She gave me such a look – ah! Such a look! From that moment I determined to be her protector against every insult, and persevered, as shall be seen in the sequel. Here, reader, let my youth, blended with extreme sensibility, plead my excuse; yet assuredly my feelings will be forgiven me.

I next ran to the house of my friend Lolkens, who happened to be the administrator of Fauconberg estate; and asking his assistance, I intimated to him my strange determination of purchasing and educating Joanna.

Having recovered from his surprise, after gazing at me silently for some time, an interview was at once proposed, and the beauteous slave, accompanied by a female relation, was produced trembling in my presence.

It now proved to be she who had privately sent me the cordial and the oranges in March, when I was nearly expiring, and which she now modestly acknowledged "was in gratitude for my expressions of compassion respecting her sad situation"; with singular delicacy, however, she rejected every proposal of becoming mine upon my terms. She was conscious, she said, "that in such a state should I soon return to Europe, she must either be parted from me for ever, or accompany me to a part of the world where the inferiority of her condition must prove greatly to the disadvantage of both herself and her benefactor, and thus in either case be miserable". Joanna firmly persisting in these sentiments, she was immediately permitted to withdraw, and return to the house of her aunt; while I could only intreat of

Mr. Lolkens his generous protection of her, and that she might at least for some time be separated from the other slaves, and continue at Paramaribo; and in this request his humanity was induced to indulge me.

On the 30th the news arrived that the rangers, having discovered a rebel village, had attacked it and carried off three prisoners, leaving four others dead upon the spot, whose right hands, chopped off and barbecued or smoke-dried, they had sent to the governor of Paramaribo as a proof of their valour and fidelity.

On receiving this intelligence, Colonel Fourgeoud immediately left the river Surinam, where he still was, and on the first of May returned to town, in expectation of his regiment being employed on actual service. But there the business ended and we still, to our utter astonishment, were allowed to linger away our time, each agreeably to his own peculiar fancy. On the 4th of May, the rangers however were reviewed in the Fort Zelandia, at which ceremony I was present, and must confess that this corps of black soldiers had a truly manly appearance: warriors whose determined and open aspect could not but give me the satisfaction of a soldier in beholding them. They here once more received the thanks of the governor for their manly behaviour and faithful conduct, particularly the taking of Boucon; besides which, they were entertained with a rural feast, at the public expense, at Paramaribo, to which were also invited their families; and at which feast several respectable people of both sexes made their appearance with pleasure, to witness the happiness of their sable friends, the day being spent in mirth and conviviality, without the least disturbance, nay even with decorum and propriety, to the great satisfaction of the inhabitants.

The *Westerlingwerf*, Captain Crass, now left the river also, bound for Holland, but first for the colony of Demerary. Thus both ships of war having sailed without us, there was some reason to suppose we were soon to be employed on actual service. There were many motives, indeed, for wishing whither that this might be the case, or that we might speedily be permitted to return to Europe. Not only our officers, but our privates, began to feel the debilitating effects of the climate, and many of that continued debauchery so common in all the ranks in the settlement. As hard labour and bad treatment constantly

JOHN GABRIEL STEDMAN

killed the poor sailors, so now our common soldiers fell the victims of idleness and licentiousness, and died frequently six or seven in a day; whence it is evident to demonstration, that all excesses, of whatever kind, are mortal to Europeans in the climate of Guiana.

But men will give lessons which they do not themselves observe. Thus, notwithstanding my former resolution of living retired, I again relapsed into a vortex of dissipation. I became a member of a drinking club, I partook of all polite and impolite amusements, and plunged into every extravagance without exception. I did not, however, escape without the punishment I deserved. I was seized suddenly with a dreadful fever; and such was its violence, that in a few days I was no more expected to recover. In this situation I lay in my hammock until the 17th, with only a soldier and my black boy to attend me, and without any other friend. Sickness being universal among the newcomers to this country, and every one of our corps having so much to do to take care of themselves, neglect was an inevitable consequence, even amongst the nearest acquaintance. This, however, is a censure which does not apply to the inhabitants, who perhaps are the most hospitable people on the globe to Europeans. These philanthropists not only supply the sick with a variety of cordials at the same time, but crowd their apartments with innumerable condolers, who from morning until night continue prescribing, insisting, bewailing, and lamenting, friend and stranger without exception; and this lasts until the patient becomes delirious and expires. Such must inevitably have been my case, between the two extremes of neglect and importunity, had it not been for the happy intervention of poor Joanna, who one morning entered my apartment, to my unspeakable joy and surprise, accompanied by one of her sisters. She informed me that she was acquainted with my forlorn situation; that if I still entertained for her the same good opinion, her only request was, that she might wait upon me till I should be recovered. I indeed gratefully accepted her offer, and by her unremitting care and attention had the good fortune so far to regain my health and spirits, as to be able, in a few days after, to take an airing in Mr. Kennedy's carriage.

Till this time I had chiefly been Joanna's friend, but now I began to feel I was her captive. I renewed my wild proposals of purchasing, educating and transporting her to Europe; which, though offered with perfect sincerity, were, by her, rejected once more, with this humble declaration:

"I am born a low contemptible slave. Were you to treat me with too much attention, you must degrade yourself with all your friends and relations, while the purchase of my freedom you will find expensive, difficult and apparently impossible. Yet though a slave, I have a soul, I hope, not inferior to that of a European, and blush not to avow the regard I retain for you, who have distinguished me so much above all others of my unhappy birth. You have, Sir, pitied me, and now, independent of every other thought, I shall have pride in throwing myself at your feet, till fate shall part us or my conduct becomes such as to give you cause to banish me from your presence."

This she uttered with a downcast look, and tears dropping on her heaving bosom, while she held her companion by the hand.

From that instant this excellent creature was mine; nor had I ever cause to repent of the step I had taken, as will more particularly appear in the course of this narrative.

I cannot omit to record, that having purchased for her presents to the value of twenty guineas, I was the next day greatly astonished to see all my gold returned upon the table, the charming Joanna having carried every article back to the merchants, who cheerfully returned her the money.

"Your generous intentions alone, Sir (she said), were sufficient: but allow me to tell you, that I cannot help considering any superfluous expense on my account as a diminution of that good opinion which I hope you have, and will ever entertain, of my disinterested disposition."

Such was the language of a slave, who had simple nature only for her instructor, the purity of whose sentiments stood in need of no comment; and these I was now determined to improve by every care.

In the evening I visited Mr. Demelly, who, with his lady, congratulated me on my recovery from sickness. At the same time, however strange it may appear to my readers, they, with a smile, wished me joy of what, with their usual good humour, they were pleased to call my conquest. One of the ladies in company assured me that while it was perhaps censured by some, it was applauded by many, and she believed in her heart it was envied by all. A decent wedding, at which many of our respectable friends made their appearance, and at which I was as happy as any bridegroom ever was, concluded the ceremony.

AFTER THE WAR: RECUPERATION AT PARAMARIBO

As I was not yet recovered, I stayed some time longer at Paramaribo. On the 21st of February, Mr Reynsdorp, the son-in-law of Mrs Godefroy, took me in his sail barge for change of air to Nuten-Schadelyk, one of his own coffee estates. The following day, sailing up Comewina River, we proceeded to the delightful cacao plantation Alkamaar, the property of the above lady, where the negro slaves are treated like children by the mistress, to whom they all look up as to their common parent. Here were no groans to be heard, no fetters to be met with, nor any marks of severity to be seen – but all was harmony and content.

On the 27th we returned to town where, the day before, a Society soldier had been shot for mutiny, and the day following a ship was burnt in the roads. This being the period of the sessions, another negro's leg was cut off for skulking from a task to which he was unequal, while two more were condemned to be hanged for running away together. The heroic behaviour of one of these men before the court particularly deserves to be noticed. He begged only to be heard for a few moments, which being granted, he proceeded thus:

"I was born in Africa, where, defending my prince during an engagement, I was made a captive and sold for a slave on the coast of Guinea by my own countrymen. One of your countrymen, who is now to be one of my judges, became my purchaser, in whose service I was treated so cruelly by his overseer that I deserted and joined the rebels in the woods. Here again I was condemned to be a slave to Bonny, their chief, who treated me with even more severity than I had experienced from the Europeans, till I was once more forced to elope, determined to shun mankind forever and inoffensively end my days in the forest. Two years had I persevered in this manner quite alone, undergoing the greatest hardships and anxiety of mind, preserving life only for the possibility of once more seeing my dear family, who were perhaps starving on my account in my own country. I say two miserable years had elapsed, when I was discovered by the rangers, taken and brought before this tribunal, who are now acquainted with the history of my wretched life, and from whom the only favour I have to ask is that I may be executed next Saturday, or as soon as it may be possibly convenient."

This speech was uttered with the utmost moderation, by one of the finest-looking negroes that was perhaps ever seen. His former master, who, as he observed, was now one of the judges, made the following laconic reply: "Rascal! That is not what we want to know; but the torture this moment shall make you confess your crimes as black as yourself, as well as those of your hateful accomplices." To which the negro, who now swelled in every vein with indignation and ineffable contempt, said *"Masera,* the tigers have trembled for these hands," holding them up; "and dare you think you can threaten me with your wretched instrument? No, I despise the utmost tortures you can now invent, as much as I do the pitiful wretch who is going to inflict them." Saying which, he threw himself down onto the rack, where amidst the most excruciating torments he remained with a smile, without uttering a syllable; nor did he ever speak again, until he ended his unhappy days at the gallows.

Having dined with Colonel Fourgeoud on the 8th of March, when we celebrated the Prince of Orange's birthday while Mr Reyndorp gave a treat to all the soldiers, he acquainted me that the rangers were now alone encamped at the Wana Creek, that the pestilential spot Devil's Harwar was at last entirely forsaken, and that the two lately raised companies of sable volunteers had taken a few prisoners and killed the officers on the Wanica path, behind Paramaribo. I was at this time a good deal better, but still, not being quite recovered, he who had formerly treated me so severely, now insisted on my staying some longer time in Paramaribo: nay, gave me an offer to return to Europe, which I absolutely refused. In short, about the middle of the month, I was as well as ever I was in my life. At this time Colonel Fourgeoud and myself were daily visitors of the ladies, in whose company no man could behave better, while I could often not avoid disgust; indeed so languid were many in their looks, and so unrestrained were some in conversation, that one even asked me, *sans ceremonie,* to supply the place of her husband. She might as well have asked me to drink, for a relish, a tumbler of salts.

On the 17th, however, my eyes were better feasted, when, going to dine with Colonel Texier of the Society troops, I first took a walk in the orange grove and the governor's gardens. Here, peeping through the foliage, I soon discovered two of the most elegant female figures after bathing, the one a fine young Samboe, the other a blooming Quadroon, which last was so very fair complexioned, that she might have passed for a native of Greece, while the roses that glowed in her cheek were equal to those that bloomed in the shrubbery. They were walking hand in hand, and conversing with smiles near a flowery bank that adorned the side of a crystal brook, in which they plunged the instant they heard me rustling the verdure.

RETURN TO EUROPE

Having at this time received a considerable present of refreshments, sent by the city of Amsterdam to the deliverers of their favourite colony, and being so near revisiting their old friends and acquaintances, all on board were in the highest flow of spirits and exulting with gladness – excepting one, from whose mind every happiness was banished.

On the 3rd June, everything being in readiness, the troops were put on board six lighters apponted to transport them to Bois-le-Duc, in which town they were next to be completed, and do the duty as part of the garrison. As we passed in the lighters through the inland towns, such as Saardam, Haarlem and Tergow, I thought them truly magnificent, particularly the glass painting in the great church of the latter; but their inhabitants, who crowded about us from curiosity to see us, appeared but a distinguishing assemblage of ill-formed and ill-dressed rabble, so much had my prejudices been changed by living among the Indians and blacks. Their eyes seemed to resemble those of a pig, their complexions were like the colour of foul linen; they seemed to have no teeth, and to be covered over with rags and dirt. This prejudice, however, was not against these people only, but against all Europeans in general, when compared to the sparkling eyes, ivory teeth, shining skin, and remarkable cleanliness of those I had left behind me. But the most ludicrous circumstance was that during all this we were never once considered the truly extraordinary figure that we made ourselves, being so much sunburnt and so pale that we were nearly the colour of dried parchment, and so thin we looked like moving skeletons; to which, I may add, that having

JOHN GABRIEL STEDMAN

lived so long in the woods, we had perfectly the appearance of wild people; and I in particular, very deservedly, obtained the characteristic title of *le Sauvage Anglais*, or the English savage.

J. B. MORETON

FROM *IN THE WEST INDIA ISLANDS*

INDIAN CUSTOMS AND MANNERS

Some master and overseers, of jealous, pimping dispositions, flog and otherwise ill treat their black wenches, when they chance to get black children. I have been often diverted, and laughing heartily, when a raw, infatuated gaukey, or a doating, debilitated debauchee has been disappointed, after all his endearing fondness and amorous exertions, with his soft, slobber-chop bundle, to get a black, instead of an olive babe. I shall annex the song of a young woman who was in this predicament:- it is in the negroe dialect, and is no less true than curious:

AIR. What care I for Mam or Dad.

Altho' a slave me is born and bred,
    My skin is black, not yellow:
I often sold my maidenhead
    To many a handsome fellow.

My massa keep me once, for true,
    And gave me clothes, wid busses:
Fine muslin coats, wid bitty, too,
    To gain my sweet embraces.

When pickinniny him come black,
    My massa starve and fum me,
He tear the coat from off my back,
    And naked him did strip me.

Him turn me out into the field,
    Wid hoe, the ground to clear-o;
Me take pickinniny on my back,
    And work him te-me weary.

Him, Obissha, him de come one night,
    And give me gown and busses;
Him get one pickanniny, white!
    Almost as white as missess.

J. B. MORETON

Then missess fum me wid long switch,
    And say him da for massa;
My massa curse her, "lying bitch!"
    And tell her, "buss my rassa!"

Me fum'd when me no condescend;
    Me fum'd too if me do it;
Me no have no one for 'tand my friend,
    So me am forc'd to do it.

Me know no law, me know no sin,
    Me is just what ebba them make me;
This is the way dem bring me in;
    So God nor devil take me!

The virtue and chastity, as well as the lives and properties of women, are at the command of the masters and overseers; they are perpetually exposed to the prostitution of them and their friends: it is pity that there is not some law to protect them from abuses so tyrannic, cruel and abominable. There was a law of the Lumbards, setting forth, That if a master debauched his slave, she was to be restored to her freedom; and, if she had a husband, him also.

    Notwithstanding all their hardships, they are fond of plays and merriment; and if not prevented by whites, according to a law of the island, they will meet on Saturday-nights, hundreds of them in gangs, and dance and sing till morning; nay, sometimes they continue their balls without intermission till Monday-morning. I have often gone, out of curiosity, to such meetings, and was highly diverted: their music is composed of any thing that makes a tinkling sound; a hollow cane, or bamboo, with holes in it, in imitation of a drum, called a gumbay: but sometimes more "gaudy balls", as they are called, are honoured with a tabret and violin; in which case, they are visited by the better sort of the neighbouring plantation negroes, and suppers and strong liquors are prepared by a few of the knowing-ones. They prepare a number of pots, some of which are good and savory; chiefly their swine, poultry, salt beef, pork, herrings, and vegetables, with roasted, barbacued and fricaseed rates, &c. &c.; all which they divide into small quantities, in calabashes, (bitts and half-bitts' worth) on which those who are able to purchase regale themselves. Their funerals and weddings are celebrated in this manner: indeed, I think I never saw anything that so nearly resembled the amusements, particularly the patrons held on Sundays, by the vulgar peasantry on the mountains in Ireland; where, to the music of a rotten bagpipe, or crazy fiddle, they dance to "tire each other down"; where they court, laugh and sing, at once; and cry, pipe and play at once; and where they gormandize and guttle, fight and quarrel at once!

When dancing, they form themselves into a circular position, adjoining some of their huts, and continue all in motion, singing so loud, that of a calm night they may be heard at about two miles distance – thus:

> Hipsaw! My deaa! You no do like a-me!
> You no jig like a-me! You no twist like a-me!
> Hipsaw! My deaa! You no shake like a-me!
> You no wind like a-me! Go, yondaa!
> Hipsaw! My deaa! You no jig like a-me!
> You no work him like a-me! You no sweet him like a-me!

Or, thus:

> Tajo, tajo, tajo! Tajo, my mackey massa!
> O! laud, O! tajo, tajo tajo!
> You work for him, mackey massa!
> A little more, my mackey massa!
>
> Tajo, tajo, tajo! My mackey massa!
> O! laud, O! tajo, tajo, tajo!
> I'll please my mackey massa!
> I'll jig to mackey massa!
> I'll sweet my mackey massa!

Thus they go on; so that it would be almost impossible for a stoic to look on without laughing. The droll capers, and wanton gestures and attitudes – the languishing glances and grimaces, so consequential and serious, of those flat-nosed damsels, timed to admiration by their jetty beau partners, are truly curious: It is very amazing to think with what agility they twist and move their joints:- I sometimes imagined they were on springs or

J. B. MORETON

hinges, from the hips downwards; whoever is most active and expert at wriggling, is reputed the best dancer. You will find amongst them many beautiful young creatures; so that you cannot possibly look on unmoved: they have too many alluring tricks to seduce and lead men astray. Perseus was moved to war by the beauty of a black woman: the great Mark Antony, once lord of the empire, could not withstand Cleopatra's jetty charms: whilst roses and lilies fade, true black, like the yew that never sheds leaves, is still the same.

> Of scorching toil regardless all the day,
> When freed from labour, cheerfully they play;
> And oft' assemble on the grassy plains,
> Expos'd to dews, foul air, and drizzly rains,
> With their hearts elate, in crowds, each in a ring,
> To dance their gumbay, and in chorus sing.
> Such scenes, I'm sure, in curious masquerade,
> By British lords and nymphs were ne'er displayed:
> When scabby Mungo, with a carv'd backside,
> Is Laura's partner, and sweet Laura's pride:
> Where Bess and Hecate, with their chigger toes,
> Mimba, crabyarv'd, and Grace with canker'd nose,
> Twist, wind and wriggle with the mackey beaux.
>
> Where Flora, Phillis, Silvia, Sall and Nell,
> In beauty's pomp their sable sex excel:
> With shifts and gowns, white hats and trinkets too,
> Skins, soft as silk, engaging glossy hue!
> And cock-up bubbies, ripe for soft delight,
> Twist, wind and turn, and turn and wind all night.
>
> When wanton Jiggo, with "side-long looks of love,"
> To mutual rapture do each other move;
> With kind compliance, and with warm desire,
> In melting pairs, they privately retire
> To lonely shades, to fences or old walls,
> To dance more pleasing jigs than at their balls:
> Whilst others slily to their huts advance,
> And twin'd in love, repeat the charming dance.
> On pork and pullets some do highly feast,
> Whilst others, hungry, can't procure a taste:

J. B. MORETON

Some gobble yams, or pepper-pot, or pease,
Or, rats and fungee, dress'd their different ways.
Whilst to the music some obedient hobble.

If you for goddesses shou'd be inclined,
There Junos and Dianas you may find;
Or, if you choose one of a royal strain,
A princess, queen, or duchess you may gain.

    Their form of marriage is nothing more than that the parents or friends of both parties meet on these festival nights, and give consent that the amorous pair may be united as long as they like each other:- ten to one, not so ceremonious, make matches without any public parade. Poor creatures! They have no idea of virtue or fidelity; the men are as fashionably wicked as white noblemen, in carrying on intrigues: some will have a dozen women in keeping at once; and the women, in return, can manage theirs as slily as a duchess. Their compliments of respect and friendship, when speaking of or to each other, is Uncle, Aunty, Granny, Tatta, Momma, Sifta, Boda. Though a white man was to give a black or mugrel £1,000 yearly, I don't think she could confine herself entirely to him only.

GEORGE COLMAN

FROM *INKLE AND YARICO*

[*As the curtain draws, Yarico and Wowski, discover'd asleep.*]

Trudge
[*Aside*] A woman! – [*Loud*] But let him come on; I'm ready – dam'me, I don't fear facing the devil himself – Faith it is a woman – fast asleep too.

Inkle
And beautiful as an angel!

Trudge
And, egad! There seems to be a nice little plump bit in the corner; only she's an angel of rather a darker sort.

Inkle
Hush keep back – she wakes. [*Yarico comes forward – Inkle and Trudge retire.*]

Song – Yarico
When the chace of day is done,
And the shaggy lion's skin,
Which for us, our warriors win,
Decks our cells, at set of sun;
Worn with toil, with sleep opprest.
I press my mossy bed, and sink to rest.

Then once more, I see our train,
With all our chace renew'd again:
    Once more, 'tis day,
    Once more, our prey
Gnashes his angry teeth, and foams in vain.
    Again, in sullen haste, he flies,
    Ta'en in the toil, again he lies,
Again he roars – and, in my slumber dies.

Inkle
Our language!

GEORGE COLMAN

Trudge
Zounds, she has thrown me into a cold sweat.

Yarico
Hark! I heard a noise! Wowski, awake! Whence can it proceed! [*She wakes Wowski, and they both come forward – Yarico towards Inkle; Wowski towards Inkle; Wowski towards Trudge.*]

Yarico
Ah! What form is this? – are you a man!

Inkle
True flesh and blood my charming heathen, I promise you.

Yarico
What harmony in his voice! What a shape! How fair his skin is too! – [*gazing*]

Trudge
This must be a lady of quality, by her staring.

Yarico
Say, stranger, whence come you?

Inkle
From a far distant island; driven on this coast by distress, and deserted by my companions.

Yarico
And do you know the danger that surrounds you here? Our woods are fill'd with beasts of prey – my country men too – (yet, I think they couldn't find the heart) – might kill you – It wou'd be a pity if you fell in their way – I think I shou'd weep if you came to any harm.

Trudge
O ho! It's time, I see, to begin making interest with the chambermaid. [*Takes Wowski apart*]

Inkle
How wild and beautiful! Sure there's magic in her shape, and

she has riveted me to the place. But where shall I look for safety? Let me fly, and avoid my death.

Yarico
Oh! no – But – [*as if puzzled*] well then, die stranger, but don't depart. – But I will try to preserve you; and if you are kill'd, Yarico must die too! Yet, 'tis I alone can save you: your death is certain without my assistance; and indeed, indeed, you shall not want it.

Inkle
My kind Yarico! What mean, then, must be us'd for my safety?

Yarico
My cave must conceal you: none dare enter it since my father was slain in battle. I will bring you food by day, then lead you to our unfrequented groves, to listen to the nightingale. If you should sleep, I'll watch you, and wake you when there's danger.

Inkle
Generous Maid! Then, to you I will owe my life; and whilst it lasts, nothing shall part us.

Yarico
And shan't it, shan't it indeed?

Inkle
No, my Yarico! For when an opportunity offers to return to my country, you shall be my companion.

Yarico
What! Cross the seas!

Inkle
Yes. Help me to discover a vessel, and you shall enjoy wonders. You shall be deck'd in silks, my brave maid, and have a horse drawn with horses to carry you.

Yarico
Nay, do not laugh at me – but is it so?

GEORGE COLMAN

Inkle
It is indeed!

Yarico
Oh wonder! I wish my countrywomen cou'd see me – But won't your warriors kill us?

Inkle
No, our only danger on land, is here.

Yarico
Then let us retire further into the cave. Come – your safety is in my keeping.

Inkle
I follow you – Yet, can you run some risque in following me?

DUET

Inkle
O say simple maid, have you form'd any notion
Of all the rude dangers in crossing the ocean?
When winds whistle shrilly, ah! Won't they remind you,
To sigh, with regret for the grot left behind you?

Yarico
Ah! No, I cou'd follow, and sail the world over,
Nor think of my grot, when I look at my lover!
The winds which blow us round us, your arms for my pillow,
Will lull us to sleep, whilst we're rocked by each billow.

Both
O say then, my true love, we will never sunder.
Nor shrink from the tempest, nor dread the big thunder:
While constant, we'll laugh at all changes of weather,
And journey over the world, both together.

[*Exeunt; as retiring further into the Cave.*]

Trudge
Why, you speak English as well as I, my little Wowski.

Wowski
Iss.

Trudge
Iss! And you learnt it from a strange man, that tumbled from a big boat, many moons ago you say?

Wowski
Iss – Teach me – Teach good many.

Trudge
Then, what the devil made'em so sorpriz'd at seeing us! Was he like me? [*Wowski shakes her head.*] Not so smart a body may-hap. Was his face, now, round, and comely, and – eh I [*Stroaking his chin*] Was it like mine?

Wowski
Like dead leaf – brown and shrivel.

Trudge
Oh oh, an old shipwreck'd sailor, I warrant. With white and grey hair, eh, my pretty beauty spot?

Wowski
Iss; all white, when night come he put it in pocket.

Trudge
Oh! wore a wig, But the old boy taught you something more than English, I believe.

Wowski
Iss.

Trudge
The devil he did. What was it?

Wowski
Teach me put dry grass, red hot, in hollow white stick.

Trudge
Aye, what was that for?

GEORGE COLMAN

Wowski
Put in my mouth – go poff, poff.

Trudge
Zounds? Did he teach you to smoke?

Wowski
Iss.

Trudge
And what became of him at last? What did your countrymen do for the poor fellow?

Wowski
Eat him one day – Our chief kill him.

Trudge
Mercy on us! What damn'd stomachs, to swallow a tough, old Tar! Though for the matter of that, there's many of our Captains would eat all they kill I believe! Ah, poor Trudge! Your killing comes next.

Wowski
No, no – not you – no – [*running to him anxiously*]

Trudge
No? What shall I do, if I get in their paws?

Wowski
I fight for you?

Trudge
Will you? Ecod, she's a brave good-natur'd wench! She'll be worth a hundred of your English wives – whenever they fight on their husband's account, it's with him instead of for him, I fancy. But how the plague am I to live here?

Wowski
I feed you – bring you kid.

GEORGE COLMAN

Song – Wowski

White man, never go away –
    Tell me why need you?
Stay with your Wowski, stay:
    Wowski will feed you.
Cold moons are now coming in:
    Ah, don't go grieve me!
I'll wrap you in leopard skin:
    White man, don't leave me.

MATTHEW G. LEWIS

THE RUNAWAY

(from *Journal of a Residence among the Negroes in the West Indies*)

Peter, Peter was a black boy;
    Peter, him pull foot one day;
Buckra girl, him Peter's joy;
    Lilly white girl entice him away.
Fye, Missy Sally, fye on you!
    Poor Blacky Peter why undo?
Oh! Peter, Peter was a bad boy;
    Peter was a runaway.

Peter, him Massa thief – Oh! fye
    Missy Sally, him say him do so.
Him money spent, Sally bid him bye,
    And from Peter away him go;
Fye, Missy Sally, fye on you!
    Poor Blacky Peter what him do?
Oh! Peter, Peter was a sad boy;
    Peter was a runaway!

Peter, him go to him Massa back;
    There him humbly own him crime:
"Massa, forgib one poor young Black!
    Oh! Massa, good Massa, forgib dis time!"
Then in come him Missy so fine, so gay,
    And to him Peter thus him say:
"Oh! Missy, good Missy, you for me pray!
    Beg Massa forgib poor runaway!

"Missy your cheek so red, so white;
    Missy, you eyes like diamond shine!
Missy, you Massa's sole delight,
    And Lilly Sally, him was mine!
Him say 'Come, Peter, wid me go,'
    Could me refuse him? Could me say 'no?'
Poor Peter – 'no' him could no say!
    So Peter, Peter ran away!"

MATTHEW G. LEWIS

Him Missy him pray; him Massa so kind
    Was moved by him prayer, and to Peter him say;
"Well, boy, for this once I forgive you! – but mind!
    With the buckra girls you no more go away!
Though fair without, they're foul within;
    Their heart is black, though white their skin.
Then Peter, Peter, with me stay;
    Peter no more run away!"

MICHAEL SCOTT

FROM *TOM CRINGLE'S LOG*

THE JOHN CANOE DANCE

He was clothed in an entire bullock's hide, horns, tail, and the other particulars, the whole of the skull being retained, and the effect of the voice growling through the jaws of the beast was most startling. His legs were enveloped in the skin of the hind-legs; while the arms were cased in that of the fore, the hands protruding a little above the hoofs, and, as he walked, reared up on his hind-legs, he used (in order to support the load of the John Canoe who had perched on his shoulders, like a monkey on a dancing bear) a strong stick, or sprit, with a crutch top on it, which he leant his breast on every now and then.

After the creature – which I will call the *Device* for shortness – had capered with its extra load, as if it had been a feather, for a minute or two, it came to a standstill, and, sticking the end of the sprit into the ground, and tucking the crutch under its chin, it motioned to one of the attendants, who thereupon handed – of all things in the world – *a fiddle to the ox*! He then shook off the John Canoe, who began to caper about as before, while the Device set up a deuced good pipe, and sung and played – barbarously enough, I will admit – to the tune of "Guinea Corn", the following ditty:

> "Massa Buccra lob for see
> Bullock caper like monkee –
> Dance, and shump and poke him toe,
> Like one humane person – just so."

And hereupon the tail of the beast, some fifty strong, music men, John Canoe and all, began to rampage about, as if they had been possessed by a devil whose name was Legion:

> "But Massa Buccra have white love,
> Soft and silken like one dove.
> To brown girl – him barley shivel! –
> To black girl – ho, Lord, de devil!"

Then a tremendous gallopading, in the which Tailtackle was nearly capsized over the wharf. He looked quietly over the edge of it.

"Boat-keeper, hand me up that switch of a stretcher." (Friend, if thou be'st not nautical, thou knowest what a rack-pin, something of the stoutest, is.)

The boy did so, and Tailtackle, after moistening well his dexter claw with tobacco juice, seized the stick with his left by the middle, and balancing it for a second or two, he began to fasten the end of it into his right fist, as if he had been screwing a bolt into a socket. Having satisfied himself that his grip was secure, he let go the hold with his left hand, and crossed his arms on his breast, with the weapon projecting over his left shoulder, like the drone of a bagpipe.

The *Device* continued his chant, giving the seaman a wide berth, however:

> "But when him once two tree year here,
> Him tink white lady wery great boder;
> De coloured peoples, never fear,
> Ah, him lob him de morest nor any oder."

Then another tumblication of the whole party.

> "But top – one time had fever catch him,
> Coloured peoples kindly watch him –
> In sick-room, nurse voice like music –
> From him hand taste sweet de physic."

Another trampoline,

> "So alway come – in two tree year,
> And so wid you, massa – never fear –
> Brown girl for cook – for wife – for nurse,
> Buccra lady – poo – no wort a curse."

"Get away, you scandalous scoundrel," cried I; "away with you, sir!"

Here the morrice dancers began to circle round old Tailtackle, keeping him on the move, spinning round like a weathercock in a whirlwind, while they shouted, "Oh, massa, one *macaroni* if you please." To get quit of their importunity, Captain Transom gave them one. "Ah, good massa, tank you, sweet massa!" And away danced John Canoe and his tail, careering up the street.

TEKAHIONWAKE (E. PAULINE JOHNSON)

A RED GIRL'S REASONING

"Be pretty good to her, Charlie, my boy, or she'll balk sure as shooting."

That was what old Jimmy Robinson said to his brand new son-in-law, while they waited for the bride to reappear.

"Oh! You bet, there's not danger of much else. I'll be good to her, help me Heaven," replies Charlie McDonald brightly.

"Yes, of course you will," answered the old man, "but don't you forget, there's a good bit of her mother in her, and," closing his left eye significantly, "you don't understand these Indians as I do."

"But I'm just as fond of them, Mr. Robinson," Charlie said assertively, "and get on with them too, now, don't I?"

"Yes, pretty well for a town boy; but when you have lived forty years among these people, as I have done; when you have had your wife as long as I have had mine – for there's no getting over it, Christine's disposition is as native as her mother's, every bit – and perhaps when you've owned for eighteen years a daughter as dutiful, as loving, as fearless, and alas! as obstinate as that little piece you are stealing away from me to-day – I tell you, youngster, you'll know more than you know now. It is kindness for kindness, bullet for bullet, blood for blood. Remember, what you are, she will be," and the old Hudson Bay trader scrutinised Charlie McDonald's face like a detective.

It was a happy, fair face, good to look at, with a certain ripple of dimples somewhere about the mouth, and eyes that laughed out the very sunniness of their owner's soul. There was not a severe nor yet a weak line anywhere. He was a well-meaning young fellow, happily dispositioned, and a great favourite with the tribe at Robinson's Post, whither he had gone in the service of Department of Agriculture, to assist the local agent through the tedium of a long census-taking.

As a boy he had had the Indian relic-hunting craze, as a youth he had studied Indian archaeology and folk-lore, as a man he consummated his predilections for Indianology by loving, winning and marrying the quiet little daughter of the English trader, who himself had married a native woman some twenty years ago. The country was all backwoods, and the Post

TEKAHIONWAKE (E. PAULINE JOHNSON)

miles and miles from even the semblance of civilisation, and the lonely young Englishman's heart had gone out to the girl who, apart from speaking a very few words of English, was utterly uncivilised and uncultured, but had withal that marvellously innate refinement so universally possessed by the higher tribes of the North American Indians.

Like all her race, observant, intuitive, having a horror of ridicule, consequently quick at acquirement and teachable in mental and social habits, she had developed from absolute pagan indifference into a sweet, elderly Christian woman, whose broken English, quiet manner, and still handsome copper-coloured face, were the joy of old Robinson's declining years.

He had given their daughter Christine all the advantages of his own learning – which, if truthfully told, was not universal; but the girl had a fair common education, and the native adaptability to progress.

She belonged to neither and still to both types of the cultured Indian. The solemn, silent, almost heavy manner of the one so commingled with the gesticulating Frenchiness and vivacity of the other, that one unfamiliar with native Canadian life would find it difficult to determine her nationality.

She looked very pretty to Charles McDonald's loving eyes, as she reappeared in the doorway, holding her mother's hand and saying some happy words of farewell. Personally she looked much the same as her sisters, all Canada through, who are the offspring of red and white parentage – olive-complexioned, grey-eyed, black-haired, with figure slight and delicate, and the wistful, unfathomable expression in her whole face that turns one so heartsick as they glance at the young Indians of to-day – it is the forerunner too frequently of "the white man's disease," consumption – but McDonald was pathetically in love, and thought her the most beautiful woman he had ever seen in his life.

There had not been much of a wedding ceremony. The priest had cantered through the service in Latin, pronounced the benediction in English, and congratulated the "happy couple" in Indian, as a compliment to the assembled tribe in the little amateur structure that did service at the post as sanctuary.

But the knot was tied as firmly and indissolubly as if all Charlie McDonald's swell city friends had crushed themselves

TEKAHIONWAKE (E. PAULINE JOHNSON)

up against the chancel to congratulate him, and in his heart he was deeply thankful to escape the flower pelting, white gloves, rice throwing, and ponderous stupidity of a breakfast, and indeed all the regulation gimcracks of the usual marriage celebrations, and it was with a hand trembling with absolute happiness that he assisted his little Indian wife into the old muddy buckboard that, hitched to an underbred-looking pony, was to convey them over the first stages of their journey. Then came more adieus, some hand clasping, old Jimmy Robinson looking very serious just at the last, Mrs. Jimmy, stout, stolid, betraying nothing of visible emotion, and then the pony, roughshod and shaggy, trudged, while mutual hand-waves were kept up until the old Hudson's Bay Post dropped out of sight, and the buckboard with its lightsome load of hearts, deliriously happy, jogged on over the uneven trail.

*

She was "all the rage" that winter at the provincial capital. The men called her a "deuced fine little woman". The ladies aid she was "just the sweetest wildflower". Whereas she was really but an ordinary, pale, dark girl who spoke slowly and with a strong accent, who danced fairly well, sang acceptably, and never stirred outside the door without her husband.

Charlie was so proud of her; he was proud that she had "taken" so well among his friends, proud that she bore herself so complacently in the drawing-rooms of the wives of pompous Government officials, but doubly proud of her almost abject devotion to him. If ever a human being was worshipped that being was Charlie McDonald; it could scarcely have been otherwise, for the almost godlike strength of his passion for that little wife of his would have mastered and melted a far more invincible citadel than an already affectionate woman's heart.

Favourites socially, McDonald and his wife went everywhere. In fashionable circles she was "new" – a potent charm to acquire popularity, and the little velvet-clad figure was always the center of interest among all the women in the room. She always dressed in velvet. No woman in Canada, has she but the faintest dash of native blood in her veins, but loves velvets and silks. As beef to the Englishman, wine to the Frenchman, fads to the Yankee, so are velvet and silk to the Indian girl, be she wild as prairie grass, be she on the borders of civilisation, or, having stepped within its boundary, mounted the steps of culture even under its superficial heights.

"Such a dolling little apple blossom," said the wife of a local M.P., who brushed up her etiquette and English once a year at Ottawa. "Does she always laugh so sweetly, and gobble you up with those great big grey eyes of hers, when you are togetheah at home, Mr. McDonald? If so, I should think youah pooah brothah would feel himself terribly *de trop*."

He laughed lightly. "Yes, Mrs. Stuart, there are not two of Christie; she is the same at home and abroad, and as for Joe, he doesn't mind us a bit; he's no end fond of her."

"I'm very glad he is. I always fancied he did not care for her, d'you know."

If ever a blunt woman existed it was Mrs. Stuart. She really meant nothing, but her remark bothered Charlie. He was fond of his brother, and jealous for Christie's popularity. So that night when he and Joe were having a pipe he said: "I've never asked you yet what you thought of her, Joe."

A brief pause, then Joe spoke. "I'm glad she loves you."

"Why?"

"Because that girl has but two possibilities regarding humanity – love or hate."

"Humph! Does she love or hate you?"

"Ask her."

"You talk bosh. If she hated you, you'd get out. If she loved you, I'd make you get out."

Joe McDonald whistled a little, then laughed.

"Now that we are on the subject, I might well ask – honestly, old man, wouldn't you and Christine prefer keeping house alone to having me always around?"

"Nonsense, sheer nonsense. Why, thunder, man, Christie's no end fond of you, and as for me – you surely don't want assurances from me?"

"No, but I often think a young couple–"

"Young couple be blowed! After a while when they want you and your old surveying chains, and spindle-legged tripod telescope kickshaws, farther west, I venture to say the little woman will cry her eyes out – won't you Christie?" This last in a higher tone, as through clouds of tobacco smoke he caught sight of his wife passing the doorway.

She entered. "Oh, no, I would not cry; I never do cry,

TEKAHIONWAKE (E. PAULINE JOHNSON)

but I would be heart-sore to lose you, Joe, and apart from that" – a little wickedly – "you may come in handy for an exchange some day, as Charlie does always say when he hoards up duplicate relics."

"Are Charlie and I duplicates?"

"Well – not exactly" – her head a little to one side, and eyeing them both merrily, while she slipped softly onto the arm of her husband's chair – "but, in the event of Charlie's failing me–" everyone laughed then. The "some day" that she spoke of was nearer than they thought. It came about in this wise.

There was a dance at the Lieutenant-Governor's, and the world and his wife were there. The nobs were in great feather that night, particularly the women, who flaunted about in new gowns and much splendour. Christie McDonald had a new gown also, but wore it with the utmost unconcern, and if she heard any flattering remarks made about her she at least appeared to disregard them.

"I never dreamed you could wear blue so splendidly," said Captain Logan, as they sat out a dance together.

"Indeed she can, though," interposed Mrs. Stuart, halting in one of her gracious sweeps down the room with her husband's private secretary. "Don't shout so, captain. I can hear every sentence you uttah – of course Mrs. McDonald can wear blue – she has a morning gown of cadet blue that she is a picture in."

"You are both very kind," said Christie. "I like blue; it is the color of all the Hudson's Bay posts, and the factor's residence is always decorated in blue."

"Is it really? How interesting – do tell us some more of your old home, Mrs. McDonald; you so seldom speak of your life at the post, and we fellows so often wish to hear of it all," said Logan eagerly.

"Why do you not ask me of it, then?"

"Well – er, I'm sure I don't know; I'm fully interested in the Ind – in your people – your mother's people, I mean, but it always seems so personal, I suppose; and– a– a–"

"Perhaps you are, like all other white people, afraid to mention my nationality to me."

The captain winced, and Mrs. Stuart laughed uneasily. Joe McDonald was not far off, and he was listening, and chuckling, and saying to himself, "That's you, Christie, lay 'em

TEKAHIONWAKE (E. PAULINE JOHNSON)

out; it won't hurt 'em to know how they appear once in a while."

"Well, Captain Logan," she was saying, "what was it you would like to hear – of my people, or my parents, or myself?"

"All, all, my dear," cried Mrs. Stuart clamorously. "I'll speak for him – tell us of yourself and your mother – your father is delightful, I am sure – but then he is only an ordinary Englishman, not half as interesting as a foreigner, or – perhaps I should say, a native."

Christie laughed. "Yes," she said, "my father often teases my mother now about how *very* native she was when he married her; then, how could she have been otherwise? She did not know a word of English, and there was not another English-speaking person besides my father and his two companions within sixty miles."

"Two companions, eh? One a Catholic priest and the other a wine merchant, I suppose, and with your father in the Hudson's Bay, they were good representatives of the pioneers in the New World," remarked Logan, waggishly.

"Oh, no, they were all Hudson's Bay men. There were no rum-sellers and no missionaries in that part of the country then."

Mrs. Stuart looked puzzled. "No *missionaries*?" she repeated with an odd intonation.

Christie's insight was quick: there was a peculiar expression of interrogation in the eyes of her listeners, and the girl's blood leapt angrily up into her temples as she said hurriedly, "I know what you are thinking. You are wondering how my parents were married–"

"Well – er, my dear, it seems peculiar – if there was no priest, and no magistrate, why– a–" Mrs. Stuart paused awkwardly.

"The marriage was performed by Indian rites," said Christie.

"Oh, do tell me about it; is the ceremony very interesting and quaint – are your chieftains anything like Buddhist priests?" It was Logan who spoke.

"Why, no," said the girl in amazement at that gentleman's ignorance. "There is no ceremony at all, save a feast. The two people just agree to live with and for each other, and the man takes his wife to his home, just as you do. There is no ritual to bind them; they need none; an Indian's word was his law in those days, you know."

Mrs. Stuart stepped backwards. "Ah!" was all she said. Logan removed his eye-glass and stared blankly at Christie. "And did McDonald marry you in this singular fashion?" he questioned.

"Oh, no, we were married by Father O'Leary. Why do you ask?"

"Because if he had, I'd have blown his brains out tomorrow."

Mrs. Stuart's partner, who had hitherto been silent, coughed and began to twirl his cuff stud nervously, but nobody took any notice of him. Christie had risen, slowly, ominously – risen, with the dignity and pride of an empress.

"Captain Logan," she said, "what do you dare to say to me? What do you dare to mean? Do you presume to think it would not have been lawful for Charlie to marry me according to my people's rites? Do you for one instant dare to question that my parents were not as legally–"

"Don't, dear, don't," interrupted Mrs. Stuart hurriedly; "it is bad enough now, goodness knows; don't make – " Then she broke off blindly. Christie's eyes glared at the mumbling woman, at her uneasy partner, at the horrified captain. Then they rested on the McDonald brothers, who stood within earshot, Joe's face scarlet, her husband's white as ashes, with something in his eyes she had never seen before. It was Joe who saved the situation. Stepping quickly across towards his sister-in-law, he offered her his arm, saying, "The next dance is ours, I think, Christie."

Then Logan pulled himself together, and attempted to carry Mrs. Stuart off for the waltz, but for once in her life that lady had lost her head. "It is shocking!" she said, "outrageously shocking! I wonder if they told Mr. McDonald before he married her!" Then looking hurriedly round, she too saw the young husband's face – and knew that they had not.

"Humph! deuced nice kettle of fish – poor old Charlie has always thought so much of honorable birth."

Logan thought he spoke in an undertone, but "poor old Charlie" heard him. He followed his wife and brother across the room. "Joe," he said, "will you see that a trap is called?" Then to Christie, "Joe will see that you get home alright." He wheeled on his heel then and left the ballroom.

Joe *did* see.

He tucked a poor, shivering, pallid little woman into a cab, and wound her bare throat up in the scarlet velvet cloak that was hanging uselessly over her arm. She crouched down beside him, saying, "I am so cold, Joe; I am so cold," but she did not seem to know enough to wrap herself up. Joe felt all through this long drive that nothing this side of Heaven would be so good as to die, and he was glad when the poor little voice at his elbow said, "What is he so angry at, Joe?"

"I don't know exactly, dear," he said gently, "but I think it was what you said about this Indian marriage."

"But why should I have not said it? Is there anything wrong about it?" she asked pitifully.

"Nothing, that I can see – there was no other way; but Charlie is very angry, and you must be brave and forgiving with him, Christie, dear."

"But I did never see him like that before, did you?"

"Once."

"When?"

"Oh, at college, one day, a boy tore his prayer-book in half, and threw it in the grate, just to be mean, you know. Our mother had given it to him at his confirmation."

"And did he look so?"

"About so, but it blew over in a day – Charlie's tempers are short and brisk. Just don't take any notice of him; run off to bed, and he'll have forgotten it by the morning."

They reached home at last. Christie said good-night quietly, going directly to her room. Joe went to his room also, filled a pipe and smoked for an hour. Across the passage, he could hear her slippered feet pacing up and down, up and down the length of her apartment. There was something panther-like in those restless footfalls, a meaning velvetyness that made him shiver, and again he wished he were dead – or elsewhere.

After a time the hall door opened, and someone came upstairs, along the passage, and to the little woman's room. As he entered, she turned and faced him.

"Christie," he said harshly, "do you know what you have done?"

"Yes," taking a step nearer him, her whole soul springing up into her eyes, "I have angered you Charlie, and–"

TEKAHIONWAKE (E. PAULINE JOHNSON)

"Angered me? You have disgraced me; and moreover, you have disgraced yourself and both your parents."

"*Disgraced?*"

"Yes, *disgraced*; you have literally declared to the whole city that your father and mother were never married, and that you are the child of – what shall we call it – love? Certainly not legality."

Across the hallway sat Joe McDonald, his blood freezing; but it leapt into every vein like fire at the awful anguish in that little voice that cried simply, "Oh! Charlie!"

"How could you do it, how could you do it, Christie, without shame either for yourself or for me, let alone your parents?"

The voice was like an angry demon's – not a trace was there in it of the yellow-haired, blue-eyed, laughing-lipped boy who had driven away so gaily to the dance five hours before.

"Shame? Why should I be ashamed of the rites of my people any more than you should be of the customs of yours – of a marriage more sacred and holy than half of your white man's mockeries?"

It was the voice of another nature in the girl – the love and the pleading were dead in it.

"Do you mean to tell me, Charlie – you who have studied my race and their laws for years – do you mean to tell me that, because there was no priest and no magistrate, my mother was not married? Do you mean to say that all my forefathers, for hundreds of years back, have been illegally born? If so, you blacken my ancestry beyond – beyond – beyond all reason."

"No, Christie, I would not be so brutal as that; but your father and mother live in more civilised times. Father O'Leary has been at the post for nearly twenty years. Why was not your father straight enough to have the ceremony performed when he *did* get the chance?"

The girl turned upon him with the face of a fury. "Do you suppose," she almost hissed, "that my mother would be married according to your *white* rites after she had been five years a wife, and I had been born in the meantime? No, a thousand times I say, no. When the priest came with his notions of Christianizing, and talked to them of re-marriage by the Church, my mother arose and said, 'Never – never – I have

TEKAHIONWAKE (E. PAULINE JOHNSON)

never had but this one husband; he has had none but me for wife, and to have you re-marry us would be to say as much to the whole world as that we had never been married before. You go away; I do not ask that *your* people be re-married; talk not so to me. I am married, and you or the Church cannot do or undo it.' "

"Your father was a fool not to insist upon the law, and so was the priest."

"Law? My people have *no* priest, and my nation cringes not to law. Our priest is purity, and our law is honour. Priest? Was there a *priest* at the most holy marriage known to humanity – that stainless marriage whose offspring is the God you white men told my pagan mother of?"

"Christie – you are *worse* than blasphemous; such a profane remark shows how little you understand the sanctity of the Christian faith–"

"I know what I *do* understand; it is that you are hating me because I told some of the beautiful customs of my people to Mrs. Stuart and those men."

"Pooh! who cares for them? It is not them; the trouble is they won't keep their mouths shut. Logan's a cad and will toss the whole tale about at the club before to-morrow night; and as for the Stuart woman, I'd like to know how I'm going to take you to Ottawa for presentation and the opening, while she is blabbing the whole miserable scandal in every drawing-room, and I'll be pointed out as a romantic fool, and you – as worse; I *can't* understand why your father didn't tell me before we were married; I at least might have warned you never to mention it." Something of recklessness rang up through his voice, just as the panther-likeness crept up from her footsteps and couched itself in hers. She spoke in tones quiet, soft, deadly.

"Before we were married! Oh! Charlie, would it have – made – any – difference?"

"God knows," he said, throwing himself into a chair, his blonde hair rumpled and wet. It was the only boyish thing about him now.

She walked towards him, then halted in the centre of the room. "Charlie McDonald," she said, and it was as if a stone had spoken, "look up." He raised his head, startled by her tone. There was a threat in her eyes that, had his rage been less courageous, his pride less bitterly wounded, would have cowed

TEKAHIONWAKE (E. PAULINE JOHNSON)

him.

"There was no such time as that before our marriage, for we *are not married now*. Stop," she said, outstretching her palms against him as he sprang to his feet, "I tell you we are not married. Why should I recognise the rites of your nation when you do not acknowledge the rites of mine? According to your own words, my parents should have gone through your church ceremony as well as through an Indian contract; according to *my* words, *we* should go through an Indian contract as well as through a church marriage. If their union is illegal, so is ours. If you think my father is living in dishonour with my mother, my people will think I am living in dishonour with you. How do I know when another nation will come and conquer you as you white men conquered us? And they will have another marriage rite to perform, and they will tell us another truth, that you are not my husband, that you are but disgracing and dishonouring me, that you are keeping me here, not as your wife, but as your – your *squaw*."

The terrible word had never passed her lips before, and the blood stained her face to her very temples. She snatched off her wedding ring and tossed it across the room, saying scornfully, "That thing is as empty to me as the Indian rites to you."

He caught her by the wrists: his small white teeth were locked tightly, his blue eyes blazed into hers.

"Christine, do you dare to doubt my honor towards you? you, whom I should have died for; do you dare to think I have kept you here, not as my wife but–"

"Oh, God! You are hurting me; you are breaking my arm," she gasped.

The door was flung open, and Joe McDonald's sinewy hands clinched like vices on his brother's shoulder.

"Charlie, you're mad, mad as the devil. Let go of her this minute."

The girl staggered backwards as the iron fingers loosed her wrists. "Oh, Joe," she cried, "I am not his wife, and he says I am born – nameless."

"Here," said Joe, shoving his brother towards the door. "Go downstairs till you can collect your senses. If ever a being acted like an infernal fool, you're the man."

The young husband looked from one to the other, dazed

TEKAHIONWAKE (E. PAULINE JOHNSON)

by his wife's insult, abandoned to a fit of ridiculously childish temper. Blind as he was with passion, he remembered long afterwards seeing them standing there, his brother's face darkened with a scowl of anger – his wife, clad in the mockery of her ball dress, her scarlet velvet cloak half covering her bare brown neck and arms, her eyes like flames of fire, her face like a piece of sculptured greystone.

Without a word he flung himself furiously from the room, and immediately afterwards they heard the heavy hall door bang behind him.

"Can I do anything for you, Christie?" asked her brother-in-law calmly.

"No, thank you – unless – I think I would like a drink of water, please."

He brought her up a goblet filled with wine; her hand did not even tremble as she took it. As for Joe, a demon arose in his soul as he noticed she kept her wrists covered.

"Do you think he will come back?" she said.

"Oh yes, of course; he'll be all right in the morning. Now go to bed like a good little girl, and – and, I say, Christie, you can call me if you want anything; I'll be right here, you know."

"Thank you, Joe; you are kind – and good."

He returned then to his apartment. His pipe was out, but he picked up a newspaper instead, threw himself into an armchair, and in a half-hour was in the land of dreams.

When Charlie came home in the morning, after a six-mile walk into the country and back again, his foolish anger was dead and buried. Logan's "poor old Charlie" did not ring so distinctly in his ears. Mrs. Stuart's horrified expression had faded considerably from his recollection. He thought only of that surprisingly tall, dark girl, whose eyes looked like coals, whose voice pierced him like a flint-tipped arrow. Ah, well, they would never quarrel again like that, he told himself. She loved him so, and would forgive him after he talked quietly to her, and told her what an ass he was. She was simple-minded and awfully ignorant to pitch those old Indian laws at him in her fury, but he could not blame her; oh, no, he could not for one moment blame her. He had been terribly severe and unreasonable, and the horrid McDonald temper had got the better of him; and he loved her so. Oh! He loved her so! She

TEKAHIONWAKE (E. PAULINE JOHNSON)

would surely feel that, and forgive him, and – he went straight to his wife's room. The blue velvet evening dress lay on the chair into which he had thrown himself when he doomed his life's happiness by those two words, "God knows". A bunch of dead daffodils and her slippers were on the floor, everything – but Christie.

He went to his brother's bedroom door.

"Joe," he called, rapping nervously thereon; "Joe, wake up; where's Christie, d'you know?"

"Good Lord, no," gasped that youth, springing out of his armchair and opening the door. As he did so a note fell from off the handle. Charlie's face blanched to his very hair while Joe read aloud, his voice weakening at every word:

"DEAR OLD JOE – I went into your room at daylight to get that picture of the Post on your bookshelves. I hope you do not mind, but I kissed your hair while you slept; it was so curly, and yellow, and soft, just like his. Good-bye, Joe.
"Christie"

And when Joe looked into his brother's face and saw the anguish settle in those laughing blue eyes, the despair that drove the dimples away from that almost girlish mouth; when he realised that this boy was but four-and-twenty years old, and that all his future was perhaps darkened and shadowed for ever, a great, deep sorrow arose in his heart, and he forgot all those things, all but the agony that rang up through the voice of the fair, handsome lad as he staggered forward, crying, "Oh! Joe – what shall I do – what shall I do?"

*

It was months and months before he found her, but during all that time he had never known a hopeless moment; discouraged he often was, but despondent, never. The sunniness of his ever-boyish heart radiated with a warmth that would have flooded a much deeper gloom than that which had settled within his eager young life. Suffer? Ah! Yes, he suffered, not with locked teeth and stony stoicism, not with the masterful self-command, the reserve, the conquered bitterness of the still-water sort of nature, that is supposed to run to such depths. He tried to be bright, and his sweet old boyish self. He took to petting dogs, looking into

TEKAHIONWAKE (E. PAULINE JOHNSON)

their large, solemn eyes with his wistful, questioning blue ones; he would kiss them, as women sometimes do, and call them "dear old fellow" in tones that had tears; and once in the course of his travels, while at a little way-station, he discovered a huge St. Bernard imprisoned by some mischance in an empty freight car; the animal was nearly dead from starvation, and it seemed to salve his own sick heart to rescue back the dog's life. Nobody claimed the big starving creature, the train hands knew nothing of its owner, and gladly handed it over to its deliverer. "Hudson," he called it, and afterwards when Joe McDonald would relate the story of his brother's life he invariably terminated it with, "And I really believe that big lumbering brute saved him." From what, he was never known to say.

But all things end, and he heard of her at last. She had never returned to the Post, as he at first thought she would, but had gone to the little town of B——, in Ontario, where she was making her living at embroidery and plain sewing.

The September sun had set redly when at last he reached the outskirts of the town, opened up the wicket gate, and walked up the weedy, unkept path leading to the cottage where she lodged.

Even through the twilight, he could see her there, leaning on the rail of the verandah – oddly enough she had about her shoulders the scarlet cloak she wore when he had flung himself so madly from the room that night.

The moment the lad saw her his heart swelled with a sudden heat, burning moisture leapt into his eyes, and clogged his long, boyish lashes. He bounded up the steps – "Christie," he said, and the word scorched his lips like an audible flame.

She turned to him, and for a second stood magnetised by his passionately wistful face; her peculiar grayish eyes seemed to drink the very life of his unquenchable love, though the tears that suddenly sprang into his seemed to absorb every pulse in his body through those hungry, pleading eyes of his that had, oh! so often, been blinded by her kisses when once her whole world lay in their blue depths.

"You will come back to me, Christie, my wife? My wife, you will let me love you again?"

She gave a singular little gasp, and shook her head. "Don't, oh! don't," he cried piteously. "You will come to me, dear? It is all such a bitter mistake – I did not understand. Oh!

TEKAHIONWAKE (E. PAULINE JOHNSON)

Christie, I did not understand, and you'll forgive me, and love me again, won't you – won't you?"

"No," said the girl with quick, indrawn breath.

He dashed the back of his hand across his wet eyelids. His lips were growing numb, and he bungled over the monosyllable "Why?"

"I do not like you," she answered quietly.

"God! Oh! God, what is there left?"

She did not appear to hear the heart-break in his voice; she stood like one wrapped in sombre thought; no blaze, no tear, nothing in her eyes; no hardness, no tenderness about her mouth. The wind was blowing her cloak aside, and the only visible human life in her whole body was once when he spoke the muscles of her brown arm seemed to contract.

"But, darling, you are mine – *mine* – we are husband and wife! Oh, heaven, you *must* love me, you *must* come to me again."

"You cannot *make* me come," said the icy voice, "neither church, nor law, nor even" – and the voice softened – "nor even love can make a slave of a red girl."

"Heaven forbid it," he faltered. "No, Christie, I will never claim you without your love. What union would that be? But, oh, Christie, you are lying to me, you are lying to yourself, you are lying to heaven."

She did not move. If only he could touch her he felt as sure of her yielding as he felt sure there was a hereafter. The memory of times when he had but to lay his hand on her hair to call a most passionate response from her filled his heart with torture that choked all words before they reached his lips; at the thought of those days he forgot she was unapproachable, forgot how forbidding were her eyes, how stony her lips. Flinging himself forward, his knee on the chair at her side, his face pressed hardly in the folds of the cloak on her shoulder, he clasped his arms about her with a boyish petulance, saying, "Christie, Christie, my little girl wife, I love you, I love you, and you are killing me."

She quivered from head to foot as his fair, wavy hair brushed her neck, his despairing face sank lower until his cheek, hot as fire, rested on the cool, olive flesh of her arms. A warm moisture oozed up through her skin, and as he felt its glow he looked up. Her teeth, white and cold, were locked over her

TEKAHIONWAKE (E. PAULINE JOHNSON)

under lip, and her eyes were as grey as stones.

"Is it all useless? All useless, dear?" he said, with lips starving for hers.

"All useless," she repeated. "I have no love for you now. You forfeited me and my heart months ago, when you said *those two words*."

His arms fell away from her wearily, he arose mechanically, he placed his little grey checked cap on the back of his yellow curls, the old-time laughter was dead in the blue eyes that now looked scared and haunted, the boyishness and the dimples crept away for ever from the lips that quivered like a child's; he turned from her, but she had looked once into his face as the Law Giver must have looked at the land of Canaan outspread at his feet. She watched him go down the long path and through the picket gate, she watched the big yellowish dog that had waited for him to lumber up to its feet – stretch – then follow him. She was conscious of but two things, the vengeful lie in her soul, and a little space on her arm that his wet lashes had brushed.

*

It was hours afterwards when he reached his room. He had said nothing, done nothing – what use were words or deeds? Old Jimmy Robinson was right; she had "balked" sure enough.

What a bare, hotelish room it was! He tossed off his coat and sat for ten minutes looking blankly at the sputtering gas jet. Then his whole life, desolate as a desert, loomed up before him with appalling distinctness. Throwing himself on the floor beside his bed, with clasped hands and arms outstretched on the white counterpane, he sobbed. "Oh! God, dear God, I thought you loved me; I thought you'd let me have her again, but you must be tired of me, tired of loving me, too. I've nothing left now, nothing! It doesn't seem that I even have you to-night."

He lifted his face then, for his dog, big and clumsy and yellow, was licking at his sleeve.

III.

EXPLORATIONS IN AFRICA AND THE NEAR EAST

Britain has a long history of interaction with Africa and the Near East, for reasons as varied as religious pilgrimage, scientific exploration or hunting expeditions. The Near East, encompassing a region stretching between India and the Eastern shores of the Mediterranean and also referred to as 'the Orient', forms one of the oldest and most popular destinations for Western travellers and colonisers. Indeed, a wealth of writing on the Near East includes work by Homer, Flaubert, Disraeli and Lawrence of Arabia.

Such writing has been essential to the way the Near East is viewed by Westerners. In his seminal text *Orientalism* (1978), Edward Said surveys depictions of the East by intellectuals, artists, commentators, politicians and writers in order to expose Western stereotypes of the Orient. He argues that such writing creates and popularises a fictional Orient, in which Easterners are depicted as lazy, gullible, cunning, lethargic, suspicious, sexually incontinent, unkind to animals and given to lying and flattery (essentially everything the proper Englishman is not). This construction of the Orient functions as a means of asserting Western superiority; as Said states, these stereotypes of the Near East depend on a *"positional superiority, which puts the Westerner in a whole series of possible relationships with the Orient without ever losing him the relative upper hand."*[1] According to Said, a catalogue of writing on the Orient does not so much reflect the reality of the Near East, but functions as an argument for Western religious, racial and cultural domination. As Billie Melman asserts, "[r]eal orientals are denied humanity, history and the authority to speak about and represent themselves, an authority which Orientalist travel writing reserves for occidentals."[2]

Lady Mary Wortley Montagu is one such occidental traveller. The wife of Edward Wortley, Ambassador Extraordinary to the Sublime Porte (Sultan Ahmet III), Montagu journeyed to Istanbul in 1717-8 and recorded her experiences in the *Turkish Embassy Letters* (published posthumously in 1763). The letters were scandalous in their day because of their access to women-only spaces such as brothels and bathhouses. As Jane

---

[1] Edward Said, *Orientalism* (London: Penguin, 2003), p.7.
[2] Billie Melman, 'The Middle East / Arabia: "the cradle of Islam" ' in Peter Hulme and Tim Youngs, *The Cambridge Companion to Travel Writing* (Cambridge: Cambridge University Press, 2002), p.107.

Robinson states, "the harems of Constantinople were hardly considered the most elegant of salons, and the company of native women, however exalted locally, must surely have been corrupting in the extreme."[3] The extract featured here shows the writer clearly taken with the host of a Turkish harem. Montagu writes, "I am not ashamed to own that I took more pleasure in looking on the beauteous Fatima than the finest piece of sculpture could ever have given me."

Fatima is representative of yet another Oriental stereotype—the lusty, lascivious native woman, the oversexed Eastern temptress who charms all with her spells. Such women feature regularly in Montagu's letters, but in ways we might not expect. Montagu's interest in women like Fatima turns her attention to Eastern polygamy, yet another Orientalist stereotype. However, Montagu celebrates polygamy instead of judging it negatively. She approves of the Muslim veil that covers female faces in the East primarily because it allows freedom to pursue extramarital interests without detection. "This perpetual Masquarade," Montagu writes, "gives them entire Liberty of following their Inclinations without Danger of Discovery... Upon the Whole, I look upon Turkish Women as the only free people in the Empire."[4]

The lusty Eastern woman is also featured in Lord Byron's *Don Juan*. Gulbeyaz, the young wife of the Sultan, is so taken with Juan after spotting him in a slave market that she orders his purchase and vows to train him in the ways of love. Apparently this is a common occurrence—Juan is but "the latest of her whims." Juan, however, still mourning the loss of his beloved wife Haidée, cannot return the Sultana's desire. Gulbeyaz resembles Fatima in both her beauty and her setting, but the poem's statements on the lasciviousness of Eastern women are much more conventional than Montagu's. 'Canto V' ends with a warning to Eastern men to keep tabs on their wives: "The Turks do well to shut—at least, sometimes— / The women up... in the East they are extremely strict, / And Wedlock and a Padlock mean the same."

The Eastern women presented in the novels of William Rufus Chetwood and Henry Brooke are better behaved than

---

[3] Jane Robinson, *Unsuitable for Ladies: An Anthology of Women Travellers* (Oxford: Oxford University Press, 1994), p.94.
[4] Qtd in ibid., pp.113-4.

those depicted by Montagu and Byron. Both Chetwood's *The Voyages, Travels and Adventures of William Owen Gwin Vaughan, Esq.* and Brooke's *The Fool of Quality* can be classified as what Roxann Wheeler terms "intermarriage novels", texts popular in the eighteenth century that depict Englishmen abroad in a positive light. The novels can be regarded as progressive in the sense that they work to erase racial and cultural divisions, not establish them; as Wheeler argues, "[u]nlike actual colonial and imperial relations, these narratives happily resolve religious conflict and dissimilar complexions through conversion and marriage."[5] The happy unions of Vaughan with Fatima and Harry Clinton with Abenaide suggest that race is not deterministic. Vaughan and Clinton are able to see past the dark complexions of their future wives, suggesting possible cultural and racial harmony.

Yet however progressive their depiction of intermarriage, Chetwood's and Brooke's texts must also be regarded as upholding ideals of imperial hegemony. Both novels assert the superiority of Western values by insisting Fatima and Abenaide convert to Christianity before marrying. While Montagu and Byron engage with the stereotype of the lascivious Eastern temptress, Chetwood and Brooke introduce an alternative stereotype—that of the pious Eastern woman eager to convert to Christianity for her white lover. As Wheeler argues, such devoted and converted women are typical of intermarriage novels: "The constraints in the characterisation over time include the Other woman's explicit passion; her actions to save the hero from the peril versus the comparative passivity of Christian heroines; the acceptance of Christianity's superiority; and the ensuing happiness of the couple."[6] Indeed, Fatima is eager to distance herself from the type of Eastern woman depicted by Montagu and Byron: as she states, "*I have found several stories in your Books of the Forwardness of* Moorish *Women; but believe me, dear* Englishman, *I hope never carry any thing but virtuous Inclinations in my Heart, which shall ever be yours.*" Religious conversion is also extended to Eastern men in Brooke's novel. The Duke and Eloisa's union can only take place after he

---

[5] Roxann Wheeler, *The Complexion of Race: Categories of Difference in Eighteenth Century British Culture* (Philadelphia: University of Pennsylvania Press, 2000), pp.139-40.
[6] Ibid., p.140.

requests "instant baptism" and is "washed by water and faith into Christ."

In addition to emphasising the superiority of Christianity, Chetwood's and Brooke's novels are also significant because of their rejection of homosexuality. In contrast to the masculine, heterosexual British male, Orientalist texts often depict Eastern men as feminine and homosexual. Two such depictions are seen in the extracts featured here; Vaughan must spurn the desires of the Moor's son (Fatima's brother), while Clinton is more than relieved when his homoerotic feelings for his best friend Abenamin are legitimised, the latter being exposed as a female in disguise. Abenamin's confession that he has a twin sister "as fair as I am black" thus doubly rights his relationship with Clinton—the fair, female Abenaide (a typical intermarriage heroine in her devotion to her white lover and his culture) forms a convenient solution to the homosexuality that strains the hegemonic boundaries of the novel. Homosexuality and religious difference are eliminated before the sanctified marriage takes place. (It is no coincidence that Abenaide resembles a "pillar of light" on her wedding day.)

Two authors—the Scottish explorer Mungo Park and the writer of popular Victorian boys' adventure stories H. Rider Haggard—represent interracial love and sex between the British and Africans. The diplomacy with which Park handles the request by a group of Moorish ladies to provide an "ocular demonstration" of whether Christian men are circumcised as Muslim men are is typical of the British approach to Africa of the time. The experiences recounted in *Travels in the Interior Districts of Africa* result from Park's 1795-7 explorations on behalf of the African Association, in which he was instructed to "ascertain the course, direction, source and terminus of the Niger River, and to make commercial and diplomatic contact with those who peopled its vicinity."[7] The Association's interest in Africa as a site of scientific knowledge and commercial potential led explorers like Park to treat Africans and African culture in a more sensitive light than previously. As Mary L. Pratt notes, while the English translator of Michel Adanson's *Voyage to Senegal* (1756) speaks of Africans as "poor and indolent," Danish physician Paul Isert is representative of a

---

[7] Qtd in Mary Louise Pratt, *Imperial Eyes: Travel Writing and Transculturation* (London: Routledge, 2002), p.70.

change in attitude when thirty years later he argues those who view Africans as "naturally lazy, obstinate, given to theft, drunknness, all the vices" will be "cured of their prejudices" upon exploration of the interior."[8] The delicacy and "jocularity" with which Park approaches the ladies' "unexpected declaration" is illustrative of his diplomatic mission.

Georgiana Cavendish's 'A Negro Song' is also illustrative of the sensitivity of Park's memoirs. The lyrics stem from Park's *Travels*, in which he records the song sung by the African women tending him. Cavendish, the Duchess of Devonshire and an active socialite and political campaigner, alters Park's lyrics to thank the "Negro" for surrogate nurturing when the white man is left with "no wife, or mother's care." Although, like the slave songs featured in Section II, the lyrics of 'A Negro Song' are distorted through their double reproduction, their inclusion here marks an important echo of African voices. That Cavendish used the song in abolition campaigns stresses the importance of this voice.

This section ends with extracts from two of H. Rider Haggard's novels. Their reading makes a strong contrast to the intermarriage novels of Chetwood and Brooke for their insistence on the romantic incompatibility of Africans and the British. Haggard's protagonist Allan Quatermain explicitly states that the two races are mismatched: although "[w]omen are women, all over the world, whatever their colour," he yet remains firmly against interracial unions: "we white men only wed white women like ourselves. Your maidens are fair, but not for us!" Tragically, Foulata, the "soft-eyed shapely Kukuana beauty" who falls in love with sailor Henry Good in *King Solomon's Mines*, agrees. Despite earlier declaring herself "my lord's handmaiden", upon her death Foulata echoes Quatermain's opinion of her unsuited relationship with Good: "I am glad to die because I know that he cannot cumber his life with such as that I am, for the sun may not mate with the darkness, nor the white with the black." Unlike the marriage of Henry Clinton and the fair Abenaide in *The Fool of Quality*, the cultural and racial differences in Haggard's novel appear too strong to overcome.

The union between Quatermain and Mameena in *Child*

---

[8] Qtd in ibid., p.70.

of Storm is similarly denied. While Foulata represents the faithful black woman who ultimately recognises her incompatibility with her white lover, Mameena is illustrative of the native temptress or dark African priestess. In the novel's dedication Haggard writes of his desire to show the Zulus "as they were, in all their superstitious madness." "[W]icked and fascinating Mameena, a kind of Zulu Helen," is this madness personified. Mameena is evil, ambitious and beautiful, and even worldly Quatermain falls prey to her magic when he agrees to declare his love for her with a very public kiss. Importantly, while Mameena personifies the superstition and witchcraft of African barbarism, her beauty stems from purely Western origins; like Helen of Troy, she resembles a Greek statue, "show[ing] no traces of the Negro type." Although her eventual union with Quatermain is refused, Mameena represents a significant character within Haggard's catalogue because of her proximity to the hero. While Quatermain usually spurns the advances of African women— *Child of Storm* again reminds readers that "snow and soot don't mix well together"—Mameena gets her kiss in the end and recurs in later stories as a fond memory of love lost.

LADY MARY WORTLEY MONTAGU
LETTER TO LADY MAR
(from the Turkish Embassy Letters)

Adrianople, 18 April 1718

I writ to you, dear sister, and to all my other English correspondents, by the last ship and only heaven can tell when I shall have another opportunity of sending you; but I cannot forbear writing though perhaps my letter may lie upon my hands this two months. To confess the truth my head is so full of my entertainment yesterday that 'tis absolutely necessary for my own response to give it some vent. Without farther preface, I will begin my story.

    I was invited to dine with the Grand Vizier's lady, and it was with a great deal of pleasure I prepared myself for an entertainment which was never given before to any Christian. I thought I should very little satisfy her curiosity, which I did not doubt was a considerable motive to the invitation, by going in a dress she was used to see, and therefore dressed myself in the court habit of Vienna, which is much more magnificent than ours. However, I chose to go incognito to avoid any disputes about ceremony, and went in a Turkish coach, only attended by my woman that held up my train and a Greek lady who was my interpretress. I was met at the court door by her black eunuch who helped me out of the coach with great respect, and conducted me through several rooms, where her she-slaves, finely dressed, were ranged on either side. In the innermost I found the lady sitting on the sofa, in a sable vest. She advanced to meet me, and presented me half a dozen of her friends with great civility. She seemed a very good woman, near fifty years old. I was surprised to observe so little magnificence in her house, the furniture being all very moderate and, except the habits and number of her slaves, nothing about her appeared expensive. She guessed at my thoughts and told me that she was not longer of an age to spend either her time or money on superfluities; that her whole expense was in charity, and her employment praying to God. There was no affectation in this speech; both she and her husband are entirely given to devotion. He never looks upon other women and, what is much more extraordinary, touches no bribes, notwithstanding the example of all his predecessors. He is so scrupulous on this point, he would not accept Mr Wortley's present till he had been assured 'over and over that 'twas a settled prerequisite of his place, at the entrance of every ambassador.

She entertained me with all kind of civility, till dinner came in, which was served, one dish at a time, to a vast number, all finely dressed after their manner, which I do not think so bad as you have perhaps heard it represented. I am a very good judge of their eating, having lived three weeks in the house of the *effendi* at Belgrade, who gave us very magnificent dinners, dressed by his own cooks which the first week pleased me extremely but, I own I then began to grow weary of it and desired our own cook might add a dish or two after our manner. But I attribute this to custom. I am very much inclined to believe an Indian that had never tasted either, would prefer their cookery to ours. Their sauces are very high, all the roast is very much done. They use a great deal of rich spice. The soup is served for the last dish and they have at least as great variety of ragouts as we have. I was very sorry I could not eat of as many as the good lady would have had me, who was very earnest in serving me of everything. The treat concluded with coffee and perfumes, which is a high mark of respect; two slaves kneeling censed my hair, clothes and handkerchief. After this ceremony she commanded her slaves to play and dance, which they did with their guitars in their hands, and she excused to me their want of skill, saying she took no care to accomplish them in that art. I returned her thanks and, soon after took my leave.

I was conducted back in the same manner I entered and would have gone straight to my own house but the Greek lady with me earnestly solicited me to visit the Kabya's lady, saying he was the second officer in the empire and ought indeed to be looked upon as the first, the Grand Vizier having only the name, while he exercised the authority. I had found so little diversion in this harem that I had no mind to go into another. But her importunity prevailed with me and I am extremely glad I was so complaisant. All things here were with quite another air then at the Grand Vizier's and the very house confessed the difference between an old devote and a young beauty. It was nicely clean and magnificent. I was met at the door by two black eunuchs who led me through a long gallery between two ranks of beautiful young girls, with their hair finely plaited almost hanging to their feet, all dressed in fine light damasks brocaded with silver. I was sorry that decency forbade to stop to consider them nearer. But that thought was lost upon my entrance into a large room or rather pavilion built round with gilded sashes, which were most of them thrown up and the trees near then gave an agreeable shade which hindered the sun from being troublesome, the jessamines and honeysuckles that twisted round their trunks shedding a soft perfume, increased by a white marble fountain playing sweet water in the lower part of the room, which fell into three of four basins with a pleasing sound. The roof was painted with all sorts of flowers falling out to gilded baskets, that seemed tumbling down.

On a sofa raised three steps and covered with fine Persian carpets, sat the Kabya's lady, leaning on cushions of white satin, embroidered, and at her feet sat two young girls, the eldest about twelve, lovely as angels, dressed perfectly rich, and almost covered in jewels. But they were hardly seen near the fair Fatima (for that is her name) so much her beauty effaced everything. I have seen all that has been called lovely either in England or Germany and must own that I never saw anything so gloriously beautiful, nor can I recollect a face that would have been taken notice of near hers. She stood up to receive me, saluting me after their fashion, putting her hand upon her heart with a sweetness full of majesty that no court breeding could ever give. She ordered cushions be given to me and took care to place me in the corner, which is the place of honour. I confess, though the Greek lady had before given me great opinion of her beauty I was so struck with admiration that I could not for some time speak to her, being wholly taken up in gazing. That whole harmony of features! That charming result of the whole! That exact proportion of the body! That lovely bloom of complexion, unsullied by art! The unutterable enchantment of her smile! But her eyes! Large and black, with all the soft languishment of the blue! Every turn of her face, discovering some new charm! After my first surprise was over I endeavoured, by nicely examining her face, to find out some imperfection, without any fruit of my search, but my being clearly convinced of the error of that vulgar notion. That a face being perfectly regular would not be agreeable; nature having done for her, with more success, what Apelles is said to have essayed, by a collection of the most exact features, to form a perfect face. And to that a behaviour so full of grace and sweetness, such easy motions, with an air so majestic, yet free from stiffness or affectation that I am persuaded, could she be suddenly transported upon the most polite throne of Europe nobody would think her other than born and bred to be a queen, though educated in a country we call barbarous. To say all in a word, our most celebrated English beauties would vanish near her.

    She was dressed in a caftan of gold brocade, flowered with silver, very well fitted to her shape, and showing to advantage the beauty of her bosom, only shaded by the thin gauze of her shift. Her drawers were pale pink, her waistcoat green and silver, her slippers white, finely embroidered, her lovely arms adorned with bracelets of diamonds; upon her head a rich Turkish handkerchief of pink and silver, her own fine black hair hanging a great length in various tresses, and on one side of her head some bodkins of jewels. I am afraid you will accuse me of extravagance in this description. I think I have read somewhere that women always speak in rapture when they speak of beauty, but I can't imagine why they should not be allowed to do so. I rather think it a virtue to be able to admire without any mixture of desire or envy. The gravest writers have spoken with great warmth of some celebrated pictures and statues. The workmanship of Heaven certainly excels all our weak intentions, and I am not ashamed to own that I took more pleasure in looking on the beauteous Fatima than the finest piece of sculpture could ever have given me. She told me the two girls at her feet were her daughters, though she appeared too young to be their mother.

    Her fair maids were ranged below the sofa, to the number of twenty, and put me in mind of the pictures of the ancient nymphs. I did not think all nature could have furnished such a scene of beauty. She made them a sign to play and dance. Four of them immediately began to play some soft airs on instruments, between a lute and a guitar, which they accompanied with their voices, while the others danced by turns. This dance was very different from what I had seen before. Nothing could be more artful or more proper to raise certain ideas; the tunes so soft, the motions so languishing, accompanied with pauses and dying eyes, half falling back and then recovering themselves in so artful a manner that I am very positive the coldest and most rigid prude upon earth could not have looked upon them without thinking of something not to be spoken of. I suppose you may have read that the Turks have no music but what is shocking to our ears, but this account is from those who have never heard any but what is played to them in the streets, and is just as reasonable as if a foreigner should take his ideas of English music from the bladder and string or marrow-bones and cleavers. I can assure you that the music is extremely pathetic; 'tis true, I am inclined to prefer the Italian, but perhaps I am partial. I am acquainted with a Greek lady who sings better than Mrs Robinson and is very well skilled in both, who gives the preference to the Turkish. 'Tis certain they have very fine natural voices; these were very agreeable.

When the dance was over, four fair slaves came into the room with silver censers in their hands and perfumed the air with amber, aloes wood and other scents. After this they served me with coffee served upon their knees in the finest japan china, with soucoups of silver gilt. The lovely Fatima entertained me all this while, in the most polite agreeable manner, calling me often guzel Sultanman, or the beautiful Sultana, and desiring my friendship with the best grace in the world, lamenting that she could not entertain me in my own language.

When I took my leave, two maids brought in a fine silver basket of embroidered handkerchiefs. She begged I would wear the richest for her sake and gave the others to my woman and interpretress. I retired through the same ceremonies as before, and could not help fancying I had been some time in Mohammed's paradise, so much was I charmed with what I had seen. I know not how the relation of it appears to you. I wish it may give you part of my pleasure for I would have my dear sister share in all the diversions of etc,

M.

WILLIAM RUFUS CHETWOOD

FROM *THE VOYAGES, TRAVELS AND ADVENTURES OF WILLIAM OWEN GWIN VAUGHAN, ESQ.*

The young *English Mahometan* often gave me some Consolation, by mingling Tears with me; but alas! that Tenderness was all he could give me, and that very secretly. My Miseries increas'd upon me, and I begg'd the Youth to procure me a Dose of *Opium*, that I might sink into an eternal Sleep, and lose my Life and Misery together; but I could not prevail upon him.

My new Beast of a Master, about a Month after the Death of his Father, was oblig'd to take a Journey to look after the Estate that was left him. I knew not how far he was to go, but I was inform'd, his Affairs would keep him in the Country Forty Days at least; so I resolv'd, in that Time, to make some Attempts to escape, tho' I lost my Life.

When he was gone, I had little Business to do, and was well us'd; for even the *Moorish* Servants were concern'd for my barbarous Treatment. When they had an Opportunity, they would come to hear me play on the flute and always bring something to make merry with.

One Evening an old Woman came to me, before the rest of the Servants, and gave me a Letter, which I open'd, and, to my Surprise, found the following Words in *English*:

SIR,
Tho' I write to you in English, I am a Moor *by Birth, and Daughter to the illustrious* Fontimama *(that was the name of my old Patron). While he was alive, I was contented with my Condition, but since the Angel of Death has taken him from me, my Brother grows most insupportably tyrannous. In short, I have heard your Story, and pity'd you, before I was capable of Love; but now I have seen you, tho' in Disguise, last Night, unknown to you, or any one but the Bearer of this, I must confess myself absolutely yours, if we can join our Hands in the holy Bands of Wedlock.*

I know you'll be surpriz'd, when I tell you, tho' all my Friends are Followers of Mahomet, *yet I am a sincere Christian in my Heart, without Baptism; and my manner of being one, I shall let you know.* Mustapha, *the Name of the* English *youth that lives in our House, taught me to speak your Language before I was seven Years old, by the*

Command of my late Father; as also to write your way. When I had learnt all that Mustapha *cou'd teach me, my Father procur'd me many books in the* English *Tongue: I read them all; some I translated into Morisco, to divert my Father; among them were several Books of your Holy Law (though unknown to any one) which I perus'd at first out of Curiosity only; but found so much sound Truth, and pure Divinity, that I began to abhor the Absurdities of the* Alcoran, *and by degrees, I hope I am come to a State of Salvation, thro' the Blood of your Prophet, that suffer'd on the Cross to save his Followers, that truly believe in him. The sensual Paradise I abhor, painted by* Mahomet *only to beguile his Adherents.*

I have found several Stories in your Books of the Forwardness of Moorish *Women; but, believe me, dear* Englishman, *I hope never carry any thing but virtuous Inclinations in my Heart, which ever shall be yours.*

P. S. I will take an Opportunity, in the Absence of my Brother, to converse with you, for I would willingly have you owe your Sense of Obligation to something else than bare Hopes of your Freedom, which we concert when I see you; and, let your Condition be what it will, I hope to bring a Dowry (I mean a worldly one) that is lawfully my own, to keep us above Want. Think favourably, and

Adieu, my Soul.

Imagine, dear Brother, the Pleasure that fill'd my Mind at the Reading of the Letter; but I must own they proceeded from the Hope of my Liberty, for Love had never laid hold of my Heart.

In the Evening, when the Servants came about me as usual, they were Amaz'd to find me so merry. I sung several *Moorish* Love-songs, that I had learnt among 'em, for their Language is very Poetical; and several *English* ones, that touch'd upon my own circumstances, which very much delighted 'em. In short, we spent the Evening in Pleasure and Mirth.

I went to rest with a Mind far more at Ease than usual; but had not slept long, before I was awak'd with a gentle Rapping at my Cell Door. When I open'd it, I perceiv'd the old Matron that brought me the Letter. Come, said she (in the *Moorish* Language, very softly) put on your Cloaths, and follow me from *Mahomet*'s Hell, into Paradise; I'll be your Conductor, tho' a Christian, as well as yourself. I dress'd myself, with a Confusion of Thought I had never felt before. I follow'd my Conductress, without well knowing what I was about; and entered into a lower Room of a Summer House, at the bottom of the Garden, in the Dark, where I heard the sweetest Voice I have ever heard in my Life (the Sound went quite thro' my Soul, and set my Body in a Tremble) bid the She-Slave make fast the Door (said the Lady) and light up Tapers. She instantly obey'd, and shew'd me the most amiable young Creature, my Eyes ever beheld. I stood like one chang'd into a Statue with Admiration, and I was not able to utter a Word for some time. I kneel'd down before her, and kiss'd her Sleeve. But she gently raised me up, with the most obliging Smile imaginable. What, Sir, said she, must I, against the Custom of your Country, declare my Passion for you, and not have a single Word in return? I reply'd the Sight of such an unexpected Angel, might well take all my faculties away. Come, said she, sit down, and partake of a small Repast I have prepar'd for you, and chear your Spirits with a cup of Wine; tho' I drink none myself (not out of any Respect to the Prophet *Mahomet*, but that I never was accustom'd to it) I know you *English* Gentlemen make it your common Drink. I begg'd to be excus'd from either, neither could I indeed, for the Sight of her, fill'd my Soul with a Profusion of Delight. (And, dear Brother, you must love, like me, before you can guess at the soft thrilling Pleasure that ran thro' my Blood.) I won't detain you with the tender things we said to each other. But sure, Novels and Romances can't produce you a Heroe that ever was so much struck at the first Sight of his adorable Mistress; 'twas then I wore the double Chains, of Love and Bondage. In short, we exchanged our Hearts, and gave one another Assurances of eternal Fidelity, that can never be shaken on my Part, or I believe on hers.

    I must beg Leave to recover myself from this Tenderness, not altogether becoming a Man, before I can pursue the Thread of my uncomfortable Story.

    Several Evenings were past thus delightfully, during the Absence of her Brother. We had many Schemes to set us at Liberty; and at last agreed, I should have a Sufficiency from her to pay my Ransom, tho' it shou'd amount to ten thousand Crowns; and when I had got my Liberty, she wou'd make use of none but her own. She had prevail'd on her Father to settle a sufficient Fortune upon her, tho' very uncustomary, that she might ever live a single Life; tho' her only Reason was, she never wou'd join in Marriage with one contrary to her own Religion; and her Father being infinitely fond of her (not knowing her true Motive) gave into her Possession secretly, the Value of Twenty Thousand Pounds, *English* money, besides several rich Jewels. The Thoughts of so much unexpected Happiness, gave another Turn to my Looks, which I could not hide; but I made the Servants and Slaves believe, the Absence of my Master occasion'd the Alteration.

HENRY BROOKE

FROM *THE FOOL OF QUALITY*

– We are your property, sir, said the lady, dispose of us as you please.

In a little time after dinner was served up, and Harry, happening to turn his head, perceived the black youth by stealth kissing the hat and pressing the gloves to his bosom that he had laid on the table.

Whatever the darkness or deformity of any aspect or person may happen to be, if the sentimental beauty of soul shall burst through the cloud upon us, the dark becomes light, the deformed quite comely, and we begin to affect what was lately our aversion. Thus it was that Harry found himself suddenly and inevitably attached by the two recent proofs that this outlandish youth had given of his affection.

Being all seated, Harry looked earnestly at the young Moor, and turning to the lady, said – I now perceive, madam, how ridiculous all sorts of prejudices are, and find that time and observation may change our opinions to the reverse of what they were. I once had an aversion to all sorts of blacks; but I avow that there is something so amiable in the face of this youth, and his eyes cast such a lustre over the darkness of his countenance, as is enough, as Shakespeare has it, to make us in love with the night, and pay no worship to the gaudy sun.

The Moor hereat smiled celestial sweetness, and joy beamed from his eyes, and throughout his dimpling aspect.

– But who can you be, my sweet fellow? said the lady; who are the picture, the image, almost the thing itself, that were so sadly in love with me five-and-thirty years ago?

– Why, madam, said our hero, you could not have been born at that early day.

– Ah, you flatterer! says she, I am turned of forty.

– But pray, madam, who was he that was so happy as to attract your infant affections?

– His name was Harry Clinton.

– Why, madam, Harry Clinton is my name,

– Harry Clinton, Harry Clinton! screamed out the lady, and started up from her chair.

– Yes, madam, I am son to the late Earl of Moreland; and I almost dare to hope that you were once the enchanting Fanny Goodall.

– Yes, my lovely kinsman, I am indeed your Fanny Goodall!

     Harry then sprung forward, and, seizing her hand, kept it dwelling on his lips. But, disengaging it, she opened her arms and clasped him to her bosom, and wept over him as a mother would over a long-lost son; while the young Moor ran and danced about the room like a mad thing, clapping hands, and springing, like an antelope, almost to the ceiling

     When they were something composed, the Moor caught the lady about the neck, and kissing her, cried – Joy, joy, my dearest madam, the greatest of all joys! Then, turning to our hero, he took each of his hands in turns, and pressed them to his lips; while Harry, kissing his forehead, cried – My brother, my brother!

     [...]

As they were settling to the tea-table – Give me leave, sir, said the duchess, to introduce my little black companion to your notice. He is a sweet fellow, I assure you, notwithstanding his complexion. He is child to our royal friend the Emperor of Morocco, who has instructed him to our guardianship for his travel and education. However he might have come by his sable outside, his father, the great Abenamin, is the least of the tawny of any man I saw in Africa, and his mother is one of the fairest and finest women that ever opened a pair of living diamonds to the light. But, my brother, I shall more particularly recommend him to your regard, by telling you that he is an exceedingly pious Christian.

     She then turned, and taking the little Abenamin by the hand, led him up and placed him before her brother; when the youth, suddenly dropping on his knees, looked up to Mr. Clinton with eyes that spoke love and reverential awe, and besought his blessing.

     The old gentleman found himself surprisingly affected, and, lifting up his hands, cried – God be gracious to you, my child, and make your soul as bright as your countenance is sable! And may the Sun of Righteousness shine with power upon you, and soon disperse or illuminate every shade that is about you! The prince embraced his legs, kissed his knees, and arose.

     [...]

In the meantime, our hero and the young prince were in close combination. Abenamin stepped about and about Harry, and toyed with him, and twisted the curls of his careless locks around his fingers, then turning and looking fondly up in his face – Ah, how fair, says he, does this black visage of mine show in those fine eyes of yours!

– It is in truth, said Harry, so fair in my eyes, that I would not exchange it for fifteen of the fairest female faces in Britain.

The prince then caught his hand, and pressed it to his bosom. – But what shall I call you? says he. You are a great lord in this country, and in my own country I am greater than a lord. But I hate the formality of titles between friends, and I will call you my Harry, provided you promise to call be your Abenamin.

– A bargain, says Harry; let us seal it with a kiss!

– No, no! says the prince, we never kiss lips in Africa; but I will kiss your head, and your hands, and your feet too, with pleasure. But tell me Harry, what makes you so mighty clever a fellow? Will you teach me to be a clever fellow also?

–Ay, that I will, says Harry, and to beat myself too, provided you promise not to hit me over hard. Abenamin laughed, and aimed a little fist as though he meant to overturn him.

[…]

Above all, Abenamin inspired mirth and good-humour throughout the family, and melancholy fled before him whenever he turned. He was daily inventive of new matters in entertainment. He danced African dances for them with wonderful action and grace, and he sung African songs that imitated and exceeded the wild and inarticulate warblings of the nightingale; so that he became the darling and little idol of the whole household.

[…]

In the meantime, our hero and Abenamin became inseparable. He made the prince a present of his little dressed jennett, and at times rode out with him, and taught him the *manege*. At other times they would run and wrestle, and play a hundred gambols through the walks and gardens.

– Did you ever see the chase of the antelope, Harry?

– Not I, truly.

– You shall not be long so, says the prince. Go, gather me all the house – man, woman, and child – before the door here. You shall be the huntsman, and I will be the antelope; and, if any of your people can catch me in a mile's running, they shall have my cap for a kerchief.

Immediately, the whole posse was summoned, to the amount of about sixty persons, male and female; and Mr. Clinton and the duchess, hearing what they were about, came laughing to the door to see the diversion.

Harry gave his royal antelope about fifty yards' law; then cried – Away! And instantly all heels and all voices were loosed after him.

The prince then turned, and bounded over a ha-ha that was sunk on the right side of the avenue; then clearing several other obstacles, whereby he threw ou the greatest number of his pursuers, he at length reached the fields, and shot away like an arrow.

Our hero's huntsman chased about nine foreign and domestic footmen, who still held the chase, though at a distance, while Abenamin led them a round of above a mile. Then, turning short homeward, he came flying up the avenue, with only the huntsman and two followers puffing far behind. At length, reaching near the door, the prince threw himself precipitately into the arms of his friend, as it were for protection, crying –Save me, my Harry! Save your little antelope!

Mr. Clinton and the duchess then successively embraced the visitor, and wished him joy. – I protest, Harry, cried Mr. Clinton, I bet a thousand pieces with you on the head of my Abenamin against your famous Polly Truck.

That night, as our hero sat with the prince in his apartment – Have you ever been in love, my Harry? says he.

– I confess, said Harry, that I have had my twitches and tendencies in that way.

He then related the tragedy of his faithful Maria, which cost the prince the drenching of a handkerchief in tears.

Ah! Exclaimed the prince, never – never will I forgive your Maria her death! Why was it not my lot, by some severer doom, to prove to you the superiority of my friendship and affection?

– What! Cried Harry, would you not leave me a single companion upon earth? When my Abenamin quits the world I shall also bid it adieu.

When their grief was over, the prince took his friend by

the hand and said – I have a sister twinned with me in the womb, and as fair as I am black. All of Africa is pleased to hail her as the beauty of the universe; but the truth is, that I think but poorly of her. The duke brought her with him to France; and should he bring her to England, beware of your heart, my Harry! For, though I am prejudiced against her, she is the idol of all others, who bow down to her as before a little divinity. This has made her excessively vain, that she holds herself of a different species from the rest of mankind, and thinks the homage of the world nothing less than her right. And now, my Harry, though I earnestly wish to be allied to you by a tie, nearer if possible than that of friendship, yet I would not wish my own happiness at the expense of your peace; and so I give you timely warning against this dangerous and haughty girl.

Our company had now been upward of six weeks at the mansion-house. Harry hitherto had never examined any part of the country, or any part of his own estate, above a mile from the house; wherefore – leaving his friend Abenamin in bed, in the presumption of his being tired with his last day's fatigue – he issued early forth, accompanied only by his huntsman and his agent's runner, who knew and was known every where.

With their staffs in their hands, they crossed and quartered the country at pleasure, without let or obstacle.

[...]

– Where is the duchess, sir, and my friend Abenamin?

–Gone, Harry, says his uncle, about breakfast-time yesterday. A courier arrived with the joyful tidings that my brother was on the road and so my sister and the prince hastened to meet him. By this time I suppose they are all on their return. And now take care of yourself Harry. The duke brings with him the sister of Abenamin, the fair princess Abenaide. The duchess tells us that a lovelier creature never beheld the light; so that you must guard your heart with double bars against the power of this beauty. She is vain and disdainful, sir – excessively vain, I am told; so that her pride will prove an antidote against the poison of her charms. However, I will haste to meet and welcome your most noble brother.

Harry was mounted on a haughty charger, that was bought when a colt in Mauritania; he was white as new-fallen snow, save a black main and tail, and three large blood-like spots on the off-shoulder. He was so perfectly instructed and subdued to the *manege*, that he seemed to have no will save the will of his rider; while Harry's least motion, like electricity, informed every joint and member.

The princess came foremost in an open chariot drawn by four spotted Arabians, and the eye could not scarce support the brightness of the wonderful beauty who sat within it.

Harry bowed twice as he approached, but she scarce deigned a perceptible nod of acknowledgment of his salute. Our hero felt himself piqued. – Proud beauty! thought he, I thank you for your timely prevention of a passion that, perhaps, might have proved unhappy to me. He then passed forward with affected carelessness to salute the duke.

When he came up, the coach stopped, and Harry, flying from his saddle, approached the window, while his steed stood trembling but motionless behind him.

– My lord, said Harry, seizing the duke's hand and respectfully kissing it, if you were sensible of the joy that my heart receives from your presence, I think it would make you nearly as happy as myself.

– My sweet fellow, said the duke, I have often heard of you at Paris, as also by the letters of my love here; my longing is at last gratified, though my wonder is increased.

– But madam, says Harry, what have you done with my little playfellow? What's become of my Abenamin?

– O, cried the duchess, laughing, he is forthcoming, I warrant you; but what has so bewitched you to him? I think you could not be fonder if he were a mistress.

– True, madam, answered Harry, sighing; I never look to have a mistress that I shall love half as well; but pray put me out of pain, and let me know where he is.

– Be pacified, said the smiling duke, he is not far off: and here is my hand and promise that you shall see him before night.

Our hero then vaulted on his horse: the coach now began to move, and Harry put his wand to the flank of his horse, who, turning his head to the carriage as of his own accord, moved sidelong toward Enfield with a proud but gentle prancing; while the duke cried out – Look, look! O the boy, the graceful, lovely boy!

While our hero attended the carriage of the duke, the princess and her train had got to the house and alighted, while Harry opened the coach-door, and handed out the noble pair, who alternately kissed and took him in their arms. Mr. Clinton then came forth and received them all with transport. But Harry, under some pretence, walked away ruminating, in order to avoid the disdainful regards of the young lady.

In the meantime, our company, rejoicing and caressing each other all the way, had got slowly, though very lovingly, to the great mansion-parlour. The duke then respectfully taking the young lady by the hand, – Permit me, brother, says he, to recommend to you my lovely ward, the fair Princess of Morocco. The lady then gently bent on one knee toward the ground, while she received the cordial blessing and salute of the old gentlemen.

They then took their seats, when Mr. Clinton, while he looked more earnestly at the princess, grew suddenly affected, and called out for a glass of fair water and hartshorn. When he drank it, he found himself in a measure restored; and lifting his hands, he cried – I protest one would think that nature had copied this lovely young creature from an image that has lain impressed upon my heart near these forty years.

– You are in the right, my brother! exclaimed the duke; it is even as you surmise. Allow me then, once more, to introduce to you the counterpart of our once adored Louisa; to introduce to you my niece, and your own offspring, my brother – even the daughter of your still living and precious Eloisa! The princess then sprung forward, and, dropping precipitately at the feet of her grandfather, she put her face between his knees, and seizing both hands, she bathed them with her tears, crying – My father! O my father! My dear, my dearest father! How inexpressibly blessed I think myself to be the offspring of such a father! Mr. Clinton then raising her, and seating her fondly on his knee, and grasping her to his bosom – I will not ask, he cried, how these miracles came about; it is enough that I feel the attraction which pulls you into my heart. And so saying, their tears flowed and mingled into a happy emotion.

Go, my angel, said Mr. Clinton, and take yonder seat, that I may view and delight my soul with your sight at leisure. My eyes begin at these years to see best at a distance. At length, the soft voice of our Harry was heard in the hall; and the duke, whispering his brother, requested him for a little time to take no notice of what had passed.

Our hero then entered, bowing respectfully and

gracefully, but carelessly, toward the side where the young princess sat. He then took his seat beside the duke, and bending fondly to him, and seizing a hand with both his hands, he pressed it to his lips and cried – Welcome, welcome, my dearest lord, to the house and the hearts of your truest lovers!

Then, giving a glance to the side where the princess sat, he caught a glimpse of her attractions, and sighing, said to himself – O the pity, the pity! But no matter; her pride shall never suffer a single charm to take place; and so thinking, he turned his eyes aside.

Meantime, Abenaide arose with as little noise as a hare from her seat; and stealing round, like a cat circumventing a mouse, she came behind Harry's chair, and reaching, and covering an eye with each of her hands, she turned his head to her, and made a sound with her lips as though she kissed him. Harry opened his eyes in utter astonishment; while in a twinkling, standing before him, she chuckled a laugh and cried – My Harry, what, have you forgotten me? Don't you remember your old playfellow, your little friend Abenamin?

Harry's eyes were now opened, in the midst of the hurry and agitation of his soul. At a glimpse he took in the whole oppression of her beauties; and casting herself, quick as a glance of lightning, at her feet, he seized the hem of her robing and glued it to his mouth.

At length, lifting up his eyes, he cried – Ah! What are all these wonders to me, or my happiness, unless my Abenamin will also become my Abenaide? –That, replied the princess, is not at my option; there sits my lord and father, at whose disposal I am.

Harry then rose, and throwing himself at the feet of his revered patron, embraced his knees in silence, while Mr. Clinton cried out – Yes, my Harry, I understand you; nothing shall ever be wanting to the happiness of my darling, that the power of his tender parent and loving uncle can effect! I can have nothing in heaven or earth that is not the property of Harry. Harry kissed his hands and sprung up.

Mr. Clinton then continued – I aver I am still in a labyrinth. Did you not say, my Abenaide, that you were also our Abenamin? – I did, my father, says she but I did not dare to avow myself. Ah! What a painful struggle did that restriction cost me, while I panted to catch and to cling on your honoured feet; while my heart swelled with affection, and my eyes with restrained tears; and while I kissed in secret the book that you read, and the ground that you trod on.

Abenaide then sat down, and Harry, lightly throwing himself on the ground beside her, looked beseechingly around, and cried – My lord – my dearest lady – our still precious Fanny Goodall – can you vouch – can ye warrant that I am safe in this matter? Then looking up to the princess, and drinking her in – No! he cried, you cannot engage it; I feel that I shall perish in the very ecstasy of the expectation of being united to her.

[...] *The Duke's story:*
On my embassy to the court of Morocco, I had several private interviews with the emperor before my credentials were opened in public. I had the good fortune to be liked by him, so that he suffered no day to pass without seeing me. His name was Abenamin; he was accounted a great captain; he exceeded all his dominions for grace of person and beauty of aspect; and that which rendered him still more singular was, that he had given liberty to all the ladies of his seraglio, and for many years had kept constant to the reigning sultana, said to be the most exquisite beauty on earth.

As we grew more intimate, in the exuberance of his affection for his empress he could not refrain from speaking of her to me; and he promised that, before I departed, I should see and converse with her – a grace, he said, never granted to any other man.

At length the day being appointed for my public entry, I rode through the city attended by a sumptuous train, and, alighting before the palace, advanced to the hall of the audience.

The emperor was seated, with his sultana at his right hand, upon a throne of ivory. As soon as I had approached the presence, and began to open my commission, the empress gave out a great shriek, and fell over in a swoon upon the bosom of her husband.

The royal Abenamin instantly turned pale as death – tore off her veil with trembling hands to give her air – and called me to his assistance, as it accounted profanation for any Moor to touch the person of the empress. But O heaven! O my friends! Think what was my astonishment when, in the pale face of the queen, I beheld the loved features of our darling Eloisa!

The court broke up in confusion, and her women came

hurrying with drops and essences. As soon as she recovered, she opened her eyes upon me, and reaching out her arms, and catching me to her, she cried – O my uncle, my dearest uncle! Am I so blessed then, as to behold you before I expire?

The monarch, in the meantime, looked upon me with a jealous eye, and twice put his hand to the haft of his dagger, but checked his rising indignation till he should have the mystery of his queen's behaviour explained. The women then raised her up and bore her to the apartment; while the emperor, turning to me with no very friendly aspect, ordered me follow him.

When I had attended a considerable time in the antechamber, he came forth with a serene and joyous countenance, and embracing me, cried – O, my friend! My dear kinsman! How transported I am to find and acknowledge you for such; the parent of my angel becomes a part of myself!

He then led me by the hand into the bed-chamber of my Eloisa, where we renewed our caresses without restraint. But the monarch, fearing that these emotions would be too much for her, told me that he had something for my private ear till dinner, and took me into an adjoining closet.

There seating, and taking me affectionately by the hand, – I will now tell you, my uncle, says he, how I came by this inestimable treasure of your niece.

I had fitted out a royal ship of my own, not as a corsair, but rather for trade in the Mediterranean. On their return from the coast of Egypt, as they passed, after a violent hurricaine, within sight of old Carthage, my people perceived at a distance a sloop stranded on a shoal of sand about a league from the shore. Immediately they sent out a boat, and took the distressed company in, consisting of my charmer, two female companions, and three servants in livery, beside the boatman.

The intendants of my ship behaved themselves with all possible respect toward the young lady and her attendants; and endeavoured to quiet her terrors by assuring her that she was free, and that their prince was a person of too much honour and humanity to derive any advantage from the disasters of the unfortunate.

The moment that they brought her before me, pale, trembling and in tears; while she dropped on her knees, and lifted to me her fine eyes in a petitioning manner; the gates of my soul opened to the sweetly affecting image, and ever after closed, of their own accord, upon it.

    – Ah! I cried; heavenly creature, calm, calm your causeless fears! I swear by our prophet, and the god of our prophet, that I would rather suffer the gaunch than put the smallest constraint on your person or inclinations. You are free, madam; you shall ever be free, save so far as I may bind you by my tender offices and affections.

    I raised her, and she grew something better assured; when, bending a knee in my turn, I kissed her robe and cried – Look not upon me as your tyrant, look not upon me as your lover; but look upon me as your friend – the tenderest and truest of friends – who shall ever be ready to sacrifice his own happiness to yours.

    From that tine I studied every amusement, every diversion, that might serve to dissipate the timid shrinkings of her remaining apprehensions; while I conducted myself toward her with a distant though fond respect, not even presuming to touch her ivory hand.

    In the meantime my soul sickened, and grew cold to all other women. If you were ever in love, my dear D'Aubigny, you know that it is a chaste as well as a tender passion. I languished indeed for her – I longed and languished to death; but then it was rather for her heart than her person I languished.

    One day, as she heaved a heavy but half-suppressed sigh – Ah, my angel! I cried; I can have no joy but yours, and yet you have griefs to which you keep your friend – your Abenamin – a stranger. – True, my lord, says she, tears breaking from her; all your bounties have not been able to silence the calls of kindred or claims of nature within me. Ah, my parents! My dear parents! I feel more for you than I feel even for myself, in being torn from you.

    The weight of her affliction fell like a mountain on my soul, and crushed me to her feet. – You would leave me then, Eloisa – you wish to leave me; but your generosity delays to tell me so, for fear of breaking my heart. Well, be it so – go from me – you know I cannot survive you; but my death is of no consequence, my Eloisa shall be happy. I will go this instant, I will dispatch my swiftest galley to Languedoc, I will write word to your parents that you are safe, that you are beloved, and yet pure and untouched, since respected as a deity. I will invite them to come and take possession of my treasures, my dominions, my heart; but should they reject my suit, I again swear by Allah to send you to them laden with wealth, though I myself should drop dead at the instant of your departure!

The noble soul of Eloisa became instantly affected. She caught a hand between both of hers, and, bathing it with tears, cried – O, now indeed you have bound me by chains infinitely stronger than all the shackles that fasten the slaves to the galleys of Africa!

I kept firm to my engagement, and in a few weeks, my winged messengers returned. But, O, the tidings, the very doleful tidings, for my beloved! They brought word that they found no creature save two ancient domestics in the great hotel, as two ravens in the midst of a lonely forest.

From these they learned that my Eloisa's mother and her little brother were dead; that her grandmother was dead; her aunt the marchioness was dead; and that the marquis had retired they knew not whither.

She wept incessantly, and I wept with her. At length she softly said – You have conquered, my lord, you have conquered; I am subdued by your weight of affliction. O that you could but conform to one article more, that we might be united as one heart, and one soul, and one sentiment for ever!

It was now, for the first time, that I dared to seize her hand; I crushed it to my lips, and thrust it to my soul. – What would you enjoin, I cried? I would do anything, dare any thing, to be united to my Eloisa; in life and death, body to body, and dust to dust, never – never to be sundered till her spirit should make the haven of my spirit hereafter!

– Ah! she suddenly exclaimed, that is the very thing I so eagerly desire. Let the God of my spirit be the God of your spirit; so shall we be united in him, and jointly partake of his blessedness through eternity.

– Ah! I cried; can I forego the divine precepts of our prophet? – Your prophet, says she, preaches only to the eye and ear, and that is all that he does or can pretend to; but CHRIST, my prophet, preaches in the heart to the affections. From him is every good motion, divine or human. He is the unknown God of your spirit, my master, my Abenamin; and you feel his precious power while you disavow his name.

I was puzzled – I was silenced. I bent a knee in reverence, kissed her hand and withdrew.

I sent for the chief of the Christian missionaries throughout the city and the country. I consulted each of them in private, but received no satisfaction from them. They all appeared equally zealous for my reformation, but attempted it by difference, and even opposite, arguments.

Some would have persuaded me to be Christian, by showing every absurdity of every religion that was not Christian. Others affirmed that my eternal salvation depended on my conformity to certain external rules and penances, while the greatest number inveighed against the Christians of every other denomination; and would have thrust me wholly from Christ, if I did not consent to receive him within the stinted pale.

I knew not what to do; I was put to a stand, and quite confounded by this multiplicity of conflicting opinions. At length a countryman of my own came to me from the desert. He had been a great sinner, but was converted by the sense of his sins; and he was revered and resorted to by all the friendless and afflicted.

I opened my soul to him, with all its doubts and difficulties. – My friend in Christ, said he, with a gentle and still voice, they have been leading you all astray, quite away from the haven that stretches forth its arms for the reception of long-toiled mariners, whom storms have at length compelled to seek a final port.

The God of your creation can alone be your redemption; the God of your nature can alone be the salvation of the nature that he imparted. But who shall convince you of this? Not all the angels in heaven, nor all the doctors upon the earth, till the Christ of your heart shall be pleased to convince you that you are, as indeed you are (however mighty a monarch), a poor, frail, erring, vile, and despicable creature; subjected to innumerable lapses and infirmities, sickness, passions, and crosses, griefs, agonies, and death. When this is effectually done, the whole of the business is done. You will call for and catch at a Saviour, in the sensibility of your want of him. When you come thus laden with your sins to him, he will in no wise cast you out. But he will take you, as Noah took the wearied dove into the ark – he will take you within the veil of his own temple of rest; and all sects, forms, and ceremonies will be as the outward courts, with which you shall have no manner of commerce or concern.

My heart felt the weight and the fullness of conviction.

I took him to my arms, and requested instant baptism. My Eloisa was called; we locked ourselves in; and I was washed by water and faith into Christ, while my kneeling angel wept a stream of delight beside me.

It is said that possession cloys, but I experienced, my dear D'Aubigny, that love never cloys. Every day with my Eloisa seemed to triumph, in heartfelt happiness, over my first bridal day. But O! what was the joy, the exultation of my fond heart, when she gave me to be the father of a little daughter of paradise!

One day, while we were toying and fooling with the smiling infant, and throwing her, as she crowed, from the one to the other – Ah! My husband! cried Eloisa, how poor I was lately; no parents, no kindred, nothing but my Abenamin upon the whole earth! And now God has been pleased to make my affliction to laugh and to give this babe for a further band, a precious link of love, between us.

[…]

The monarch then, deeply musing and heavily sighing, began – I am now, my dearest friends, friends beloved above the world, and all that it contains – I am now to open to you my inmost heart, and to reveal a purpose whereon I have been ruminating these many months, but could not hit on an expedient for bringing it to pass. How opportunely has our JESUS sent you to us on this occasion!

I have but two children living; my Abenaide, and a son by a former woman of my seraglio. His name is Abencerrage; he is a youth renowned in the field, but of a proud and impetuous demeanour. He had long conceived an illicit passion for his young and lovely sister. At length the fire broke forth, and he lately attempted to carry her away.

I would have instantly put him to death, had I any other heir to succeed to my dominions. I therefore contented myself with banishing him from my court and my presence; though I am sensible that this has not availed for the extinguishing of his horrid flame.

Now, my friends, should I die, or should this violent boy break into rebellion – for he is the favourite of the licentious soldiery – I tremble to think what would become of my bright-eyed dove within the talons of such a vulture.

This, together with my eager desire of quitting the

kingdom of infidels, and of joining with the blessed society of Christian people, has, after many struggles, determined me to abdicate my throne, as soon as I can amass and transmit a fund sufficient for supporting Eloisa and myself, with becoming dignity, in her native country.

– Ah, my lord! I cried, clasping him passionately in my arms, regard not your treasures, delay not a moment for that! Your Eloisa's relations, both by father and mother, are possessed of princely fortunes, and they will be all freely at the disposal of your majesty.

– Ah, my D'Aubigny! said he, I am not yet so duly mortified a Christian as needlessly to elect a state of dependence, or willingly to descend at once from the king to the beggar. I have, however, been preparing: I have already converted a large part of my effects into bills and jewels, of high value but light portage, to the amount, as I think, of about forty millions of French money. This I will transmit by you; and, as soon as I shall have compassed an equal sum, I will stay no longer in Africa; I will fly to your bosoms, my precious friends.

In the mean time this violent and unprincipled boy gives no rest to my apprehensions. It is therefore necessary that I commit my Abenaide to your trust. It is necessary, I say, that I tear away my choicest limb, the dearest part of my vitals! Support me, CHRIST, in the trial: but it must be gone through.

This, however, must be done with all possible privacy. I am persuaded that my young villain has his spies in and about my palace. I shall therefore request my dear aunt to disguise my little girl in boy's apparel, and to blacken every part of her complexion, that she may pass unnoticed, as your page, through the midst of my attendants.

At length the time approached, and pressed for my departure; but how to part was the question. All attendants were ordered to avoid their presence far away. Our metamorphosed Abenaide stood weeping beside us, while her father and mother crushed us successively to their bosoms. All was passion, a gush of tears, but not a word was uttered on any part.

[...]

Soon after, a post-chaise whirled into the court, and Harry flying out, caught Clement and Arabella into his strict embrace. He then hurried them in, where Mr. Clinton received, and caressed, and introduced them to the duke and duchess as persons of great merit, and his highly valued friends. He then presented to them his Abenaide, who saluted Clement, and embraced Arabella with an affectionate familiarity.

– Oh sir! cried our hero, kissing his uncle's hand, am I to be the last person in the world whom you will honour with a salute from your bewitching daughter? – I ask your pardon, my lord, said Mr. Clinton solemnly; allow me then, at length, to repair my omission, by presenting to your earlship her little highness Abenaide.

The duke and duchess and Meekly laughed; but Harry was not a whit the slower in laying hold of his advantage.

He kissed her forehead, her eyes, her cheeks; and lastly dwelt upon her lips, as though he would have infused his soul between them. – Harry, Harry! cried Mr. Clinton, I will never introduce you to my girl again, unless you promise not to kiss so hard, and bring so much blood into her face.

[…]

Dinner was then served. During the repast the duke said – Let us not, my brother, keep our Harry in pain; why should we delay the happiness of children so very dear to us? With regard to your child's marriage to some mighty prince, as your son-in-law hinted, I think her more ennobled and more illustrious by her marriage with our hero here, who purchased her at his peril, than if she were mated to the greatest potentate on earth.

– You must excuse me, my noble brother, said Mr. Clinton; I will have no clandestine doings in this business. My girl shall be married in the face and witnessing of thousands; lest hereafter this young rogue should have the effrontery to deny her. What day of the week is this? Thursday I think; let Monday se'nnight be the day.

Harry rose, and pressed and kissed the hand of the duke, with rapture, and then kissed the hand of his patron in silent submission.

In the meantime, all preparations were pushed into forwardness by Mr. Clinton. The many shops of the many towns within many miles around were emptied of their boards and sheeting, their knives and forks, &c. Hundreds of tables and forms were framed, hundreds of tents were erected. Proclamation was made in every village, and all the people within ten miles were invited to the wedding.

When the day approached, one hundred oxen were

slain, one hundred sheep, with fifty fat deer, &c. &c. The spits fried and the cauldrons smoked over the fires of many a field.

At length the auspicious morning arose; and Harry and his bride were already up and dressed in their respective apartments.

The princess was habited, after the Persian fashion, in a vest of silver brocading, scalloped over a petticoat of the same fabric, that flowed in a train behind. A scarf of a cerulean tint flew between her right shoulder and her left hip, being buttoned at each end by a rose of rubies; her shining tresses of jetty black, bound together at her neck beneath a huge amethyst, fell down in luxuriant ringlets, and shaded and revealed by turns the fine bend of her tapering waist; a coronet of diamonds, through which there waved a white branch of the feathers of the ostrich, was inserted on the left decline of her lovely head; and a stomacher of inestimable brilliance rose beneath her dazzling bosom, and by a fluctuating blaze of unremitted light, checked and turned the eye away from too presumptuous a gaze.

Our hero coming forth, beheld her, as a pillar of light just issuing from her antechamber. He stepped back as she advanced, and fixed his eyes upon her in mute astonishment; then springing forward, he fell prostrate and kissed the hem of her robing.

GEORGIANA CAVENDISH, DUCHESS OF DEVONSHIRE

A NEGRO SONG
(adapted from Mr. Park's Travels)

I.
The loud wind roar'd, the rain fell fast;
The White Man yielded to the blast:
He sat him down, beneath our tree;
For weary, sad and faint was he;
And ah, no wife, or mother's care,
For him, the milk or corn prepare:

CHORUS
The White Man, shall our pity share;
Alas, no wife or mother's care,
For him, the milk or corn prepare.

II.
The storm is o'er; the tempest past;
And Mercy's voice has hush'd the blast.
The wind is heard in whispers low;
The White Man, far away must go; –
But ever in his heart will bear
Remembrance of the Negro's care.

CHORUS
Go, White Man, go; – but with thee bear
The Negro's wish, the Negro's prayer;
Remembrance of the Negro's care.

MUNGO PARK

FROM *TRAVELS IN THE INTERIOR DISTRICTS OF AFRICA*

About this time, all the women of the camp had their feet, and the ends of their fingers, stained a dark saffron colour. I could never ascertain whether this was done from motives of religion, or by way of ornament. The curiosity of the Moorish ladies had been very troublesome to me ever since my arrival at Benowm; and on the evening of the 25th (whether from the instigation of others, or impelled by their own ungovernable curiosity, or merely out of frolic, I cannot affirm) a party of them came into my hut, and gave me plainly to understand that the object of their visit was to ascertain, by actual inspection, whether the rite of circumcision extended to the Nazerenes as well as to the followers of Mahomet. The reader will easily judge of my surprise at this unexpected declaration; and in order to avoid the proposed scrutiny, I thought it best to treat the business jocularly. I observed to them that it was not customary in my country to give ocular demonstration in such cases, before so many beautiful women; but that if all of them would retire, except the young lady to whom I pointed (selecting the youngest and handsomest), I would satisfy her curiosity. The ladies enjoyed the jest, and went away laughing heartily; and the youngest damsel herself to whom I had given the preference (though she did not avail herself of the privilege of inspection) seemed no way to displeased at the compliment; for she soon afterwards sent me some meal and milk for my supper.

GEORGE GORDON, LORD BYRON
FROM *DON JUAN, 'CANTO V'*

[*into the harem…*]

    91
Before they entered, Baba paused to hint
   To Juan some slight lessons as his guide.
"If you could just contrive," he said, "to stint
   That somewhat manly majesty of stride,
'Twould be as well, and (though there's not much in't)
   To swing a little less from side to side,
Which has at times an aspect of the oddest;
And also could you look a little modest,

    92
'Twould be convenient, for these mutes have eyes
   Like needles, which may pierce those petticoats;
And if they should discover your disguise,
   You know how near us the deep Bosphorous floats,
And you may chance ere morning rise,
   To find our way to Marmora without boats,
Stitched up in sacks, a mode of navigation
A good deal practised here upon occasion."

    93
With this encouragement, he led the way
   Into a room still nobler that the last.
A rich confusion formed a disarray
   In such sort that the eye along it cast
Could hardly carry anything away –
   Object on object flashed so bright and fast,
A dazzling mass of gems and gold and glitter,
Magnificently mingled in litter.

    94
Wealth had done wonders, taste not much. Such things
   Occur in orient palaces and even
In the more chastened domes of western kings
   (Of which I have also seen some six or seven),
Where I can't say or gold or diamond flings

GEORGE GORDON, LORD BYRON

Great lustre. There is much to be forgiven:
Groups of bad statues, tables, chairs and pictures,
On which I cannot pause to make my strictures.

    95
In this imperial hall at distance lay
  Under a canopy and there reclined
Quite in a confidential queenly way,
  A lady. Baba stopped and kneeling signed
To Juan, who though not much used to pray,
  Knelt down by instinct wondering in his mind
What all this meant, while Baba bowed and bended
His head, until the ceremony ended.

    96
The lady, rising up with such an air
  As Venus rose with from the wave, on them
Bent like an antelope a Paphian pair
  Of eyes, which put out each surrounding gem,
And raising up an arm, as moonlight fair,
  She signed to Baba, who kissed the hem
Of her deep purple, and speaking low,
Pointed to Juan, who remained below.

    97
Her presence was as lofty as her state;
  Her beauty of that overpowering kind,
Whose force description only would abate.
  I'd rather leave it much to your own mind
That lessen it by what I could relate
  Of forms and features. It would strike you blind
Could I do justice to the full detail;
So, luckily for both, my phrases fail.

    98
This much, however I may add: her years
  Were ripe, they might make six and twenty springs,
But there are forms which Time to touch forbears
  And turns aside his scythe to vulgar things,
Such as was Mary's, Queen of Scots. True, tears

GEORGE GORDON, LORD BYRON

And love destroy, and sapping sorrow wrings
Charms from the charmer, yet some never grow
Ugly, for instance, Ninon de l'Enclos.

    99
She spake some words to her attendants, who
  Composed a choir of girls, ten or a dozen,
And were all clad alike; like Juan too,
  Who wore their uniform, by Baba chosen.
They formed a very nymph-like looking crew,
  Which might have called Diana's chorus 'cousin',
As far as outward show may correspond;
I won't be bail for anything beyond.

    100
They bowed obeisance and withdrew, retiring.
  But not by the same door through which we came in
Baba and Juan, which last stood admiring
  At some small distance all he saw within
This strange saloon, much fitted for inspiring
  Marvel and praise, for both or none things win.
And I must say, I ne'er could see the very
Great happiness of the *nil admirari*.

    101
"Not to admire is all the art I know"
  (Plain truth, dear Murray, needs few flowers of speech)
"To make men happy, or to keep them so"
  (So take it in the very words of Creech).
Thus Horace wrote all we know long ago,
  And thus Pope quotes the precept to re-teach
From his translation, but had none admired,
Would Pope have sung, or Horace have been inspired?

    102
Baba, when all the damsels were withdrawn,
  Motioned to Juan to approach and then
A second time desired to kneel down
  And kiss the lady's foot, which maxim when
He heard repeated, Juan with a frown
  Drew himself up to his full height again

GEORGE GORDON, LORD BYRON

And said it grieved him, but he could not stoop
To any show, unless it shod the Pope.

103

Baba, indignant at this ill-timed pride
   Made fierce remonstrances, and then a threat
He muttered (but the last was given aside)
   About a bowstring – quite in vain. Not yet
Would Juan bend, though 'twere to Mahomet's bride.
   There's nothing in the world like etiquette
In kingly chambers or imperial halls,
As also at the race and county balls.

104

He stood like Atlas, with a world of words
   About his ears, and nathless would not bend.
The blood of all his line's Castilian lords
   Boiled in his veins, and rather than descend
To stain his pedigree, a thousand swords
   A thousand times of him had made an end.
At length perceiving the 'foot' could not stand,
Baba proposed that he should kiss the hand.

105

Here was an honourable compromise,
   A halfway house of diplomatic rest,
Where they might meet in much more peaceful guise;
   And Juan now his willingness exprest
To use all fit and proper courtesies,
   Adding that this was commonest and best,
For through the South the custom still commands
The gentleman to kiss the lady's hands.

106

And he advanced, though with but a bad grace,
   Though on more thoroughbred or fairer fingers
No lips e'er left their transitory trace.
   On such as these the lip too fondly lingers
And for one kiss would fain imprint a brace,
   As you will see, if she you love shall bring hers
In contact. And sometimes even a fair stranger's

GEORGE GORDON, LORD BYRON

An almost twelvemonth's constancy endangers.

    107
The lady eyed him o'er and o'er and bade
  Baba retire, which he obeyed in style,
As if well used to the retreating trade;
  And taking hints in good part all the while,
He whispered to Juan not to be afraid
  And looking on him with a sort of smile,
Took leave, with such a face of satisfaction,
As good men wear who have done a virtuous action.

    108
When he was gone, there was a sudden change.
  I know not what might be the lady's thought,
But o'er her bright brow flashed a tumult strange,
  And into her clear cheek the blood was brought,
Blood-red as sunset summer clouds which range
  The verge of heaven; and in her large eyes wrought
A mixture of sensations might be scanned,
Of half voluptuousness and half command.

    109
Her form had all the softness of her sex,
  Her features all the sweetness of the devil,
When he put on the cherub to perplex
  Eve and paved (God knows how) the road to evil.
The sun himself was scare more free from specks
  Than she from aught at which the eye could cavil;
Yet somehow there was something somewhere wanting,
As if she rather ordered than was granting.

    110
Something imperial or imperious threw
  A chain o'er all she did; that is, a chain
Was thrown as 'twere about the neck of you.
  And rapture's self will seem almost a pain
With aught which looks like despotism in view.
  Our souls at least are free, and 'tis in vain
We would against them make the flesh obey;
The spirit in the end will have its way.

GEORGE GORDON, LORD BYRON

111

Her very smile was haughty, though not so sweet;
   Her very nod was not an inclination.
There was a self-will even in her small feet.
   As though they were quite conscious of her station;
They trod as upon necks. And to complete
   Her state (it is the custom of the nation),
A poniard decked her girdle, as the sign
She was a sultan's bride (thank heaven, not mine).

112

"To hear and to obey" had been from birth
   The law of all around her; to fulfil
All phantasies which yielded joy or mirth
   Had been her slaves' chief pleasure, as her will.
Her blood was high, her beauty scarce of earth;
   Judge then if her caprices e'er stood still.
Had she but been a Christian, I've a notion
We should have found our perpetual motion.

113

Whate'er she saw and coveted was brought;
   Whatever she did not see, if she supposed
It might be seen, with diligence was sought,
   And when 'twas found straightaway the bargain closed.
There was no end unto the things she bought,
   Nor to the trouble which her fancies caused.
Yet even her tyranny had such a grace,
The women pardoned all except her face.

114

Juan, the latest of her whims, had caught
   Her eye in passing on his way to sale.
She ordered him directly to be bought,
   And Baba, who had ne'er been known to fail
In any kind of mischief to be wrought,
   At all such auctions knew how to prevail.
She had no prudence, but he had; and this
Explains the guard which Juan took amiss.

GEORGE GORDON, LORD BYRON

115

His youth and features favoured the disguise,
   And should you ask how she, a sultan's bride,
Could risk or compass such strange phantasies,
   This I must leave sultans to decide.
Emperors are only husbands in wives' eyes,
   And kings and consorts oft are mystified,
As we may ascertain with due precision,
Some by experience, others by tradition.

116

But to the main point, where we have been tending,
   She now conceived all difficulties past
And deemed herself extremely condescending
   When, being made her property at last,
Without more preface, in her blue eyes blending
   Passion and power, a glance on him she cast,
And merely saying, "Christian, canst thou love?"
Conceived that phrase was quite enough to move.

117

And so it was, in proper time and place;
   But Juan, who had still his mind o'erflowing
With Haidee's isle and soft Ionian face,
   Felt the warm blood, which in his face was glowing,
Rush back upon his heart, which filled apace,
   And left his cheeks as pale as snowdrops blowing.
These words went through his soul like Arab spears,
So that he spoke not, but burst into tears.

118

She was a good deal shocked; not shocked at tears,
   For women shed and use them at their liking.
But there is something when man's eye appears
   Wet, still more disagreeable and striking.
A woman's teardrop melts, a man's half sears
   Like molten lead, as if you thrust a pike in
His heart to force it out, for (to be shorter)
To them 'tis a relief, to us a torture.

GEORGE GORDON, LORD BYRON

119

And she would have consoled, but knew not how;
   Having no equals, nothing which had e'er
Infected her with sympathy till now,
   And never having dreamt what 'twas to bear
Aught of a serious sorrowing kind, although
   There might arise some pouting petty care
To cross her brow, she wondered how so near
Her eyes another's eye could shed a tear.

120

But nature teaches more than power can spoil;
   And when a strong although a strange sensation
Moves, female hearts are such a genial soil
   For kinder feelings, whatsoe'er their nation,
They naturally pour the "wine and oil",
   Samaritans in every situation.
And thus Gulbeyaz, though she knew not why,
Felt an odd glistening moisture in her eye.

121

But tears stop like all things else; and soon
   Juan, who for an instant had been moved
To such a sorrow by the intrusive tone
   Of one who dared to ask if he had loved,
Called back the stoic to his eyes, which shone
   Bright with the very weakness he reproved.
And although sensitive to beauty, he
Felt most indignant still at not being free.

122

Gulbeyaz, for the first time in her days,
   Was much embarrassed, never having met
In all her life with aught save prayers and praise;
   And as she also risked her life to get
Him whom she meant to tutor in love's ways
   Into a comfortable tête à tête,
To lose the hour would make her quite a martyr,
And they had wasted now almost a quarter.

GEORGE GORDON, LORD BYRON

123

I also would suggest the fitting time
  To gentlemen in any such like case,
That is to stay, in a meridian clime
  (With us there is more law given to the chase),
But here a small delay forms a great crime.
  So recollect that the extremest grace
Is just two minutes for your declaration;
A moment more would hurt your reputation.

124

Juan's was good and might have been still better,
  But he had got Haidee into his head.
However strange, he could not forget her,
  Which made him seem exceedingly ill-bred.
Gulbeyaz, who looked on him as her debtor
  For having had him to her palace led,
Began to blush up to the eyes and then
Grow deadly pale and then blush back again.

125

At length, in an imperial way, she laid
  Her hand on his and bending on him eyes,
Which needed not an empire to persuade,
  Looked into his for love, where none replies.
Her brow grew black, but she would not upbraid,
  That being the last thing a proud woman tries.
She rose and pausing one chaste moment, threw
Herself upon his breast, and there she grew.

126

This was an awkward test, as Juan found,
  But he was steeled by sorrow, wrath and pride.
With gentle force her white arms he unwound
  And seated her all drooping by his side.
Then rising haughtily he glanced around
  And looking coldly in her face, he cried,
"The prisoned eagle will not pair. Nor I
Serve a sultana's sensual phantasy.

GEORGE GORDON, LORD BYRON

127

"Thou ask'st if I can love; be this the proof
  How much I *have* loved – that I love not thee!
In this vile garb, the distaff, web and woof
  Were fitter for me. Love is for the free!
I am not dazzled by this splendid roof.
  Whate'er thy power, and great it seems to be,
Heads bow, knees bend, eyes watch around a throne,
And hands obey – our hearts are still our own."

128

This was a truth to us extremely trite,
  Not so to her, who ne'er had heard such things.
She deemed her least command must yield delight,
  Earth being only made for queens and kings.
If hearts lay on the left side or the right
  She hardly knew; to such perfection brings
Legitimacy its born votaries when
Aware of their due royal rights o'er men.

129

Besides, as has been said, she was so fair
  As even in a much humbler lot had made
A kingdom or confusion anywhere,
  And also, as may be presumed, she laid
Some stress on charms, which seldom are, if e'er,
  By their possessor thrown into the shade.
She thought hers gave a double "right divine",
And half of that opinion's also mine.

130

Remember or (if you cannot) imagine,
  Ye who have kept your chastity when young,
While some more desperate dowager has been waging
  Love with you and been in the dog days stung
By your refusal, recollect her raging!
  Or recollect all that was said or sung
On such a subject; then suppose the face
Of a young downright beauty in this case.

131

Suppose, but you already have supposed,
  The spouse of Potiphar, the Lady Booby,
Phedra, and all which story has disclosed
  Of good examples. Pity that so few by
Poets and private tutors are exposed,
  To educate – ye youth of Europe – you by!
But when you have supposed the few we know,
You can't suppose Gulbeyaz' angry brow.

132

A tigress robbed of young, a lioness,
  Or any interesting beast of prey,
Are similes at hand for the distress
  Of ladies who cannot have their own way;
But though my turn will not be served with less,
  These don't express one half what I should say.
For what is stealing young ones, few of many,
To cutting short their hopes of having any?

133

The love of offspring's Nature's general law,
  From tigresses and cubs to ducks and ducklings.
There's nothing whets the beak or arms the claw
  Like an invasion of their babes and sucklings.
And all who have seen a human nursery, saw
  How mothers love their children's squalls and chucklings.
And this extreme effect (to tire no longer
Your patience) shows the cause must still be stronger.

134

If I said fire flashed from Gulbeyaz' eyes,
  'Twere nothing, for her eyes flashed always fire
Or said her cheeks assumed the deepest dyes,
  I should but bring disgrace upon the dyer,
So supernatural was her passion's rise,
  For ne'er till now she knew a checked desire.
Even ye who know what a checked woman is
(Enough, God knows!) would much fall short of this.

GEORGE GORDON, LORD BYRON

135

Her rage was but a minute's and 'twas well –
  A moment's more had slain her; but the while
It lasted 'twas like a short glimpse of hell.
  Nought's more sublime than energetic bile,
Though horrible to see, yet grand to tell,
  Like ocean warring 'gainst a rocky isle;
And the deep passions flashing through her form
Made her a beautiful embodied storm.

136

A vulgar tempest 'twere to a typhoon
  To match a common fury with her rage,
And yet she did not want to reach the moon,
  Like moderate Hotspur on the immortal page.
Her anger pitched into a lower tune,
  Perhaps the fault of her soft sex and age.
Her wish was but to "kill, kill, kill" like Lear's
And then her thirst of blood was quenched in tears.

137

A storm it raged, and like the storm it passed,
  Passed without words; in fact she could not speak.
And then her sex's shame broke in at last,
  A sentiment till then in her but weak,
But now it flowed in natural and fast,
  As water through an unexpected leak,
For she felt humbled; and humiliation
Is sometimes good for people in her situation.

138

It teaches them that they are flesh and blood,
  It also gently hints to them that others,
Although of clay, are yet not quite of mud,
  That urns and pipkins are but fragile brothers,
And works of the same pottery, bad or good,
  Though not all born of the same sires and mothers.
It teaches – heaven knows only what it teaches,
But sometimes it may mend, and often reaches.

GEORGE GORDON, LORD BYRON

139

Her first thought was to cut off Juan's head;
   Her second, to cut only his – acquaintance;
Her third, to ask him where he had been bred,
   Her fourth, to rally him into repentance;
Her fifth, to call her maids and go to bed;
   Her sixth, to stab herself; her seventh, to sentence
The lash to Baba; but her grand resource
Was to sit down again, and cry of course.

H. RIDER HAGGARD

FROM *KING SOLOMON'S MINES*

The great space in front of the king's kraal bore a very different appearance from that which it had presented on the previous evening. In place of the grim ranks of serried warriors were company after company of Kukuana girls, not over-dressed, so far as clothing went, but each crowned with a wreath of flowers, and holding a lily palm leaf in one hand and a white arum lily in the other. In the centre of the open moonlit space sat Twala the king, with old Gagool at his feet, attended by Infadoos, the boy Scragga, and twelve guards. There were also present about a score of chiefs, amongst whom I recognised most of our friends from the night before.

Twala greeted us with much apparent cordiality, though I saw him fix his eye viciously on Umbopa.

"Welcome, white men from the Stars," he said; "this is another sight from that which your eyes gazed on by the light of last night's moon, but it is not so good a sight. Girls are pleasant, and were it not for such as these," and he pointed round him, "we should none of us be here this day; but men are better. Kisses and the tender words of women are sweet, but the sound of the clashing of the spears of warriors, and the smell of men's blood, are sweeter far! Would ye have wives from among our people, white men? If so, choose the fairest here, and ye shall have them, as many as ye will," and he paused for an answer.

As the prospect did not seem to be without attractions for Good, who, like most sailors, is of a susceptible nature; being elderly and wise, and foreseeing the endless complications that anything of that sort would involve, for women bring trouble so surely as the night follows the day, I put in a hasty answer – "Thanks to thee, O king, but we white men only wed white women like ourselves. Your maidens are fair, but they are not for us!"

The king laughed. "It is well. In our land there is a proverb which runs, 'Love her who is present, for be sure she who is absent is false to thee'; but perhaps these things are not so in the Stars. In a land where men are white all things are possible. So be it, white men; the girls will not go begging! Welcome again; and welcome, too, thou black one; if Gagool here had won her way, though wouldst have been stiff and cold by now. It is lucky for thee that thou too camest from the Stars; ha! ha!"

"I can kill thee before thou killest me, O king," was Ignosi's calm answer, "and thou shalt be as stiff before my limbs cease to bend."

Twala started. "Thou speakest boldly, boy," he replied angrily; "presume not too far."

"He may well be bold in whose lips are truth. The truth is a sharp spear which flies home and misses not. It is a message from the 'Stars', O king."

Twala scowled, and his eye gleamed fiercely, but he said nothing more.

"Let the dance begin," he cried, and then the flower-crowned girls sprang forward in companies, singing a sweet song and waving delicate palms and white lilies. On they danced, looking faint and spiritual in the delicate sad light of the risen moon; now whirling round and round, now meeting in mimic warfare, swaying, eddying here and there, coming forward, falling back in an ordered confusion delightful to witness. At last they paused, and a beautiful young woman sprang out from the ranks and began to pirouette in front of us with a grace and vigour which would have put most ballet girls to shame. At length she retired exhausted, and another took her place, then another and another, but none of them, in grace, skill or personal attractions, came up to the first.

When the chosen girls had all danced, the king lifted his hand.

"Which deem ye the fairest, white men?" he asked.

"The first," said I unthinkingly. Next second I regretted it, for I remembered that Infadoos had told us that the fairest woman must be offered up as a sacrifice.

"Then is my mind as your minds, and my eyes are your eyes. She is the fairest; and a sorry thing it is for her, for she must die!"

"*Ay, must die!*" piped out Gagool, casting a glance of her quick eyes in the direction of the poor girl, who, as yet ignorant of the awful fate in store for her, was standing some ten yards off in front of a company of maidens, engaged in nervously picking a flower from her wreath to pieces, petal by petal.

"Why, O king?" said I, restraining my indignation with difficulty; "the girl has danced well, and pleased us; she is fair too; it would be hard to reward her with death."

Twala laughed as he answered – "It is our custom, and the figures who sit in stone yonder," and he pointed towards the three distant peaks, "must have their due. Did I fail to put the fairest girl to death to-day, misfortune would fall upon me and my house. Thus runs the prophecy of my people: 'If the king offer not a sacrifice of a fair girl, on the day of the dance of the maidens, to the Old Ones who sit and watch on the mountains, then shall he fall, and his house.' Look ye, white men, my brother who reigned before me offered not the sacrifice, because of the tears of the women, and he fell, and I reigned in his stead. It is finished; she must die!" Then turning to the guards – "Bring her hither; Scragga, make sharp thy spear."

Two of the men stepped forward, and as they advanced, the girl, for the first time realising her impending fate, screamed aloud and turned to fly. But the strong hands caught her fast, and brought her, struggling and weeping, before us.

"What is thy name, girl?" piped Gagool. "What! Wilt thou not answer? Shall the king's son do his work at once?"

At this hint, Scragga, looking more evil than ever, advanced a step and lifted his great spear, and at that moment I saw Good's hand creep to the revolver. The poor girl caught the faint glint of steel through her tears, and it sobered her anguish. She ceased struggling, and clasping her hands convulsively, stood shuddering from head to foot.

"See," cried Scragga in high glee, "she shrinks from the sight of my plaything even before she has tasted it," and he tapped the broad blade of his spear.

"If ever I get the chance you shall pay for that, you young hound!" I heard Good mutter beneath his breath.

"Now that thou art quiet, give us thy name, my dear. Come, speak out, and fear not," said Gagool in mockery.

"Oh, mother," answered the girl in trembling accents, "my name is Foutala, of the house of Suko. Oh, mother, why must I die? I have done no wrong!"

"Be comforted," went on the old woman in her hateful tone of mockery. "Thou must die, indeed, as a sacrifice to the Old Ones who sit yonder," and she pointed to the peaks; "but it is better to sleep in the night than to toil in the daytime; it is better to die than to live, and thou shalt die by the royal hand of the king's own son."

The girl Foutala wrung her hands in anguish, and cried aloud, "Oh, cruel! And I so young! What have I done that I should never again see the sun rise out of the night, or the stars come following on his track in the evening, that I may no more gather the flowers when the dew is heavy, or listen to the laughing of the waters? Woe is me, that I shall never see my father's hut again, nor feel my mother's kiss, nor tend the lamb that is sick! Woe is me, that no lover shall put his arm around me and look into my eyes, nor shall men children be born of me! Oh, cruel, cruel!"

And again she wrung her hands and turned her tear-stained, flower-crowned face to heaven, looking so lovely in her despair – for she was indeed a beautiful woman – that assuredly the sight of her would have melted the heart of any less cruel than were the three fiends before us. Prince Arthur's appeal to the ruffians who came to blind him was not more touching that that of this savage girl.

But it did not move Gagool or Gagool's master, though I saw signs of pity amongst the guards behind, and on the faces of the chiefs; and as for Good, he made a fierce snort of indignation, and made a motion as though to go to her assistance. With all a woman's quickness, the doomed girl interpreted what was passing in his mind, and by a sudden movement flung herself before him, and clasped his "beautiful white legs" with her hands.

"Oh, white father from the Stars!" she cried, "throw over me the mantle of thy protection; let me creep into the shadow of thy strength, that I may be saved. Oh, keep me from these cruel men and from the mercies of Gagool!"

"All right, my hearty, I'll look after you," sang out Good, in nervous Saxon.

"Come, get up, there's a good girl," and he stooped and caught her hand.

[…] *Good falls sick:*
Twala's death at the hands of Sir Henry had put an end to all further chance of disturbance; for Scragga had been his only son, and there was no rival claimant to the throne left alive.

I remarked that Ignosi had swum to power through blood. The old chief shrugged his shoulders. "Yes," he answered; "but the Kukuana people can only be kept cool by letting their blood flow sometimes. Many were killed, indeed, but the women were left, and others would soon grow up to take the places of the fallen. After this the land would be quiet for a while."

Afterwards, in the course of the morning we had a short visit from Ignosi. On whose brows the royal diadem was now bound. As I contemplated him advancing with kingly dignity, an obsequious guard following in his steps, I could not help recalling to my mind the tall Zulu who had presented himself to us at Durban some few months back, asking to be taken into our service, and reflecting on the strange revolutions of the wheel of fortune.

"Hail, O king!" I said, rising.

"Yes Macumazahn. King at last, by the might of your three right hands," was the ready answer.

All was, he said, going on well; and he hoped to arrange a great feast in two weeks' time in order to show himself to the people.

I asked him what he had settled to do with Gagool.

"She is the evil genius of the land," he answered, "and I shall kill her, and all the witch-doctors with her! She has lived so long that none can remember when she was not old, and she it is who has always trained witch-hunters, and made the land wicked in the sight of the heavens above."

"Yet she knows much," I replied; "it is easier to destroy knowledge, Ignosi, than to gather it."

"That is so," he said thoughtfully. "She, and she only, knows the secret of the 'Three Witches' yonder, whither the great road runs, where the kings are buried, and the Silent Ones sit."

"Yes, and the diamonds are. Forget not thy promise Ignosi; thou must lead us to the mines, even if thou hast to spare Gagool alive to show the way."

"I will not forget, Macumazahn, and I will think on what thou sayest."

After Ignosi's visit I went to see Good, and found him quite delirious. The fever set up by his wound seemed to have taken a firm hold of his system, and to be complicated by an internal injury. For four or five days his condition was most critical; indeed I believe that had it not been for Foutala's indefatigable nursing he must have died.

Women are women, all the world over, whatever their colour. Yet somehow it seemed curious to watch this dusky beauty bending night and day over the fevered man's couch and performing all the merciful errands of a sick-room swiftly, gently, and with as fine an instinct for it as that of a trained hospital nurse. For the first night or two I tried to help her, and so did Sir Henry as soon as his stiffness allowed him to move, but Foutala bore our interference with impatience, and finally insisted upon our leaving him to her, saying that our movements made him restless, which I think was true. Day and night she watched him and tended him, giving him his only medicine, a native cooling drink made of milk, in which was infused juice from the bulb of a species of tulip, and keeping the flies from settling on him. I can see the whole picture now as it appeared night after night by the light of our primitive lamp; Good tossing to and fro, his features emaciated, his eyes shining large and luminous, and jabbering nonsense by the yard; and seated on the ground by his side, her back resting against the wall of the hut, the soft-eyed shapely Kukuana beauty, her face, weary as it was, animated by a look of infinite compassion – or was it more than compassion?

For two days we thought that he must die, and crept about with heavy hearts.

Only Foutala would not believe it.

"He will live," she said.

For three hundred yards or more around Twala's chief hut, where the sufferer lay, there was silence; for by the king's order all who lived in the habitations behind it, except Sir Henry and myself, had been removed, lest any noise should come to the sick man's ears. One night, it was the fifth of Good's illness, as was my habit, I went across to see how he was getting on before turning in for a few hours.

I entered the hut carefully. The lamp placed upon the floor showed the figure of God, tossing no more, but lying quite still.

So it had come at last! In the bitterness of my heart I gave something like a sob.

"Hush-h-h!" came from the patch of dark shadow behind Good's head.

Then, creeping closer, I saw that he was not dead, but sleeping soundly, with Foutala's taper fingers clasped tightly in his poor white hand. The crisis had passed, and he would live. He slept like that for eighteen hours; I scarcely like to say it, for fear I should not be believed, but during that entire period did this devoted girl sit by him, fearing that if she moved and drew away her hand it would wake him. What she must have suffered from cramp and weariness, to say nothing of want of food, nobody will ever know; but it is the fact that, when at last he woke, she had to be carried away – her limbs were so stiff she could not move them.

After the turn had once been taken, Good's recovery was rapid and complete. It was not till he was nearly well that Sir Henry told him all he owed to Foutala; and when he came to the story of how she sat by his side for eighteen hours, fearing lest by moving she should wake him, the honest sailor's eyes filled with tears. He turned and went straight to the hut where Foutala was preparing the mid-day meal, for we were back in our old quarters now, taking me with him to interpret in case he could not make his meaning clear to her, though I am bound to say that she understood him marvellously as a rule, considering how extremely limited was his foreign vocabulary.

"Tell her," said Good, "that I owe her my life, and that I will never forget her kindness."

I interpreted, and under her dark skin she actually seemed to blush.

Turning to him with one of those swift and graceful motions that in her always reminded me of the flight of a wild bird, Foutala answered softly, glancing at him with her large brown eyes – "Nay, my lord; my lord forgets! Did he not save my life, and am I not my lord's handmaiden?"

It will be observed that the young lady appeared entirely to have forgotten the share which Sir Henry and myself had taken in her preservation from Twala's clutches. But that is the way of women! I remember my dear wife was just the same. Well, I retired from that little interview sad at heart. I did not like Miss Foutala's soft glances, for I knew the fatal amorous propensities of sailors in general, and of Good in particular.

There are two things in the world, as I have found it, which cannot be prevented; you cannot keep a Zulu from fighting, or a sailor from falling in love upon the slightest provocation!

It was a few days after this last occurrence that Ignosi held his great "indaba", or council, and was formally recognised as king by the "indunas", or head men, of Kukuanaland. The spectacle was a most imposing one, including as it did a grand review of troops. On this day the remaining fragments of the Greys were formally paraded, and in the face of the army thanked for their splendid conduct in the great battle. To each man the king made a large present of cattle, promoting them one and all to the rank of officers in the new corps of Greys which was in process of formation. An order was also promulgated throughout the length and breadth of Kukuanaland that, whilst we honoured the country by our presence, we three were to be greeted with the royal salute, and to be treated with the same ceremony and respect that was by custom accorded to the king. Also the power of life and death was publicly conferred upon us. Ignosi, too, in the presence of his people, reaffirmed the promises which he had made, to the effect that no man's blood would be shed without trial, and that witch-hunting should cease in the land.

When the ceremony was over we waited upon Ignosi, and informed him that we were now anxious to investigate the mystery of the mines to which Solomon's Road ran, asking him if he had discovered anything about them.

"My friends," he answered, "I have discovered this. It is there that the three great figures sit, who here were called the 'Silent Ones' and to whom Twala would have offered the girl Foulata as a sacrifice. It is here, too, in a great cave deep as the mountain, that the kings of the land are buried; there ye shall find Twala's body, sitting with those that went before him. There, also, is a deep pit, which, at some time, long-dead men dug out, mayhap for the stones ye speak of, such as I have heard men in Natal tell of at Kimberley. There, too, in the Place of Death is a secret chamber, known to none but the King and Gagool. But Twala who knew it, is dead, and I know it not, nor know I what is in it. Yet there is a legend in the land that once, many generations gone, a white man crossed mountains, and was led by a woman to the secret chamber, and shown the wealth hidden in it. But before he could take it, she betrayed him, and he was driven by the king of the day back out of the mountains, and since then no man has entered the place."

[…] *The place of death:*
"I have done the bidding of many kings, Infadoos, till in the end they did mine. *Ha! ha!* I go to look upon their faces once more, and Twala's also! Come on, come on, here is the lamp," and she

drew a large gourd full of oil, and fitted with a rush wick, from under her fur cloak.

"Art thou coming, Foutala?" asked Good in his villainous kitchen Kukana, in which he had been improving himself under that young lady's tuition.

"I fear, my lord," the girl answered timidly.

"Then give me the basket."

"Nay my lord, whither thou goest there will I go also."

"The deuce you will!" I thought to myself; "that may be awkward if we ever get out of this."

Without further ado Gagool plunged into the passage, which was wide enough to admit of two walking abreast, and quite dark. We followed the sound of her voice as she piped to us to come on, in some fear and trembling, which was not allayed by the flutter of a sudden rush of wings.

"Hullo! What's that?" hallooed Good; "somebody hit me in the face."

"Bats," said I; "on you go."

When, so far as we could judge, we had gone some fifty paces, we perceived that the passage was growing faintly in light. Another minute, and we were in perhaps the most wonderful place that the eyes of the living man have beheld.

Let the reader picture to himself the hall of the vastest cathedral he ever stood in, windowless indeed, but dimly lighted from above, presumably by shafts connected with the outer air and driven in the roof, which arched away a hundred feet above our heads, and he will get some idea of the enormous cave in which we found ourselves, with the difference that this cathedral designed by nature was loftier and wider than any built by man. But its stupendous size was the least of the wonders of the place, for running in rows down its length were gigantic pillars of what looked ice, but were, in reality, huge stalactites. It is impossible for me to convey any idea of the overpowering beauty and grandeur of these pillars of white spar, some of which were not less than twenty feet in diameter at the base, and sprang up in the lofty and yet delicate beauty sheer to the distant roof. Others again were in the process of formation. On the rock floor there was in these cases what looked, Sir Henry said, exactly like a broken column in an old Grecian temple, whilst high above, depending from the roof, the point of a huge icicle could be dimly seen.

Even as we gazed we could hear the process going on, for presently with a tiny splash a drop of water would fall from the far-off icicle onto the column below. On some columns the drops only fell once in two or three minutes, and in these cases it would be an interesting calculation to discover how long, at that rate of dripping, it would take to form a pillar, say eighty feet high by ten in diameter. That the process, in at least one example, was incalculably slow, the following example will suffice to show. Cut on one of these pillars we discovered the rude likeness of a mummy, by the head of which appeared to be the figure of an Egyptian god, doubtless the handiwork of some old-world labourer in the mine.

[…]

It was all done in four seconds.

Then we turned to Foulata. The poor girl was stabbed in the body, and I saw that she could not live long.

"Ah! Bougwan, I die!" gasped the beautiful creature. "She crept out – Gagool; I did not see her, I was faint – and the door began to fall; then she came back, and was looking up the path – I saw her come in through the slowly falling door, and caught her and held her, and she stabbed me, and I die, Bougwan!"

"Poor girl! Poor girl!" Good cried; and then, as he could do nothing else, he fell to kissing her.

"Bougwan," she said, after a pause, "is Macumazahn there? It grows so dark, I cannot see."

"Here I am, Foulata."

"Macumazahn, be my tongue for a moment, I pray thee, for Bougwan cannot understand me, and before I go into darkness I would speak a word."

"Say on, Foulata, I will render it."

"Say to my lord Bougwan, that – I love him, and that I am glad to die because I know that he cannot cumber his life with such as I am, for the sun may not mate with the darkness, nor the white with the black.

"Say that, since I saw him, at times I have felt as though there were a bird in my bosom, which one day would fly hence and sing elsewhere. Even now, though I cannot lift my hand, and my brain grows cold, I do not feel as though my heart were dying; it is so full of love that it could live a thousand years, and yet be young. Say that if I live again, mayhap I shall see him in the Stars, and that – I will search them all, though perchance there I should still be black and he would – still be white. Say – nay, Macumazahn. Say no more, save that I love – oh, hold me closer Bougwan, I cannot feel thine arms – *oh! oh!*"

"She is dead – she is dead!" exclaimed Good, rising in grief, the tears running down his honest face.

"You need not let that trouble you, old fellow," said Sir Henry.

"Eh!" said Good; what do you mean?"

"I mean that you will soon be in a position to join her. Man, don't you see that we are buried alive?"

FROM *CHILD OF STORM*

[*from the Author's dedication, to James Stuart, Esq., Late Assistant Secretary for Native Affairs, Natal*]

I must admit that my acquaintance with this people dates from a period which closed almost before your day. What I know of them I gathered at the time when Cetewayo, of whom my volume tells, was in his glory, previous to the evil hour in which he found himself driven by the clamour of his regiments, cut off, as they were, through the annexation of the Transvaal from their hereditary trade of war, to match himself against the British strength. I learned it all by personal observation in the 'seventies, or from the lips of the great Shepstone, my chief and friend, and from my colleagues Osborn, Fynney, Clarke and others, every one of them long since "gone down".

Perhaps it may be as well that this is so, at any rate in the case of one who desires to write of the Zulus as a reigning nation, which they have now ceased to be, and to try and show them as they were, in all their superstitious madness and bloodstained grandeur.

Yet they had virtues as well as vices.

To serve their Country in arms, to die for it and for the King; such was their primitive ideal. If they were fierce they were loyal, and feared neither wounds nor doom; if they listened to the dark redes of the witch-doctor, the trumpet-call of duty sounded still louder in their ears; if, chanting their terrible "Ingoma", at the King's bidding they went forth to slay unsparingly, at least they were not mean or vulgar, From those who continually must face the last great issues of life and death meanness and vulgarity are far removed. These qualities belong to the safe and crowded haunts of civilised men, not to the kraals of Bantu savages, where, at any rate of old, they might be sought in vain.

Now everything is changed, or so I hear, and doubtless in the balance this is best. Still we may wonder what are the thoughts that pass through the mind of some ancient warrior of Caha's or Dingaan's time as he suns himself crouched on the ground, for example, where once stood the royal kraal, Duguza, and watches men and women of the Zulu blood passing homeward from the cities or the mines, bemused, some of them, with the white man's smuggled liquor, grotesque with the white man's cast-off garments, hiding perhaps, in their blankets examples of the white man's doubtful photographs – and then shuts his sunken eyes and remembers the plumed and kilted regiments making that same ground shake as, with a thunder of salute, line upon line, company upon company, they rushed out to battle.

Well, because the latter does not attract me, it is of this former time that I have tried to write – the time of the Impis and the witch-finders and the rival princes of the royal house.

[*from the Author's Note*]

Mr Allan Quatermain's story of the wicked and fascinating Mameena, a kind of Zulu Helen, has, it should be stated, a broad foundation in historical fact. Leaving Mameena and her wiles on one side, the tale of the struggle between the Princes Cetewayo and Umbelazi for succession to the throne of Zululand is true.

When the differences between these sons of his became intolerable, because of the tumult which they were causing in his country, King Panda, their father, the son of Senzangakona, and the brother of the great Chaka and of Dingaan, who had ruled before him, did say that "when two young bulls quarrel they had better fight it out." So, at least, I was told by the late Mr. F. B. Fynney, my colleague at the time of the annexation of the Transvaal in 1877, who, as Zulu Border Agent, with the exceptions of the late Sir Theophilus Shepstone and the late Sir Melmoth Osborn, perhaps knew more of the land and people than anyone else of his period.

As a result of this hint given by a maddened king, the great battle of the Tugela was fought at Endondakusaka in December, 1856, between the *Usutu* party, commanded by Cetewayo, and the adherents of Umbelazi the Handsome, his brother, who was known among the Zulus as *Indhlovu-ene-Sihlonti*, or the "Elephant with the tuft of hair," from a little lock of hair which grew down low upon his back.

[*from Allan Quatermain's story*]
Now, although I take it out of its strict chronological order, the first of these histories that I wish to preserve is in the main that of an extremely beautiful woman – with the exception of a certain Nada, called "the Lily", of whom I hope to speak some day, I think the most beautiful that ever lived among the Zulus. Also she was, I think, the most able, the most wicked, and the most ambitious, Her attractive name – for it was very attractive as the Zulus said it, especially those of them who were in love with her – was Mameena, daughter of Umbezi. Her other name was Child of Storm (*Ingane-ye-Sipepo*, or more freely and shortly, *O-we-Zulu*), but the word "Ma-mee-na" had its origin in the sound of the wind that wailed about the hut when she was born.

Since I have been settled in England I have read – of course in translation – the story of Helen of Troy, as told by the Greek poet, Homer. Well, Mameena reminds me very much of Helen, or rather Helen reminds me of Mameena. At any rate, there was this in common between them, although one of them was black, or, rather, copper-coloured, and the other white – they both were lovely; moreover, they both were faithless, and brought men by hundreds to their deaths. There, perhaps, the resemblance ends, since Mameena had much more fire and grit than Helen could boast, who, unless Homer misrepresents her, must have been but a poor thing after all. Beauty Itself, which those old rascals of Greek gods made use of to bait their snares set for the lives and honour of men, such was Helen, no more; that is, as I understand her, who have not had the advantage of a classical education. Now, Mameena, although she was superstitious – a common weakness of great minds – acknowledging no gods in particular, as we understand them, set her own snares, with varying success but a very definite object, namely, that of becoming the first woman in the world as she knew it – the stormy, bloodstained world of the Zulus.

But the reader shall judge for himself, if ever such a person should chance to cast his eye upon this history.

[…]

For a while I contemplated the roof and sides of the hut by the light which entered it through the smoke-vent and the door-hole, wondering whose it might be and how I came there.

Then I tried to sit up, and instantly was seized with agony in the region of the ribs, which I found were bound about with broad strips of soft tanned hide. Clearly they, or some of them, were broken.

What had broken them? I asked myself, and in a flash everything came back to me. So I had escaped with my life, as the old dwarf, "Opener-of-Roads", had told me that I should. Certainly he was an excellent prophet; and if he spoke truth in this matter, why not in others? What was I to make of it all? How could a black savage, however ancient, foresee the future?

By induction from the past, I supposed; and yet what amount of induction would suffice to show him the details of a forthcoming accident that was to happen to me through the agency of a wild beast with a peculiarly shaped horn? I gave it up, as before and since that day I have found it necessary to do in the case of many other events in life. Indeed, the question is one that I have often had cause to ask where Kafir "witch-doctors" or prophets are concerned, notably in the insistence of a certain Mavovo, of whom I hope to tell one day, whose predictions saved my life and those of my companions.

Just then I heard the sound of someone creeping through the bee-hole of the hut, and half-closed my eyes, as I did not feel inclined for conversation. The person came in and stood over me, and somehow – by instinct, I suppose – I became aware that the visitor was a woman. Very slowly I lifted my eyelids, just enough to enable me to see her.

There, standing before me in a beam of golden light that, passing through the smoke-hole, pierced the soft gloom of the hut, stood the most beautiful creature that I had ever seen – that is, if it be admitted that a person who is black, or rather copper-coloured, can be beautiful.

She was a little above the medium height, not more, with a figure that, so far as I am a judge of such matters, was absolutely perfect – that of a Greek statue indeed. On this point I had an opportunity of forming an opinion, since, except for her little head apron and a single string of large blue beads about her throat, her costume was – well, that of a Greek statue. Her features showed no trace of the negro type; on the contrary, they were singularly well cut, the nose being straight and fine and the pouting mouth that just showed the ivory teeth between very small. Then the eyes, large, dark, liquid, like those of a buck, set beneath a smooth, broad forehead on which the curling, not woolly, hair grew low. This hair, by the way, was not dressed up in any of the eccentric native fashions, but simple parted in the middle and tied in a big knot over the nape of the neck, the little ears peeping out through its tresses. The hands, like the feet, were very small and delicate, and the curves of the bust soft and full without being coarse, or even showing the promise of coarseness.

A lovely woman, truly; and yet there was something not quite pleasing about the beautiful face; something, notwithstanding its childlike outline, which reminded me of a flower breaking into bloom, that one does not associate with youth and innocence. I tried to analyse what this might be, and came to the conclusion that without being hard, it was too clever and, in a sense, too reflective. I felt even that the brain within the shapely head was keen and bright and polished steel; that this woman was made to rule, not to be man's toy, or even his loving companion, but to use him for her ends.

She dropped her chin till it hid the little, dimple-like depression below her throat, which was one of her charms, and began not to look at, but to study me, seeing which I shut my eyes tight and waited. Evidently she thought that I was still in my swoon, for now she spoke to herself in a low voice that was soft and sweet as honey.

"A small man," she said; "Saduko would make two of him and the other" – who was he, I wondered – "three. His hair, too, is ugly; he cuts it short and it sticks up like that on a cat's back. *Iya!*" (i.e. Piff!), and she moved her hand contemptuously, "a feather of a man. But white – white, one of those who rule. Why, they all know that he is their master. They call him 'He-who-never-Sleeps'. They say that he has the courage of a lioness with young – he who got away when Dingaan killed *Piti* and the Boers; they say that he is quick and cunning as a snake, and that Panda and his great *indunas* think more of him than of any white man they know. He is unmarried also, though they say, too, that twice he had a wife, who died, and now he does not turn to look at women, which is strange in any man, and shows that he will escape trouble and succeed. Still, it must be remembered that they are all ugly down here in Zululand, cows, or heifers who will be cows. *Piff*! no more."

She paused for a little while, then went on in her dreamy, reflective voice:

"Now, if he met a woman who is not merely a cow or a heifer, a woman cleverer than himself, even if she were not white, I wonder – "

At this point I thought it well to wake up. Turning my head I yawned, opened my eyes and looked at her vaguely, seeing which her expression changed in a flash from that of brooding power to one of moved and anxious girlhood; in short, it became sweetly feminine.

"You are Mameena," I said; "is it not so?"

"Oh, yes, *Inkoosi*," she answered, "that is my poor name. But how did you hear it, and how do you know me?"

"I heard it from one Saduko" – here she frowned a little – "and others, and I knew you because you are so beautiful"– an incautious speech at which she broke into a dazzling smile and tossed her deer-like head.

"Am I?" she asked. "I never knew it, who am only a common Zulu girl to whom it please the great white chief to say kind things, for which I thank him"; and she made a graceful little reverence, just bending one knee. "But," she went on quickly, "whatever else I be, I am of no knowledge, not fit to tend you who are hurt. Shall I go and send my oldest mother?"

"Do you mean her whom your father calls the 'Worn-out-Old-Cow,' and whose ear he shot off?"

"Yes, it must be she from the description," she answered with a little shake of laughter, "though I have never heard him give her that name."

"Or if you did, you have forgotten it," I said dryly. "Well, I think not, thank you. Why trouble her, when you will do quite as well? If there is milk in that gourd, perhaps you will give me a drink of it."

She flew to the bowl like a swallow, and next moment was kneeling at my side and holding it to my lips with one hand, while with the other she supported my head.

"I am honoured," she said. "I only came to the hut the

moment before you woke, and seeing you lost in a swoon, I wept – look, my eyes are still wet (they were, though she how she made them so I do not know) – for I feared lest that sleep should be but the beginning of the last."

"Quite so," I said; "it is very good of you. And now, since your fears are groundless – thanks be to heaven – sit down if you will, and tell me the story of how I came here."

She sat down, not, as I noted, as a Kafir woman ordinarily does, in a kneeling position, but on a stool.

"You were brought into the kraal, *Inkoosi*," she said, "on a litter of boughs. My heart stood still when I saw that litter coming; it was not mere heart; it was cold iron, because I thought the dead or injured man was – " and she paused.

"Saduko?" I suggested.

"Not at all, *Inkoosi* – my father."

"Well it wasn't either of them," I said, "so you must have felt happy."

"Happy! *Inkoosi*, when the guest of our house had been wounded, perhaps to death – the guest of whom I have heard so much, although by misfortune I was absent when he arrived."

[...]

"Oh, Macumazahn, will you take me? My father would not trust me with you."

"Yes, I dare say," I answered; "but the question is, could I trust myself with you?"

"What do you mean?" she asked. "Oh, I understand. Then, after all, I am more to you than a black stone to play with?"

I think it was that unlucky joke of mine which first set Mameena thinking, "like a white ant in its tunnel", as Saduko said. At least, after it her manner towards me changed; she became very deferential; she listened to my words as though they were all wisdom; I caught her looking at me with her soft eyes as though I were quite an admirable object. She began to talk to me of her difficulties, her troubles and her ambitions. She asked me for my advice as to Saduko. On this point I replied to her that, if she loved him, and her father would allow it, presumably she ought to marry him.

"I like him well enough, Macumazahn, although he wearies me at times; but love – oh tell me, *what* is love?" Then she clasped her slim hands and gazed at me like a fawn.

"Upon my word, young woman," I replied, "that is a matter upon which I thought you more competent to instruct me."

"Oh, Macumazahn," she said almost in a whisper, and letting her hand droop like a fading lily, "you have never given me the chance have you?" And she laughed a little, looking extremely attractive.

"Good gracious!" – or, rather, its Zulu equivalent – I answered, for I began to feel nervous. "What do you mean, Mameena? How could I – " There I stopped.

"I do not know what I mean, Macumazahn," she exclaimed wildly, "but I know well enough what you mean – that you are white as snow and that snow and soot don't mix well together."

"No," I answered gravely, "snow is good to look at, and so is soot, but mingled they make an ugly colour. Not that you are like soot," I added hastily, fearing to hurt her feelings. "That is your hue" – and I touched a copper bangle she was wearing – "a very lovely hue, Mameena, like everything else about you."

"Lovely," she said, beginning to weep a little, which upset me very much, for if there is one thing I hate, it is to see a woman cry. "How can a poor Zulu girl be lovely? Oh, Machumazahn, the spirits have hardly dealt with me, who have given me the colour of my people and the heart of yours. If I were white, now, what you are pleased to call this loveliness of mine would be of some use to me, for then – then – oh, cannot you guess, Macumazahn?"

I shook my head and said that I could not, and next moment was sorry, for she proceeded to explain.

Sinking to her knees – for we were quite alone in the big hut and there was no one else about, all the other women were engaged in rural or domestic tasks, for which Mameena declared she had no time, as her business was to look after me – she rested her shapely head upon my knees and began to talk in a low, sweet voice that sometimes broke into a sob.

"Then I will tell you – I will tell you; yes, even if you hate me afterwards. I could teach you what love is very well, Macumazahn, you are quite right – because I love you." (*Sob.*) "No, you shall not stir until you have heard me out." Here she flung her arms about my legs and held them tight, so that without using great violence it was absolutely impossible for me to move. "When I saw you first, all shattered and senseless, snow seemed to fall upon my heart, and it stopped for a little while and has never been the same since. I think that something is growing in it, Macumazahn, that makes it big." (*Sob.*) "I used to like Saduko, but afterwards I did not like him at all – no, nor Masapo either – you know, he is the big chief who lives over the mountain, a very rich and powerful man who, I believe, would like to marry me. Well, as I went on nursing you my heart grew bigger and bigger, and now you can see it has burst." (*Sob.*) "Nay, stay still and do not try to speak. You *shall* hear me out. It is the least you can do, seeing that you have caused me all this pain. If you did not want me to love you, why did you not curse at me and strike me, as I am told white men do to Kafir girls?" She rose and went on:

"Now, hearken. Although I am the colour of copper, I am comely, I am well-bred also; there is no higher blood than ours in Zululand, both on my father's and my mother's side, and, Macumazahn, I have a fire in me that shows me things. I can be great, and I long for greatness. Take me to wife, Macumazahn, and I swear to you that in ten years I will make you king of the Zulus. Forget your pale women and wed yourself to the fire which burns in me, and it shall eat up all that stands between you and the Crown, as flame eats up dry grass. More, I will make you happy. If you choose to take other wives, I will not be jealous, because I know that I should hold your spirit, and that, compared to me, they would be nothing in your thought – "

"But Mameena," I broke in, "I don't want to be king of the Zulus."

"Oh, yes, yes, you do, for every man wants power, and it is better to rule over a brave, black people – thousands and thousands of them – than to be no one among the whites. Think, think! There is wealth in the land. By your skill and knowledge the *amabuto* (regiments) could be improved; with the wealth you would arm them with guns – yes, and 'by-and-byes' also with the throat of thunder" (that is, or was, the Kafir name for cannon). "They would be invincible. Chaka's kingdom would be nothing to ours, for a hundred thousand warriors would sleep on their spears, waiting for your word. If you wished it even you could sweep our Natal and make the whites there your subjects, too. Or perhaps it would be safer to let them be, lest others should come across the green water to help them, and to strike northwards, where I am told there are great lands as rich and fair, in which no one would dispute our sovereignty – "

"But, Mameena," I gasped, for this girls's titanic ambition literally overwhelmed me, "surely you are mad! How would you do all those things?"

"I am not mad," she answered; "I am only what is called great, and you know well enough that I can do them, not by myself, who am but a woman and tied with the ropes that bid women, but with you to cut those ropes and help me. I have a plan which will not fail. But, Macumazahn," she added in a changed voice, "until I know that you will be my partner in it I will not tell it even to you, for perhaps you might talk – in your sleep, and then the fires in my breast would soon go out – for ever."

"I might talk now, for the matter of that, Mameena."

"No; for men like you do not tell tales of foolish girls who chance to love them. But if the plan began to work, and you hear say that kings or princes died, it might be otherwise. You might say, 'I think I know now where the witch lives who causes these evils' – in your sleep, Macumazahn."

"Mameena," I said, "tell me no more. Setting your dreams on one side, can I be false to my friend, Saduko, who talks to me day and night of you."

"Saduko! *Piff!*" she exclaimed, with that expressive gesture of the hand.

"And can I be false," I continued, seeing that Saduko was no good card to play, "to my friend, Umbezi, your father?"

"My father!" she laughed. "Why, would it not please him to grow great in your shadow? Only yesterday he told me to marry you, if I could, for then he would find a stick indeed to lean on, and be rid of Saduko's trembling."

Evidently, Umbezi was a worse card even than Saduko. So I played another.

"And can I help you, Mameena, to tread a road that at the best must be red with blood?"

"Why not," she asked, "since with or without you I am destined to tread that road, the only difference being that with you it will lead to glory and without you perhaps to the jackals and the vultures? Blood! *Piff!* What is blood in Zululand?"

This card having also failed, I tabled my last.

"Glory or no glory, I do not wish to share it, Mameena. I will not war among a people who have entertained me with hospitality, or plot the downfall of their Great Ones. As you told me just now, I am nobody – just one grain of sands upon a white shore – but I had rather be that than a haunted rock which draws the heavens' lightnings and is drenched with sacrifice. I seek no throne over black or white, Mameena, who walk my own path to a quiet grave that shall perhaps not be without honour of its own, though other than you seek. I will keep your counsel, Mameena, but because you are so beautiful and so wise, and because you say you are fond of me – for which I thank you – I pray you put away these fearful dreams of yours that in the end, whether they succeed or fail, will send you shivering from the world to give account of them to the Watcher-on-high."

"Not so, O Macumazahn," she said with a proud little laugh. "When your Watcher sowed my seed – if thus he did – he sowed the dreams that are part of me also, and I shall only bring him back his own, with the flower and the fruit by way of interest. But that is finished. You refuse the greatness. Now, tell me, if I sink those dreams in a great water, tying about the stone of forgetfulness and saying: 'Sleep there, O dreams; it is not your hour' – if I do this, and stand before you just a woman who loves and swears by the spirits of her fathers never to think or do that which has not your blessing – will you love me a little, Macumazahn?"

Now I was silent, for she had driven me to the last ditch, and I knew not what to say. Moreover, I will confess my weakness – I was strangely moved. This beautiful girl with the "fire in her heart", this woman who was different from all other women that I had ever known, seemed to have twisted her slender fingers into my heart-strings and to be drawing me closer towards her. It was a great temptation, and I bethought me of old Zikali's saying in the Black Kloof, and seemed to hear his giant laugh.

She glided up to me, she threw her arms about me and kissed me on the lips, and I think I kissed her back, but really I am not sure what I did or said for my head swam. When it cleared again she was standing in front of me, looking at me reflectively.

"Now, Macumazhan," she said, with a smile that both mocked and dazzled, "the poor black girl has you, the wise, experienced white man, in her net, and I will show you that she can be generous. Do you think that I do not read your heart, that I do not know that you believe I am dragging you down to your shame and ruin? Well, I spare you, Macumazahn, since you have kissed me and spoken words which already you may have forgotten, but which I do not forget. Go your road, Macumazahn, and I go mine, since the proud white man shall not be stained with my black touch. Go your road; but one thing I forbid you – to believe that you have been listening to lies, and that I have merely played off a woman's arts upon you for my own ends. I love you, Macumazahn, as you will never be loved until you die, and I shall never love another man, however many I shall marry. Moreover, you shall promise me one thing – that once in my life, and once only, if I wish it, you shall kiss me again before all men. And now, lest you should be moved to folly and forget your white man's pride, I bid you farewell, O Macumazahn. When we meet again it will be as friends only."

Then she went, leaving me feeling smaller that ever I felt in my life, before or since – even smaller than when I walked into the presence of old Zikali the Wise. Why, I wondered, had she first made a fool of me, and then thrown away the fruits of my folly? To this hour I cannot quite answer the question, though I believe the explanation to be that she did really care for me, and was anxious not to involve me in trouble and her plottings; also she may have been wise enough to see that our natures were as oil and water and would not blend.

[...]

"There is a man whom I do not hate, whom I have never hated, whom I think I love because he would not love me. He sits there," and to my utter dismay, and the intense interest of the company, she pointed to me, Allan Quatermain!

"Well, once by my 'magic', of which you have heard so much, I got the better of this man against his will and judgement, and, because of that soft heart of mine, I let him go; yes, I let the rare fish go when he was on my hook. It is well that I should have let him go, since, had I kept him, a fine story would have been spoiled and I should have become nothing but a white hunter's servant. To be thrust away behind the door when the white *Inkosikazi* came to eat his meat – I, Mameena, who never loved to stand out of sight behind a door. Well, when he was at my feet and I spared him, he made me a promise, which yet I think he will keep now when we part for a little while. Macumazahn, did you not promise to kiss me once more upon the lips whenever and wherever I should ask you?"

"I did," I answered in a hollow voice, for in truth her eyes held me as they had held Saduko.

"Then come now, Macumazahn, and give me that farewell kiss. The King will permit it, and since I have now no husband, who take Death to husband, there is none to say you nay."

I rose. It seemed to me that I could not help myself. I went to her, this woman surrounded by implacable enemies, this woman who had played for great stakes and lost them, and who knew so well how to lose. I stood before her, ashamed and yet not ashamed, for something of her greatness, evil though it might be, drove me out of my shame, and I knew that my foolishness was lost in vast tragedy.

Slowly she lifted her languid arm and threw it about my neck; slowly she bent her red lips to mine and kissed me, once upon the mouth and once upon the forehead. But between those two kisses she did a thing so swiftly that my eyes could scarce follow what she did. It seemed to me that she had brushed her left hand across her lips, and that I say her throat rise as though she swallowed something. Then she thrust me from her, saying:

"Farewell, O Macumazahn, you will never forget this kiss of mine; and when we meet again we shall have much to talk of, for between now and then your story will be long. Farewell, Zikali. I pray that all your planning may succeed, since those you hate are those I hate, and I bear you no grudge because you told the truth at last. Farewell, Prince Cetewayo. You will never be the man your brother would have been, and your lot is very evil, you who are doomed to pull down a House built by One who was great. Farewell, Saduko, the fool who threw away your fortune for a woman's eyes, as though the world were not full of women. Nandie the Sweet and Forgiving will nurse you until your haunted end. Oh! why does Umbelazi lean over your shoulder, Saduko, and look at me so strangely? Farewell, Panda the Shadow. Now let loose your slayers. Oh! let them loose swiftly, lest they should be balked of my blood!"

Panda lifter his hand and the executioners leapt forward, but ere ever they reached her, Mameena shivered, threw wide her arms and fell back – dead. The poisonous drug she had taken worked swiftly and well.

Such was the end of Mameena, Child of Storm.